# INDUSTRIAL DEVELOPMENT AND MANUFACTURING IN THE ANTEBELLUM GULF SOUTH

# INDUSTRIAL DEVELOPMENT AND MANUFACTURING IN THE ANTEBELLUM GULF SOUTH

## A REEVALUATION

MICHAEL S. FRAWLEY

LOUISIANA STATE UNIVERSITY PRESS BATON ROUGE

Published by Louisiana State University Press

Manufactured in the United States of America
First printing

DESIGNER: Mandy McDonald Scallan
TYPEFACE: Whitman
PRINTER AND BINDER: Sheridan Books

Maps created by Mary Lee Eggart

Library of Congress Cataloging-in-Publication Data
Names: Frawley, Michael S., 1978– author.
Title: Industrial development and manufacturing in the Antebellum Gulf South : a reevaluation / Michael S. Frawley.
Description: Baton Rouge : Louisiana State University Press, [2019] | Includes bibliographical references and index.
Identifiers: LCCN 2018046167| ISBN 9780807170687 (cloth : alk. paper) | ISBN 9780807171394 (pdf) | ISBN 9780807171400 (epub)
Subjects: LCSH: Industrialization—Gulf States—History—19th century. | Economic development—Gulf States—History—19th century. | Manufacturing industries—Gulf States—History—19th century. | Gulf States—Economic conditions—History—19th century. | Southern States—History—1775–1865.
Classification: LCC HC107.A13 F73 2019 | DDC 338.976009/034—dc23
LC record available at https://lccn.loc.gov/2018046167

The paper in this book meets the guidelines for permanence and durability of the Committee on Production Guidelines for Book Longevity of the Council on Library Resources.♾

*For Melissa*

# CONTENTS

# ACKNOWLEDGMENTS

As I look back now on all of the time and effort that it took to complete this work, I cannot help but be reminded of all those people who gave their time, expertise, and support to help me finish this endeavor. I have been extremely fortunate that I have so many wonderful friends, teachers, and family who were willing to at least feign interest in my work while I endlessly droned on about maps, tables, charts, and the importance of industry in the antebellum Gulf South.

First, none of this would have been possible without the help and support of the Louisiana State University Department of History. The faculty of the department were always willing to stop and talk, give me tips on writing and research, and challenge me to explore paths that I had never thought to take. Victor Stater and Suzanne Marchand opened their home many times to my wife and me and taught me the joys of an academic life. Moreover, I will always remember my discussions on Caribbean slavery with Paul Hoffman, and our search for that perfect number. Hopefully someday I will find it. Gaines Foster and William J. Cooper always were willing to go the extra mile to help me reach my goals, and their comments on early versions of this manuscript were invaluable. Moreover, I want to thank them for putting up with all of the numbers in which this work attempts to drown readers. The Geography Department at LSU, and especially Craig Colten, greatly supported my work as I attempted to combine history and geography. GIS is something more historians should take advantage of when studying historical problems.

Paul Paskoff read and commented on large parts of this work, and for once, shockingly, I do not know what to say, as words alone cannot express my gratitude. I learned more in my conversations with Paul at Louie's, Burgersmith, and Community Coffee than I did in any archive.

Anything worthwhile in this book was inspired by him. Even when I felt that I no longer could keep my head above water, he assured me that I was doing important work and that I was equal to the task. Paul sharpened my arguments and made me see avenues of research that I had not even considered. Moreover, he pushed me into using maps to make my data easier for the general public to understand, something that makes this work much better. Everything good that has happened in my career thus far, I credit to him. He is not just my mentor, he is also my friend. Paul, thank you.

I also had the good fortune to have many colleagues who were a constant source of support throughout this process. Adam Pratt waded through an avalanche of statistics, reading parts of this work as it was being written, and providing me with valuable feedback. Michael Robinson, Nathan Buman, and Kat Sawyer were always available to just sit down and talk, either about our work or about the trials and tribulations of academia. Chris Childers served as a shining example of what it means to be a scholar, and if my work is half as good as his recent book I will have accomplished a great deal. Katie Eskridge had the pleasure of sharing an office with me, and I am sure that she is scarred for life from that experience. I hope that you can still smell the McDonald's french fries I insisted on eating in the office just to drive you crazy. Finally, Jason Wolfe, and his wife Ali, made my time in Baton Rouge not just instructive, but fun. Even as we have gone on our separate career paths, their continued friendship has been more valuable to me than I will ever be able to express.

At this point, most authors writing their acknowledgments take the time to thank all of the libraries and archives that they worked in, and I am no different. As part of this book, I performed research that was taxing not just to me but to the staff of the archives. Retrieving rolls of microfilm constantly just to see me find only one issue of a newspaper and returning it must have been frustrating to the staff. But the staff of the Mississippi State Archives, the Alabama State Archives, and the Texas State Archives, not only did this work with a smile on their face, they went out of their way to make suggestions of archival sources in their repositories that could be of use to me. The staff of the archives of the Harvard Business School taught me the ins and outs of the R. G. Dun collection, which this book could not have been written without. The staff at facilities such as this do not get half of the credit and thanks that they truly deserve. Moreover, I had the help of a very talented cartographer to create the maps and charts that are at the heart of this book. While I have never met Mary Lee Eggart, I will be forever in your debt.

While the ink was still drying on my diploma, the History Department at the University of Texas of the Permian Basin took me on as a Senior Lecturer. Derek Catsam, Ana Martinez-Catsam, Roland Spickermann, Diana Hinton, Chad Vanderford, and Lanita Akins plucked me out of a pile of applicants, and for that, I will always be grateful. While lecturers are supposed to focus on teaching, they all encouraged me to push forward and finish this book. Diana Hinton even gave me money from her research funds to finance one last trip to the Harvard Business School Archives, which was instrumental in finishing my work. Roland and his wife Loraine opened their home to my wife and me as we got acclimated to West Texas, while Derek and Ana always had time to check in on me, and on my progress, and talk about what it meant to be a historian in academia today. My biggest regret is not being able to spend more time getting to know Chad Vanderford, who passed away as I was finishing this manuscript. We both came out of the same program at LSU, and our talks about football and politics will always stay with me. Now secure in an assistant professorship and working on the tenure track, I know I will always have the department's support and encouragement.

Outside of the History Department I have many very dear friends here at UTPB. The English Department has been wonderful to me. Nichole Rougeau-Vanderford and Clark Moreland listened to me vent on many occasions, while my next-door neighbor, Sheena Stief, not only put up with my insanity, she indexed this book. Dan and Michelle Keast, and Frank and Karen Eychaner, all have helped me grow and develop into the teacher and writer I am today through many nights at the local beer garden. A special mention needs to be made here to four of my best friends here in the Petroplex, Bill and Rachel Harlow, and John and Laurie Wilks. You four have helped me through all of the ups and downs that come with a job like this, and I will always value sitting on the back porch of one of your homes discussing the absurdity that is life. I suppose I can even overlook their A&M ties, as we still beat them in football every year. All in all, I have found a home here at UTPB.

I would also like to thank the LSU Press for taking on this project. Rand Dotson has been very supportive of my work. I was always worried about how I was going to deal with the large amount of data that I used in this book. His suggestion of creating a website for the data was amazing, and having that outlet to discuss the book has really helped me to get my ideas out to the public. He also stuck with me when this manuscript took longer to complete than I originally thought it would. Also, I now understand the importance of a good copyeditor, and Gary Von Euer has been amazing. He has enhanced this work in so many ways, and I will always be in his debt for his hard work on my behalf.

Of course, without my parents I would not be where I am today. My mother, Kathy, instilled in me from a very young age a love of reading that inspired me to join the academic world. I still would rather sit down and read a book than do almost anything else. She also believed that I could be anything I wanted to be and that I could accomplish any goal I set for myself. Mom, I would apologize here for all of the trouble I caused you growing up, but as we both know, I am not really sorry, as it was always fun. My love of the Civil War I have to credit to my father, Leo. I still have his copy of Bruce Catton's three-volume *The Army of the Potomac* sitting above my desk. I read it for the first time when I was around nine or ten years old and have returned to its pages many times over the years. Moreover, the example he set for me has made me the person I am today. Thus, if anyone reading this has a problem with how I act today, blame him. My brother, Dan, made my childhood eventful, if not fun, and his quiet, steady support means more to me than he will ever know. My in-laws, Peggy and Chester Proba, welcomed me into their home and made me part of the family, and for that I will always be grateful. A great deal of this manuscript was written in a recliner in the corner of their living room over the holidays that I spent there. Finally, to my sister-in-law Allison, my mother always told me that if I could not say anything nice, do not say anything at all, so . . .

Finally, to my wife Melissa, I do not know where to begin. She listened to me read aloud every single word in this book. She has supported me through this entire process as an editor, proofreader, and armchair psychologist. I moved us halfway across the country to pursue my dreams, from the winters of northwestern Pennsylvania to the summer heat of Louisiana to the desert of West Texas, and she never missed a beat. She has not made a single complaint about moving nor raised any questions about where. She has always been prepared for the next adventure; as long as we are together, it does not matter to her. I could not ask for a better companion. She is not only my wife, she is my best friend, and nothing I have ever strived for in my life could have been achieved without her help and support. Now, if she could just get the cats to leave the hamsters alone . . . in theory, our lives should be perfect, and in actual practice, they already are.

# INDUSTRIAL DEVELOPMENT AND MANUFACTURING IN THE ANTEBELLUM GULF SOUTH

# 1

## CLOUDED VISION

### Perceptions of Industry on the Eve of the War

Frederick Law Olmsted, the famous designer of New York City's Central Park, made his living before the Civil War as a writer of travel books, a very popular genre at the time. In the aftermath of the Compromise of 1850, many northerners were interested in what the South was really like. Henry Jarvis Raymond, the cofounder of the *New York Daily Times*, commissioned Olmsted to explore the South and write about what he experienced.[1] Because Olmsted supposedly "had no opinion on its [slavery's] economic merit," Raymond thought him well suited for this assignment.[2] Thus, on December 11, 1852, Olmsted began his journey south. As he sent his reports back he offered what he represented to be an accurate picture of what southern life was like and how the region functioned socially, politically, and economically. During his excursion he observed southern society and recorded his observations, showing slavery to be holding back southern progress at every turn. Olmsted's work became one of the most well-known and widely read accounts of the antebellum South. The North at this time was like a supersaturated solution just waiting for some crystal of information around which to solidify its opinion of the South. Olmsted's stories, which began to appear in the *New York Daily Times* in February 1854, confirmed northerners' views of southern ignorance and backwardness.

Olmsted was a product of his society and he did have preconceptions. He saw the free North and its society as virtuous and progressive and the slave-based society of the South as immoral and backward. Olmsted's travels were purported to have crossed the South, and "cross" it he

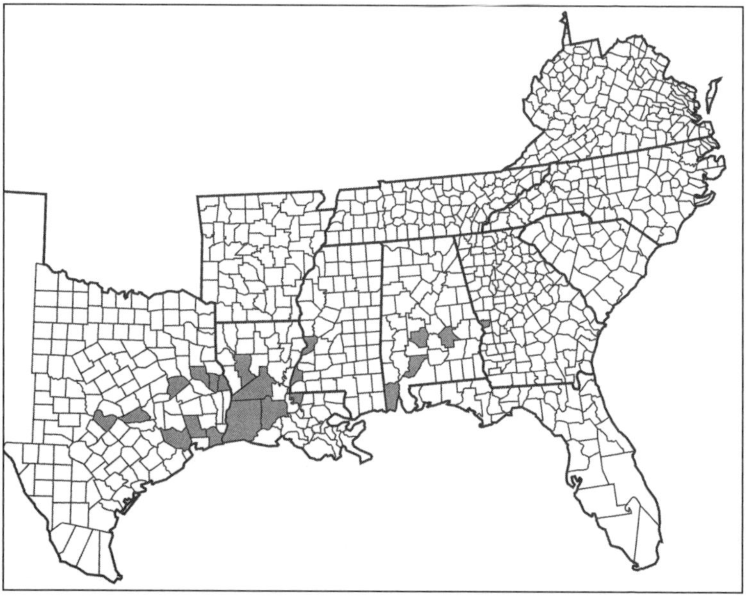

MAP 1.1. Counties Olmsted traveled through according to his accounts.
*Source:* Olmsted, *The Cotton Kingdom*, passim.

did. But he really experienced very little of the region (see Map 1.1). He traveled to perhaps forty counties in the slave states, less than 5 percent of the total number of counties in these states. Yet he drew conclusions about all of southern slave society from his tiny bit of exposure to it. Moreover, northerners, who had no experience with the South, believed his reports.

He did find some of what he saw in his travels to be commendable. For example, the nicest house in the Alabama hill country was owned by a man who was a marked exception to Olmsted's conception of a typical southerner: he grew no cotton, owned a sawmill, was the postmaster for the local area, and had been in the state legislature.[3] Passing through Montgomery, Alabama, he commented on how pleasant and prosperous the town was, but asserted that its happy condition resulted from the fact that most of the people living there were northern- or foreign-born.[4] But for the most part, Olmsted found everything about the South to be deplorable. Mobile, populated mostly by southerners, presented a sharp contrast to Montgomery. Olmsted described it as a dirty town with very high prices. The city's only assets, its one hotel and the beginnings of a shipbuilding industry, were, of course, owned and operated by northern men or foreign-born merchants.[5] Similarly, San Augustine, Texas, settled by migrants from the lower South, was a filthy, drunken, violent place with no redeeming qualities at all.[6] Olmsted insisted that during all of his travels in East Texas he never saw a single person read and that the entire population was mired in ignorance.[7] One of the most important cities in the Southwest at this time, Vicksburg, barely rated a mention from Olmsted beyond a complaint about the condition of its dock facilities.[8] The city of Natchez was not any better, as "the houses and shops within the town are generally small, and always inelegant."[9] He stopped at no smaller towns or villages in Mississippi and none at all in Tennessee because all of the inhabitants there were in his estimation dirty, toothless, ignorant, or flea-ridden. Olmsted found what he was looking for in his travels, a region backward and blighted, lacking in virtue and industry. Of course, it was slavery that held the region back.

Later, at the Southern Commercial Convention in 1855, Albert Pike, an Arkansas newspaper editor, gave a speech warning that an agrarian South should not be dependent on the North for all of its manufactured goods.[10] His concern was not uncommon among southerners who saw the South as a region of large fields of cotton worked by slave labor, with little in the way of industry. One of the best-known accounts of the South written before the war is Hinton Helper's *The Impending Crisis*. Helper was adamant that slavery and slave owners were destroying the South economically and industrially and that, "in a commercial, mechanical, manufactural, financial, and literary point of view, we are helpless as babes."[11] Attacking his own home, his words carried more weight, making him a turncoat in the eyes of much of the white South.[12] His view was supported both by northern abolitionists, who saw slavery as incompatible with industrial development, and southerners, who believed that industry disrupted the region's agricultural way of life.[13] In 1860, when recording census data for Attala County, Mississippi, Census Marshal James J. Durham described the underlying situation: "This is a country adapted to farming and but little of the Industrial pursuit is followed by our citizens."[14] For many, then, the South was an agrarian paradise and industry was something to be pursued at a later date, should that prove necessary. As historian Ronald Lewis observed, "The roar of a blast furnace, or the din of a cotton factory, was more likely to jar the southern imagination than to capture it, given the South's traditional idealization of itself as an Arcadian paradise."[15] Thus the moonlight and magnolia image of the South, popularized in *Gone With the Wind*, has long been the commonly held view of the antebellum South. But is it correct?

Others at the time, such as Thomas Kettell, a magazine editor and author in the 1850s, believed the South was making strides in its development, even if the North was getting rich from manufacturing and marketing southern cotton. Southerners had a great deal of capital available, and the raw materials that they exported could be used by local firms instead. Also, manufactured items imported by the South could be made at home for a domestic market that already existed. Kettell asserted that "the figures show that it [the South] is fast supplanting Northern and imported goods with its own industry."[16] Moreover, he insisted, if the North worked to end slavery, the economic disturbances caused by abolition would cripple both sections.[17] His ideas appeared in other works, such as that of J. D. B. De Bow, and circulated widely throughout the region and the nation.[18]

In the same vein as Kettell, De Bow was an antebellum southern industrial booster. *De Bow's Review*, one of the most widely circulated journals in the region, published many articles on the benefits of developing the South's nascent industrial capacity. In February 1850, for example, De Bow printed an article from "A Mississippi Planter," who stated: "*The South ought to supply the North with Cotton manufactures;* and it is a matter of wonder, that northern capitalists have not availed themselves of the superior advantages offered them in the cotton growing regions for manufacturing purposes."[19] The planter went on to explain:

> As it is, a planter desires a bale of cotton made into cloth. He gins and bales it, drags it, often, sixty or seventy miles to a shipping

> point; it goes to New Orleans, thence to Boston, and finally to Lowell. It is manufactured, sent back to Boston, thence to New Orleans, thence to the point of original shipment, and is once more hauled through the mud to the cabin of the planter.[20]

Both De Bow and this planter clearly saw great potential for southern manufacturing. De Bow also published a three-volume work on industry in the South based on the 1850 census, of which he was superintendent, which indicated that manufacturing was developing in the region. He even created a plan for planters to encourage industry by assigning a certain number of hands to manufacturing to keep them from sitting idle during off seasons, thereby doubling the value of their labor.[21] At least some southerners, then, saw industry as vital to the South and believed that the area's economic system could support development without causing any major upheaval. But if this was true, why has the *Gone With the Wind* view of the South become so entrenched and persistent?

The image of a rusticated, unindustrialized South was not confined to Americans before the war. John Cairnes, an Englishman, wrote that slavery and manufacturing were incompatible in the South and that industry was "at variances with the best interests, material as well as moral, of its inhabitants."[22] Slaves could never be used in industry, Cairnes asserted, because of the fear of revolt by large gatherings of such workers.[23] In the end, this prewar vision of the South disappeared into the smoke of the Civil War and came out the other side confirmed, even strengthened; the South had no industry at all.

To counter the pastoral image of the South and change minds in hopes of drumming up business, many southern manufacturers used newspapers to urge industrialization. But they fought against a very strong current when they published their pleas for the South to embrace manufacturing. Southern firms tried to convince consumers that goods manufactured at home were just as good as anything being produced in the North. A Houston, Texas, newspaper ran at the top of its advertisement section a banner reading, "ENCOURAGE Southern Manufactures!"[24] Other papers in the region printed advertisements containing personal statements from owners of manufacturing concerns asking for customers to support southern industry, such as, "Hurrah For Home Manufacture! Certain Downfall of Abolitionism!"[25] One manufacturer went so far as to call northern-made goods a "sham" when compared to southern products, while another explained: "We know that strong efforts are being made to prejudice the minds of the people against all manufacturing establishments South of Mason and Dixon's line, but if purchasers will give our Furniture an impartial examination, we feel assured that the style and price will satisfy them that it is to their interest to patronize home institutions."[26]

Many southerners thought that these manufacturers were aberrations to be tolerated in small numbers but would never really affect the region's society or economy. Perhaps the perceived marginalization of manufacturing suggests that southern industry and society did not possess the "creative tension" needed to develop a southern manufacturing sector.[27] But, the South fought four years of civil war, and it needed industry to do so.

The extent of the South's industrial base on the eve of the Civil War needs to be reexamined. This can be done by going beyond the 1860 census numbers to show how extensive its industry truly was. If there were more manufacturing firms than the census and the Old South's conventional wisdom suggests, it would change our understanding of how the late antebellum southern economy functioned and allow a reevaluation of the presumed depressive effect that the South's slavery system had on industrialization. In fact, industrial concerns were just as important to the antebellum South as they were to any other part of the nation. Further, these firms were not aberrations on the southern landscape; they were firmly integrated into southern society. Manufacturing firms, much as farms or plantations, did not exist in an economic or environmental vacuum devoid of context. That is, they existed and operated in and over a large geographic region, and therefore a geographical perspective is the most appropriate one from which to study them.

In 1860, the Gulf South was the richest part of the region. The capital needed for industry existed in states such as Alabama, Mississippi, and Texas. By studying these states we can determine the nature and scope of manufacturing and consider it in geographic and statistical terms.[28]

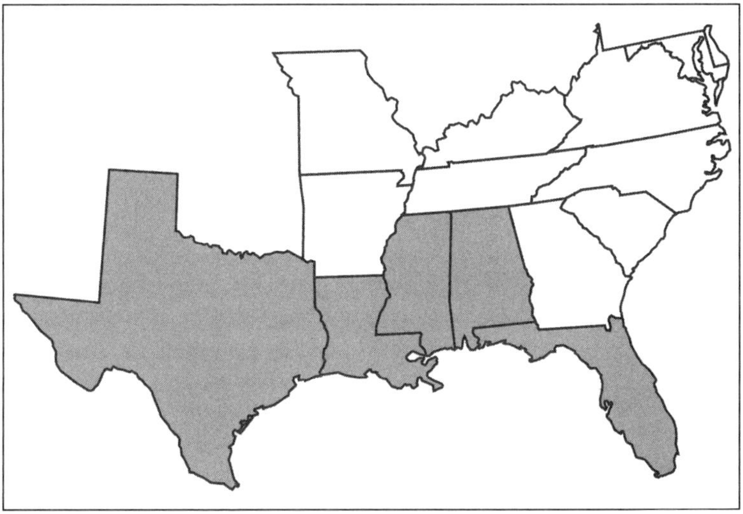

MAP 1.2. The Gulf South as a subset of the slave states in 1860, including the states focused on here—Alabama, Mississippi, and Texas.

The Gulf South was a relatively homogenous area. Map 1.2 shows these states in relation to the rest of the slave states in 1860. All had similar patterns of development and extensive ties with one another and the rest of the South.[29] Thus, by looking at manufacturing geographically, we can determine how industrial concerns interacted with each other and analyze the relationships that existed between the location of manufacturing establishments and markets, resources, and transportations facilities.[30]

The Gulf South, like the rest of the nation, had varying degrees of industry. In places where intensive industrialization occurred, it depended upon the availability of transportation facilities, markets, complementary concerns, labor, and the presence of exploitable resources, such as coal and iron, and, in the case of textile manufacturing, cotton. Most development in a given area was externally stimulated and "typically leads to a concentration of investments upon one or two areas."[31] The existence of these factors is most readily appreciated when considered geographically. Maps produced with Geographical Information System

(GIS) software can display these relationships and concentrations while also showing the actual extent of industry in these states.[32]

GIS analysis has not traditionally been turned to the question of antebellum southern industrialization, as it has been to study southern agriculture. But whether industry or agriculture, "discussion or analysis of any area of substantial size is made easier through the simple act of studying it piece by piece."[33] Moreover, a further advantage to such an approach is that "The field of cartography is not limited to showing graphic representations of reality; it offers other types of maps whose versatility permits display of a wide variety of quantitative information, not simply numbers of people or animals, or amounts of crops, but of abstractions, such as ratios, densities, and proportions."[34]

The reluctance of historians to adopt this approach has deprived them of some obvious benefits, and by taking advantage of what GIS-generated maps can offer, we can find new insights into southern industry.

The South was not an industrial juggernaut capable of matching the output of the northern states in 1860; "southern industrial accomplishments should not be exaggerated [and] any evaluation of the region's industrial achievements or its capability at the time of secession hinges crucially on the reference standard."[35] The standard by which to judge the industrial capacity of the South will not solely be that of the North. The main standard used will be the traditional view of the South, first drawn before the war and preserved by historians to form our current picture of what the South was before the conflict.[36] Lewis's characterization of the southern imagination has become ingrained in the scholarship of southern industry, and any attempt to alter this view must deal with how this happened.

Most portrayals done after the war show a prostrate South, completely destroyed by the Union army. That view is changing, though, as the destruction of agriculture, public property, and railroads was not nearly as extensive as many believed.[37] But southern industry was in a shambles because of targeted violence by Union forces and overuse, and it took decades to recover.[38] The most convenient explanation, though, was not the problems created by the war, but the slave-based society of the former Confederate states. Also, southerners had to deal with the psychological trauma of being the only Americans to be on the losing side of the war.[39] Taken together, these points developed into a drive to explain all the problems of the postwar South in such a way as to allow the reintegration of the region into mainstream American society. So, very early on a solution to these problems was created: the "Lost Cause" narrative and Ulrich B. Phillips's school on the history of slavery.

The "Lost Cause" mythology took root immediately after the end of the war as a way of coping with defeat. The earliest use of this term was in an 1866 book by Edward Alfred Pollard. Pollard, using the 1860 census returns as his data set, described a South that was outnumbered and outproduced at the outset of the struggle.[40] But in Pollard's opinion, the war still had to be fought in defense of principles: "Two great political schools of American—that of the Consolidation and that of the States Rights—were founded on different estimates of the relations of the General Government of the States. All other controversies in the political history of the country were subordinate and incidental to this great division of parties."[41]

Historians who subscribed to this view of the region ignored any existing manufacturing because the South was destined to lose anyway. The "Lost Cause" became so ingrained in the South after the war that southern apologists never considered industry, because there was no need to look at something that had not existed.[42] Because of this belief, and the industrial backwardness of the postwar South, historians ignored manufacturing in the antebellum South for almost one hundred years.

Next, U. B. Phillips's work on American slavery became the standard for how slavery, slaves, and slave owners were viewed. Phillips believed that slavery was a backward economic system and that, given time, it would have collapsed under its own weight.[43] The South's slave-based economy was stuck in a never-ending cycle in which owners used their money to buy land and slaves, which they then used to make more money, which in turn was further invested in additional land and slaves.[44] As far as Phillips was concerned there was nothing more worthwhile to invest in than slaves in the antebellum South.[45] Slavery therefore held back southern industrial development because no one with money to invest placed their capital willingly in manufacturing. Phillips's view kept intact the traditional view of the South as an agrarian paradise. Also, this explained why so little economic development occurred in the immediate postwar South, and why so few manufacturing concerns, such as cotton mills, were founded before the 1880s: "Planters did not take kindly to manufacturing; their rural habits of life ran against it—possibly they had the tribeman's instinctive dislike for unaccustomed ways."[46] The agricultural focus of slave owners made the South backward, which carried over to make the postwar South just as backward.

But industry did exist in the antebellum South. The only problem with southern manufacturing before the war was that it lagged far behind that in the North. Capital investment in the South in 1860 was on the same level as that of the North in 1850 and was continuing to grow.[47] Unfortunately, the South has never really been considered in any way other than in a direct comparison to the North. This does nothing to show the development of southern industry, but just that it was not as strong as its northern counterpart. The dichotomy between the views of Hawk and Beard in the study of southern industry can be seen throughout the historiography of antebellum southern industry. Discerning which side is correct is one of the driving forces behind this work.

Scholars have generally studied the subject of southern industry in two ways. The earlier approach was qualitative, even anecdotal, in character, exemplified by Eugene Genovese's *Political Economy of Slavery*.[48] Genovese argued that the South's slave-based economy was precapitalist and was incapable of becoming industrialized like the North.[49] His contention became widely accepted and has held back the study of southern manufacturing, as it explained very neatly how the South lost the war and preserved its agrarian traditions. Genovese's work, and others like it, looked at small parts of the southern industrial base, focusing on the writings during the prewar period, including industrialists, newspaper editors, and slave owners, as they explained their perceptions of manufacturing.[50] Although these monographs provided an idea of how some southerners viewed industry, their lack of a large quantitative statistical base of evidence does not afford a systematic, comprehensive view of the extent and intensity of manufacturing in the South.

In a second, later approach, historians did compile quantitative data to study the antebellum South. This data reinforced the idea that the South was held back by its slave-based economy. The South's staple crops flowed out of the region for the purchase of goods and services, while the North supplied the South with transportation, marketing, insurance, and industrial goods.[51] All the South needed was a few places along its borders to gather and ship out cotton and sugar.[52] These statistics then confirmed Genovese's view. Beginning in the 1950s and 1960s, cliometrics was turned to the study of antebellum southern economics and slavery and historians began to alter the traditional view.[53] Robert Fogel and Stanley Engerman's painstaking work, *Time on the Cross*, showed slavery to be extremely profitable, and thus it was not going to disappear on its own.[54] Moreover, slaves made good agricultural workers and their labor created a large amount of wealth for their owners. Even though the South was an agricultural area, "its manufacturing and trade were highly enough developed to place it among the forefront of nations in these respects."[55] Unfortunately, because the South was so far behind the North in industry and commerce, many dismissed this development as inconsequential. Statistics now were being applied to the study of the antebellum southern economy, but the old disagreements still cropped up.

But numbers paint a different picture. For example, there were large numbers of slaves living in southern cities. These urban slaves could be, and were, used as industrial workers by southern industrialists even though many white urban residents felt uncomfortable about their presence in the workplace.[56] Further, southern planters worked to create slave-based manufacturing concerns in the region, investing surplus capital in these firms. Thus, slaves were well suited for industrial pursuits. But at times, the need for agricultural labor made the cost of workers for manufacturing concerns too high, stunting industrial growth.[57] Overall, then, we are back to where we started in the earliest historiography of southern industry. The South, because of a myriad of reasons related to slavery, did not have an industrial base from which to fight the Civil War. But after the Panic of 1837, planters invested in industry, at least locally, to attempt to keep from ever going through something like the Panic again. Moreover, the full extent and results of this investment have never been systematically studied in detail for the entire Gulf South.[58]

Thus, southern planters, who controlled most of the region's capital, had a choice to make: purchase more land and slaves or invest in other concerns and diversify their holdings. Many planters took the first option more often, because it proved safer and better known, and so, "the Southern economy grew, but it did not develop."[59] Southern agriculture produced more per capita in 1860 than in 1800, but the increase resulted from better organization and the larger size of plantations, not from the adoption of new machines or techniques.[60] The South, perhaps, did not want or need to keep up with the changes the North so readily adopted.

Gavin Wright's work, *Old South, New South: Revolutions in the Southern Economy Since the Civil War,* echoes these views. Wright argues that southerners favored investment in highly mobile objects, slaves, that could move with their owners and shaped southern investment patterns, as "Slave owners had little attachment or loyalty to local areas."[61] With that mindset, investment in things that could not be moved to follow the progress of cotton, such as industrial firms, did not appeal to these men, stunting growth in the region, something that a larger view of southern industry bears out. Moreover, Wright shows that the effects of this investment had far-reaching implications for the region. To really understand how historians studied industry, though, we need to return to the first real statistical studies of the subject.

Bateman and Weiss undertook the first systematic cliometric study of southern industry in their now classic book, *A Deplorable Scarcity: The Failure of Industrialization in the Slave Economy.*[62] While not the last book to be written chronologically, this work, and others in the same vein by this pair, became the accepted view of the level of industrialization in the antebellum South.[63] Because of this, a detailed look at how they came to their conclusions is important to any work on antebellum southern manufacturing. As they state, the study of southern industry before this work "evolved more from historiographical inferences than from direct examination or analysis of this region's industrial status before the Civil War."[64] Bateman and Weiss, as the title of their book suggests, concluded that the South did not have a large industrial base because slavery inhibited its formation by diverting capital and talent from manufacturing to plantation agriculture, making slave-based agriculture the driving force in the southern economy.[65] But southern industrial firms were, overall, small, making them easy to overlook when studying the area. Thus, careful work is needed to discover all of the manufacturing concerns in the region.

The South did have industry before the war but lagged far behind the North. This imbalance worsened after the war. According to Bateman and Weiss, this disparity suggested that something was fundamentally wrong with the antebellum southern economy.[66] For example, at the beginning of the Civil War, the South and the West were relatively equal in their levels of industrialization. During and after the conflict, though, the West surged ahead while the South became a backwater. Before the conflict, "there is little to suggest that the West was poised to become a major industrial region while the South was destined to remain dependent on agriculture."[67] They put forward six reasons as to why the South's industrial development was so stunted: limited market size, the comparative advantage of agriculture, social and political barriers, slavery, entrepreneurial inability, and income distribution.[68]

The availability of markets proved an important consideration for southern industrialists. If they could not sell what they produced, they would quickly go out of business. If the market size was too small, manufacturing may have been stunted. All manufacturers, not just southern ones, faced this problem. Smaller markets caused industry not to operate at full capacity at all times, but that does not mean that firms could not operate.[69] Southern industry was being built up around local consumption; there was very little need for external support and markets for this level of development.[70] Although concerns in the South did not, for the most part, take full advantage of economies of scale, very few places anywhere in the country at this time did, so market size did not hold back southern manufacturing.[71] Also, as Bateman and Weiss pointed out: "Virtually nothing is known regarding the structure of industrial markets before the Civil War."[72]

Southern manufacturing faced many other obstacles that Bateman and Weiss studied in great detail. They wrote about the problems caused by monopolies, which were detrimental to development because the lack of competition slowed innovation. Monopolies, though, were common throughout the nation before the war, and industry continued to expand and capital and labor were both available in sufficient quantities to support manufacturing.[73] Planters, however, who controlled much of the region's labor and capital, had to be willing to support industry.[74] Slaves were a form of both capital and labor, and while there were some drawbacks to this system, it could easily coexist with industrial development.[75] In the end, after numerous reasons were considered as to why industrial development was slow, slavery was yet again the answer that a new generation of historians settled on to explain why manufacturing was not as developed in the South as it was in the North. This conclusion is not surprising based on how industry and economic development have been studied by historians. Slavery was not supposed to be modern enough to support industrial development. As Walter Johnson so succinctly explains, "it is hard to think about slavery as capitalism . . . slavery is, in some sense, 'unthinkable' in the historical terms that frame western political economy."[76]

Many people in the antebellum United States believed that slaves could not perform industrial tasks, or that enslaved workers stopped native whites or immigrants from wanting to do the same work. Slaves, however, were good industrial workers for the firms that used them.[77] For example, the Tredegar Iron Works, in Richmond, Virginia, used slaves alongside white workers profitably and was one of the largest manufacturers of its kind in the nation.[78] Now perhaps slave labor was overcapitalized. Once a slave was purchased you could not lay them off during slow times, they had to be taken care of forever or sold, and capital, as a result, became tied up in the labor force. As Bateman and Weiss explain, "Proponents of one of the most enduring arguments accounting for Southern industrial backwardness claim that by absorbing Southern savings, slavery prevented accumulation of nonhuman capital and inhibited the emergence of a large manufacturing sector."[79] Overcapitalization decreased the amount of money available for investment, but not enough to stop southern industrialization.[80] Moreover, slavery was not going to end. Other uses for slave labor would be found to keep it alive, or conditions would change in some unforeseeable way, because "both slavery and free labor met the demands of entrepreneurs for flexibility."[81]

Overall, as argued in *A Deplorable Scarcity*, there were few obvious reasons for industry not to have developed in the South: the rates of return on manufacturing investments were high, there were sufficient markets, protection from outside competition existed, scale was not a problem, and labor and capital were available.[82] So finally, Bateman and Weiss concluded that there should have been more industry in the antebellum South than was present, and the only explanation for the lack of industrial investment came from slaveholders themselves. They poured all of their capital into land and slaves. U. B. Phillips's refrain was repeating itself in a new form.[83] As Bateman and Weiss succinctly explain, "While the South was not merely so devoid of industry as conventionally believed, it no doubt could have done better. That it did not, largely reflects upon the behavior of southern investors."[84]

There are, however, problems with their work. Bateman and Weiss used the 1860 manufacturing census, both the published compilation and the original manuscript schedules, to create their data set. They believed the census was the most complete set of data available to study the extent of southern industrialization.[85] They created two samples from this data, a primary one of two hundred concerns for each state, and a secondary one of the top 1 percent of all firms, based on production in each state, with a minimum of twenty concerns selected. Moreover, they assumed that the census did not omit any significant number of firms and that their sample was therefore truly representative of the total number of manufacturers.[86] They used these samples not just for *A Deplorable Scarcity*, but for many other works as well.

Omission of establishments by enumerators in the manuscript schedule of manufacturing was unlikely to have occurred randomly. Consequently, a random sample drawn from the census of manufacturers would unavoidably reproduce omissions of establishments and therefore not fairly reflect the actual number of manufacturing firms and the intensity of manufacturing in the South. Bateman and Weiss also excluded many categories, especially primary processing firms, from their work because such enterprises were not industrial in their opinion, while others, such as ginning, sugar refining, and rice cleaning, because they were done on plantations, went unreported completely.[87] Bateman and Weiss questioned many parts of the original census records, such as capital figures, wages, and employees, and also the accuracy of the census summaries compiled from the manuscript census, but they did not ask if there were any industrial firms missing.[88] They explained away the errors they found: "In some cases, census errors cancel each other out while in others they compound themselves. Indeed, it is our judgment that the samples themselves provide a better description of the parent population than do the published census summaries."[89] Moreover, Bateman and Weiss also believed that this data could be used for many different applications, such as an exploration of market development in the antebellum South.[90]

Some historians have debated the validity of Bateman and Weiss's sample, and the use of sampling, in general.[91] Richard Vedder and Lowell Gallaway questioned the use of a sample when the information for the entire population was readily available and suggested that the sample seemed to be skewed toward helping Bateman and Weiss make their case.[92] Others question not the sample itself, but Bateman and Weiss's starting assumptions, because they "based their exploration on a wage-labor driven, Northern-derived understanding of industrialization that does not fully consider a mix of free and enslaved labor."[93] Moreover, *A Deplorable Scarcity* did not take into account the geographic location of the firms studied. Industrial firms are not just numbers on a chart; they relate to one another over space and grow in relationship to each other. Bateman and Weiss ignored these relationships completely. Engerman asks: "The data for 1840 and 1860 are, by now, familiar, as is their [Bateman and Weiss] interpretations . . . . Are there any other regional data which can be used for suggestive inferences on Southern growth?"[94] The answer to Engerman's question is emphatically yes, and, for reasons listed above, a more detailed look at all of the available data on southern industry is warranted. This work provides that closer, more detailed look. Bateman and Weiss's sample is not representative of the industry that actually existed and is skewed toward the larger manufacturing establishments that census takers found easier to find and record. Bateman and Weiss themselves lament that, "No one has ever completely told the story of the transformation from an agrarian to an industrial economy."[95] Now this narrative will be written. First will be a review of the manufacturing firms that existed in 1860, not just from the census records, but from all available sources. Then a review needs to be done of the base this industry was built upon and how manufacturing developed in the region. Finally, the true value of this industry can be discussed, showing how important it was to southern society. Moreover, all of this will be done from a geographic perspective.

R. Ogilvie Buchanan, in his landmark work of economic geography, stated: "Man himself decides which, if any, of the possibilities he will attempt to exploit, and how, if at all, he will attempt to overcome the difficulties."[96] The South used slave labor to overcome its labor difficulties, and in the opinion of many, held back industrial development. A finding that more industry than previously believed existed in the antebellum South has a significance for historians' understanding of how the late antebellum southern economy functioned and creates a need to reevaluate the presumed depressive effect that the South's slavery system had on industrialization. Moreover, the advantages of studying antebellum industry by applying a historical geographic approach using GIS are manyfold, as "economic development shows the combined effect of physical environment, technology, and social institutions."[97] Bateman and Weiss believed that the "roots of retardation had indeed been planted before the Civil War," and many other historians concurred that it was not until after the war that a "New" South developed, one more open to modern ways and industrial development.[98] Richard Brown agreed, explaining, "Modern America is generally said to have emerged some time between 1865 and the First World War, the decades when telegraphy and the railroads reached full development and when the ascendancy of the national government became secure."[99] John Majewski saw an antebellum

South full of "economic black holes" caused by slavery.[100] But more recently, historians, including Lewis, Steven Collins, and Jonathan Wells, have shown that the "New" South had extensive prewar roots.[101] This work will contribute to our understanding of the origins of this industrial "New" South, one that began its development well before the outbreak of hostilities, living by industrialist William Gregg's motto of "The Plow, the Anvil, and the Loom."[102]

# 2

## GULF SOUTH INDUSTRIAL FIRMS

### Location, Organization, and Ownership

Speaking before the pivotal 2nd session of the 36th Congress on January 15, 1861, Representative John Reagan of Texas explained the benefits that the South would receive by leaving the Union. "It will compel us," he stated, "to manufacture for ourselves, to build up our own commerce, our own great cities, our own railroads and canals."[1] Based on the returns from the 1860 census, Reagan's reasoning was correct. The South did not have a great deal of industry. But, like many politicians, perhaps the representative did not really understand what was going on back home as he served in Washington, DC. Much of the Gulf South was a frontier area in 1860 when the census was taken. According to the compiled returns, many parts of the region had no manufacturing to speak of, and the areas that did report industrial firms had very few. Southerners, though, were rational economic actors, just like any other people across the nation. Migrants moved to the Gulf South to create a better life for themselves and their families. They needed manufactured goods to run their farms and businesses, and many discovered that they could make things for themselves, and for others, rather than pay the cost to have necessary items shipped from the more industrialized East. A man named T. Suggs, in Palestine, Texas, where Reagan made his home, took advantage of this need, as his steam sawmill was "selling all lumber they can make."[2] This case study shows a larger trend in Gulf South manufacturing on the eve of the war that Reagan would have applauded, if he had taken the time to look for it.[3]

Reagan, and earlier Olmsted, however, were wrong. Many cities and towns in the South boasted cultural amenities and manufacturing firms. Those who believed that the South was developing, such as J. D. B. De Bow, reported on firms being founded throughout the region. De Bow believed that "no country has ever acquired permanent wealth by exporting its unmanufactured products," and thus he pushed for industrial development in the South.[4] Another industrial booster and a textile mill owner himself, William Gregg, touted the importance of the textile industry: "cotton manufacturers have been the pioneers which have introduced and given impetus to all other branches of mechanism in Great Britain, the continent, and this country."[5] These manufacturing endeavors were beginning to alter the southern landscape. Machines transformed the relationship between workers and employers and even the concept of labor itself.[6] The antebellum South underwent rapid economic development, and that tide of development eroded political and cultural opposition to industrial enterprise.[7]

Before any real discussion of manufacturing in the Gulf South can begin, though, there needs to be some discussion of terminology. *Manufacturing* and*industry,* in many places in this study, will be used relatively interchangeably. This is because the Gulf South was an economy in a state of flux. The region was undergoing industrial development. The term *development* alone suggests a system in a state of change, with no clear picture of what it will become. Thus, some of the firms listed would, as in any society, grow into larger firms, especially when undergoing the stresses of war, while others, who did not take advantage of new developments, would fade away. The term *industrial* may suggest new machines and new technologies to many people, but there is little way of knowing what machines and technologies these firms were using. Based on advertisements in southern newspapers, technology was available for most lines of business, and at least some took advantage.[8] Thus, while the census may list a saddler or a shoemaker, businesses that have existed for hundreds of years, the description does not go beyond that as record keepers were still coming to grips with how to collect data on this new and developing part of American society. The census at this time did not differentiate all of these concerns, which appeared on the same ledgers, and so this work will consider them all to be a part of industry

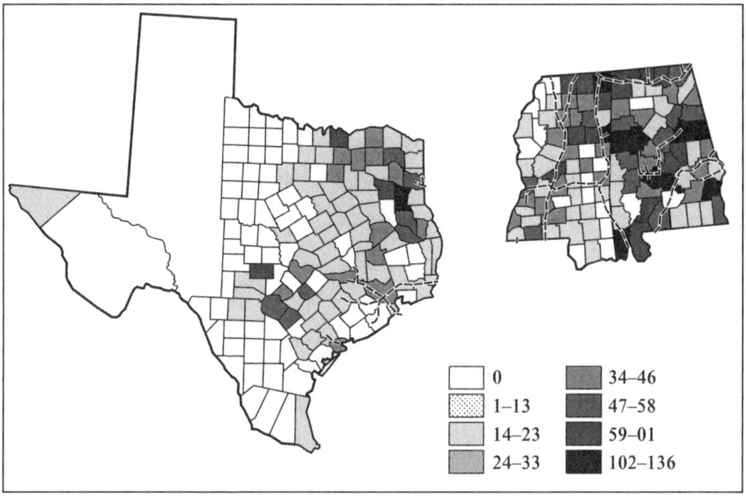


MAP 2.1. Manufacturing firms listed in the 1860 Census for Alabama, Mississippi, and Texas.
*Source:* Census of 1860 Manufacturing Schedules.

in the antebellum Gulf South. What we do know is that the level of production needed to be listed in the census goes beyond home production and perhaps plants the seeds of an industrial future.

Informed observers of the antebellum South considered "the census of 1860 [to be] a proper and suitable starting point" for studying the industrial base of the region.[9] Map 2.1 shows the locations of industrial firms across most of the Gulf South, based on the 1860 manufacturing census schedules. This map depicts a region scarcely devoid of manufacturing concerns. Manufactories engaged in many lines of business, including foundries, machine shops, clothing manufacturers, and a large variety of mills. Many of these concerns were located on railroad lines and in market centers, helping southern towns and cities to grow into economic centers. Urban areas in turn contributed to the growth of these firms by affording them readily accessible markets. Although the South had far fewer firms than the North, this map shows that industrial enterprise was anything but scarce in the Gulf South. But while the census found more industry than Olmsted reported on in his travels,

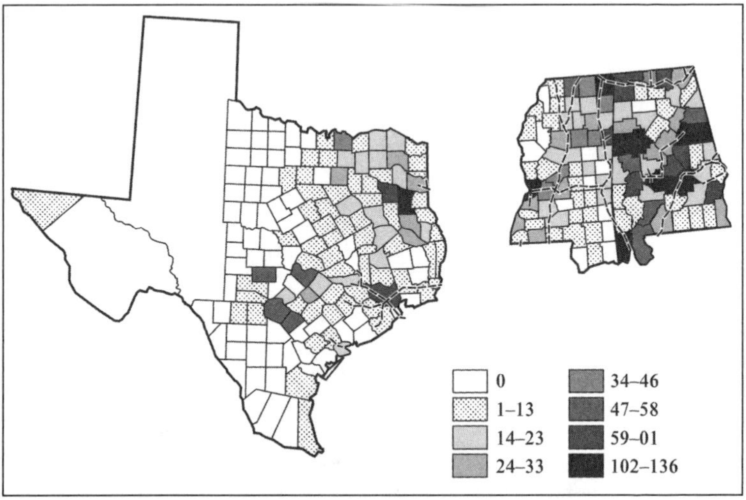


MAP 2.2. Manufacturing firms in 1860, derived from all sources.
*Sources:* Census of 1860 Manufacturing Schedules, newspapers, county directories, journals, and the R. G. Dun Credit Reports.

the South, when compared to other parts of the country, nevertheless seemed like an industrial "Sahara."[10]

Even though census marshals supposedly performed their duties "with fidelity and zeal," historians discovered many problems with the 1860 census enumerations.[11] Some census takers simply missed firms that operated in their assigned areas, while other unaccounted-for concerns were in locations that the marshals never reached. Moreover, some firm owners attempted to evade the census because they feared what the information would be used for, such as future attempts at taxation by the federal government.[12] These deficiencies resulted in an undercounting of manufacturing firms in the Gulf South and, it follows, an understatement of the region's industrial capacity. Although missing from the census returns, the identities of many of these unenumerated firms are recoverable through the use of other, contemporaneous, sources such as newspapers, city directories, credit reports, and local histories.

The 1860 census lists 3,280 manufacturing firms in Alabama, Mississippi, and Texas. When the 788 firms found in other sources are added to the census concerns, the new total is 4,068, an increase of 19.4 percent over the total reported in the census records alone. The geography presented by Map 2.2 is a composite picture of manufacturing in the Gulf South, based on evidence drawn from every reliable source in addition to the census.[13] This map reveals that industry in the Gulf South was more widespread than suggested by the census.

There were counties in the Gulf South for which few, if any, records of manufacturing are available. Newspapers were lost to fires, floods, or carelessness, and some firms may never have been recorded at all in any source. If anything, the number of industrial concerns, as shown in the map and in Table 2.1, most likely understates the extent of manufacturing in the region.

Table 2.2 provides a breakdown of how some of these new firms were listed in the available sources. As the table shows, there is not a great deal of overlap among the census, newspaper advertisements, and the Dun reports. Thus, most of the firms listed in sources other than the

TABLE 2.1. Manufacturing firms in 1860

| | Census | Other sources | Total |
|---|---|---|---|
| Alabama | 1,407 (76.3%) | 436 (23.7%) | 1,843 |
| Mississippi | 882 (82.9%) | 182 (17.1%) | 1,064 |
| Texas | 991 (85.4%) | 170 (14.6%) | 1,161 |
| Total | 3,280 (80.6%) | 788 (19.4%) | 4,068 |

*Sources*: Census of 1860 Manufacturing Schedules, newspapers, county directories, journals, and the R. G. Dun Credit Reports.

*General note*: Numbers in parentheses are the percentage of each states' total number of firms, those enumerated by the census plus those found in noncensus sources. Thus, for example, 23.7 percent of Alabama's 1,843 firms were found in noncensus sources but were not listed in the census. See Appendix C, available at drmichaelfrawley.com, for a breakdown of firms omitted from the census by county for Alabama, Mississippi, and Texas.

TABLE 2.2. Synoptic table of firms listed and unlisted in census

| | Number of firms in census | Number of firms not in census but in newspaper | Number of firms not in census or newspaper but in R. G. Dun reports | Number of firms not in census but in newspaper and R. G. Dun reports |
|---|---|---|---|---|
| Alabama | 1,407 | 218 | 52 | 34 |
| Mississippi | 882 | 56 | 66 | 9 |
| Texas | 991 | 136 | 34 | 1 |
| Total | 3,280 | 410 | 152 | 44 |

*Sources:* Census of 1860 Manufacturing Schedules, newspapers, and the R. G. Dun Credit Reports.

census were those missed by the marshals. One reason for the omission of a firm from the census was the set of guidelines to be followed by the census marshals. Inclusion in the census required that a firm have an annual output of at least $500.[14] The purpose of that restriction, according to the marshal's instructions, was to exclude small household production from the manufacturing schedules, as well as firms not considered substantial enough to be recorded. To keep this production amount in perspective, we can look at the most well-known product of the antebellum South, cotton. The price of cotton in 1860 was about 13 cents per pound. According to the 1860 census the average bale of cotton weighed 400 pounds.[15] This means that one bale of cotton was worth about $52. To get to the $500 that a manufacturing firm had to produce to be included in the census, a cotton farmer would have had to grow just over nine-and-a-half bales. Thus, because newspaper advertisements and listings in the Dun reports did not include production numbers, marshals may have left out some of these firms intentionally because they did not reach the $500 threshold.

The listing of a firm in the Dun reports indicates that a business with an interest in a southern concern's credit-worthiness had asked the R. G. Dun Company to investigate.[16] Most likely, such southern firms were fairly substantial. That is, their business would have been producing at least $500 worth of products and therefore should have been in-

TABLE 2.3. Mobile, Alabama businesses in the Dun reports but omitted in the census, for 1860

| Company name | Line of business |
|---|---|
| Beach, Ela, & Company | Saddle and harness |
| A&S Metzgar | Carriages |
| Michael Hines | Machinist & blacksmith |
| Theo Byrnes | Saddler |
| JC McGuire | Blacksmith |
| F Winter & GB Miller | Furniture |
| EJ Rollings | Carriage maker |
| Mobile and Ohio Railroad | Railroad |
| Geo Spanagel | Furniture |
| Bowen & Gillman | Cabinetmaker |
| W Welch & Company | Carriage makers |
| GK Palmes | Coach maker |
| JF Jewett | Steam lumber mill |
| John Suter | Cabinetmaker |
| J Fichet | Shoes and leather |
| F Jones | Blacksmith |
| John Ryan | Shoemaker |
| JM & T Meaher | Sawmill and shipbuilding |
| JW Porter & Company | Sash and door factory |

*Sources:* Alabama, vol. 17, pp. 38–318, R. G. Dun & Co. Credit Report Volumes, Baker Library Historical Collections, Harvard Business School.

cluded in the census schedule. Moreover, the Dun reports have entries in them for counties about which the census recorded nothing, such as DeSoto and Coahoma counties in Mississippi, Clarke in Alabama, and Bosque and Brazoria in Texas. Credit reporters, it seems, were more willing to go into certain areas than were census marshals. Moreover, areas well represented in the census had many firms missed by marshals that were included in the reports of Dun's correspondents. For example, as Table 2.3 shows, the marshals missed nineteen firms in Mobile, Alabama, for which businessmen requested credit reports. For this reason, and others as well, the Dun reports are a valuable resource in any effort to reconstruct a record of the antebellum southern industrial base. Dun's efforts also provide a window into the character of industry in the Gulf South, especially about the ownership and forms of organization of industrial concerns.

Newspaper advertisements were relatively inexpensive. In 1860, the *Daily Confederation* of Montgomery, Alabama, for example, charged $5 to run a "1 square advertisement" for one month in its daily edition and $2.50 for one square for a month in its weekly edition.[17] Firms that were producing less than $500 worth of goods, however, would most likely have avoided the expense of advertising. Perhaps some firms advertising in local newspapers aspired to turn out at least $500 worth of products and used advertisements in an attempt to carve out a spot in the local market to reach that goal. But a six-month run of advertisements in a daily newspaper cost $30. That expense amounted to 6 percent of the annual output of a firm that manufactured $500 worth of goods, an all but prohibitive expense for a small enterprise. Although a few concerns found in these other sources may have fallen below the $500 threshold for inclusion in the census, it is reasonable to assume that most should have been recorded by the census marshals.

Moreover, much like the Dun reports, advertisements in newspapers offer insights into the extent and types of industry in the antebellum Gulf South, quite apart from a determination of what firms were missing from the census schedules. Some editors in 1860 created columns in their newspapers' advertisement sections specifically dedicated to home industry so that southern consumers could find southern manufacturers from which to purchase goods.[18] Many newspapers touted industrial growth in the South, either as good in its own right or as protection against perceived northern economic aggression. These papers reported on manufacturing in their local areas and applauded the efforts of entrepreneurs to invest in it and expand existing firms.[19] For example, manufacturers in northeastern Alabama found out from their local newspapers that they could get southern-built steam engines in nearby Columbus, Georgia.[20] The Central Railroad Company used the *Weekly Houston Telegraph* to announce that its local rail yards were now producing their own rolling stock. A grist mill manufacturer in Clinton, Mississippi, advertised in the *Vicksburg Whig* that he was able to supply the area with all sizes of mills and provided a list of the prices for mills of varying types and sizes.[21] The Southern Agricultural Implement Factory of Jackson, Mississippi, supplied much of the state with plows and cultivators and ran ads in newspapers throughout Mississippi touting its products.[22] The editors of the *Vicksburg Whig* even printed an article about a newly run advertisement by the Vicksburg Foundry, applauding the firm's impressive size:

> We invite attention to the advertisement of the Vicksburg Foundry by A.B. Reading. We believe this foundry is as large, if not larger, than any other in the southern country. We doubt whether New Orleans can furnish its equal in point of size, or capability to turn out a large amount of work. A boiler yard has lately been added to it, where our planters can have their boilers either made or repaired. Mr. Reading is now prepared to build a steam engine every week, besides furnishing all the mill and gin work that may be called for.[23]

Curiously, the census listed this concern as merely a foundry, neglecting the firm's other, extensive industrial activity. Many newspaper editors, planters, and industrialists used newspapers to promote the industrial economy of the South and the founding of firms across the region.[24]

Map 2.3 shows where firms missing in the census were located and concentrated. As the map indicates, the counties with the most firms missing from the census fall into two main categories. Some of the missing concerns were in areas far from railroad and river transportation. Most likely census marshals missed these firms because of the difficulty and expense involved in getting to outlying areas. The counties that were easier to reach were consequently more thoroughly covered by the census. But census enumerators also failed to record firms that operated in well-surveyed areas. As Table 2.4 illustrates, some fairly large cities, such as Vicksburg and Natchez, Mississippi, supported a great deal of manufacturing that census marshals did not find. The fifteen manufac-

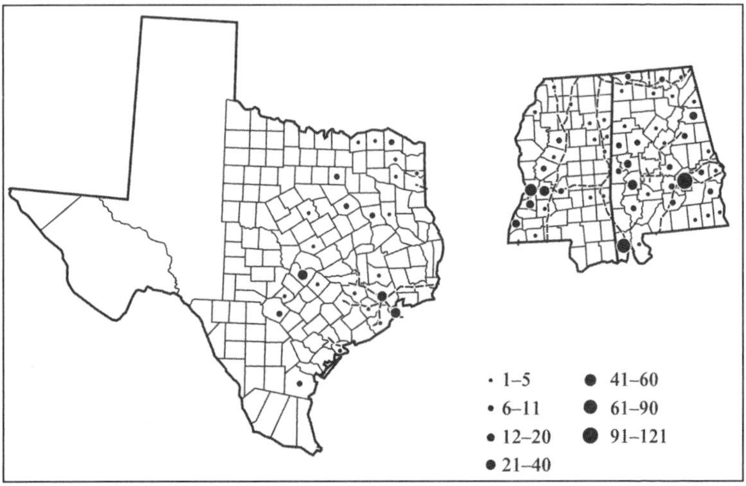


MAP 2.3. Number and locations of manufacturing firms not listed in the 1860 Census.

*Sources:* Newspapers, county directories, journals, local histories, and the R. G. Dun Credit Reports.

turing firms reported by the census for Adams County, in which Natchez was located, accounted for only 47 percent of the thirty-two firms operating within the county. The census's coverage for Vicksburg's Warren County was even worse, capturing less than one-third of the county's seventy-seven manufacturing firms.

The census listed the Spangler Manufacturing Company, founded by S. Spangler of Vicksburg, as a mill. But local histories show that, along with being a lumber and grist mill, the firm also produced sashes, doors, and blinds.[25] The Dun reports also vetted many firms in Vicksburg missed by the census, including one that turned out railroad products for the Vicksburg, Shreveport, and Texas Railroad.[26] The census also missed George Smith, a Vicksburg foundry owner with an important contract to make fittings for the city's gas works.[27] In Natchez, firms missing from the census enumerations included a substantial wagon and carriage factory owned by A. R. Tyler, another carriage manufactory owned by George G. Dickerman, and a cabinet shop owned by

TABLE 2.4. Census coverage and omission of manufacturing firms in two urban Mississippi counties in 1860

| | Census | Other sources | Total |
|---|---|---|---|
| Adams County, Mississippi (Natchez) | 15 (47%) | 17 (53%) | 32 |
| Warren County, Mississippi (Vicksburg) | 24 (31%) | 53 (69%) | 77 |

*Sources:* Census of 1860 Manufacturing Schedules for Adams and Warren County, Mississippi, local newspapers, local histories, and the R. G. Dun Credit reports.

*General note:* Figures in parentheses are the percentages of each city's total number of firms. Thus, as the text points out, of Adams County's total of 32 firms, only 47% were enumerated in the census.

Henry Keim, whose "future looked bright."[28] Also omitted were important firms such as James Orr's wagon and plow factory and Andrew Boyer's wagon firm.[29] In Texas, such as in Harris County, major firms were also missed, such as Alexander McGowan's Houston foundry or Andrew Gammell's gunsmithy.[30] While McGowan's company survived the war, Gammell was killed at the Battle of Shiloh.[31] The firms missed by the census marshals were not just small concerns with no impact; the people living in these cities recognized them, through newspapers and credit reports, as important parts of their communities.

The census did, of course, identify many large manufacturing firms that operated in the Gulf South. Such firms served as examples to would-be industrialists and as engines to drive further development. The best-known industrialist in the region may have been Daniel Pratt. Credit correspondents hired by Dun discussed the creditworthiness of Pratt's factory at Prattville in Autauga County, Alabama. Contrary to what Olmsted might have thought about this area because 57 percent of its population was enslaved, the report on Pratt described him as being "quite responsible" and as having "the best gin factory in America."[32] An advertisement in the August 28, 1860, issue of the *Southern Statesman* explains the successfulness of Pratt's concerns. Pratt's twenty-nine years of experience had created a firm that had a gross income of $742,514.35 in 1860, spread across the numerous concerns of his Prattville complex.[33] Pratt's success suggests that, under the right guidance, southern industry could develop and prosper. Of course, firms like Pratt's did not appear overnight, and as he and other manufacturers were well aware, industrial development took time and required investment in supporting enterprises, especially in transportation infrastructure.[34]

Manufacturing was becoming important enough in the region to influence public policy. Beginning in 1852, the Mississippi state legislature passed laws to "encourage the establishment of manufacturing enterprises."[35] By then, Jackson, the state capital, had become a center of trade and industry, home to such enterprises as carriage manufactories, boot and shoe factories, and iron works. James Stevens, a machinist in the city who also owned a foundry, was "good" and "been in bus sever years" *[sic]*.[36] Phillip & Kells ran a very large plow factory in Jackson and their business was worth $40,000 in 1860.[37] With all of the cotton grown in the area, James Hewes's cotton gin factory was very prosperous and was worth $10,000 at the outbreak of the war.[38] Moreover, these were just a few of the concerns active in the city at this time. Jackson was, of course, hardly alone in its industrial activity, and new concerns were being founded across the Gulf South by individual proprietors, partnerships, and companies (see Table 2.5).

Unfortunately, the census did not explicitly record the form of organization or type of ownership of the firms reported in it. The Dun reports also neglected to report this information. Consequently, we can only infer ownership type by the name of the firm and the list of its proprietors. Firm size also influenced the organizational form of a business. We can reasonably assume that an individual owned a smaller firm with one listed proprietor and no business name. In fact, as the table indicates, individuals owned most firms in the Gulf South in 1860. Firms owned by two proprietors were generally simple partnerships and made up 14 percent of the census total. The largest firms, with business names listed and perhaps the suffix "Company" or "Inc.," were likely to have been corporations. Such concerns constituted only 10 percent of the total.

For concerns not listed in the census, individual proprietorships

TABLE 2.5. Distribution of firms by form of organization, 1860, from census

| | Individual | Partnership | Company | Total |
|---|---|---|---|---|
| Alabama | 1,048 (74.5%) | 180 (12.8%) | 179 (12.7%) | 1,407 |
| Mississippi | 711 (80.6%) | 115 (13%) | 56 (6.4%) | 882 |
| Texas | 729 (73.6%) | 165 (16.6%) | 97 (9.8%) | 991 |
| Total | 2,488 (76%) | 460 (14%) | 332 (10%) | 3,280 |

*Source:* Census of 1860 Manufacturing Schedules.

*General note:* Figures in parentheses are the percentages of each state's total number of firms, as recorded in the census.

were also the dominant form of business, accounting for almost 63 percent of all manufacturing firms in Alabama, Mississippi, and Texas (Table 2.6). Surprisingly, though, the second-most missed type of firm was the company. While only 10% of the firms listed in the census records were companies, 17.5% of firms missed by the census were of that type. More surprising is the fact that the census marshals in Alabama, Mississippi, and Texas together failed to report close to a third (30.7 percent) of all companies operating in the region in 1860. The corresponding levels of omissions for individual proprietorships and partnerships were 18 percent and 18.6 percent, respectively (Table 2.7). This distribution shows that concerns missed by census marshals in the Gulf South were not insubstantial ones. Moreover, many of these firms were listed in the Dun reports, which indicates that businessmen in the North knew of their existence and requested information on them. Northern creditors called for investigations of all types of firms in the region. However, southern companies, which may have hoped to do business over a wider area than would a firm owned by an individual or a partnership, would naturally have received a great deal of attention. One such firm, Samuel Coale and Company's steam mill in Clarke County, Alabama, was worth "some $15000 or $20000Ð and according to its Dun report, was "good for all contracts."[39] Yet, somehow the census marshals overlooked the firm. Census marshals missed not only small firms, but a large number of important ones as well.

TABLE 2.6. Distribution of firms by ownership type, 1860, from noncensus sources

| | Individual | Partnership | Company | Total |
|---|---|---|---|---|
| Alabama | 279 (64%) | 66 (15.1%) | 91 (20.9%) | 436 |
| Mississippi | 148 (81.3%) | 16 (8.8%) | 18 (9.9%) | 182 |
| Texas | 118 (69.4%) | 23 (13.5%) | 29 (17.1%) | 170 |
| Total | 545 (69.2%) | 105 (13.3%) | 138 (17.5%) | 788 |

*Sources:* Newspapers, county directories, journals, and the R. G. Dun Credit Reports.

*General note:* Figures in parentheses are the percentages of each state's total number of firms by ownership type.

TABLE 2.7. Levels of omission of manufacturing concerns by organizational type in Alabama, Mississippi, and Texas in 1860

| | Individual | Partnership | Company | Total |
|---|---|---|---|---|
| Alabama | 1,327 (21%) | 246 (26.8%) | 270 (33.7%) | 1,843 (23.7%) |
| Mississippi | 859 (17.2%) | 131 (12.2%) | 74 (24.3%) | 1,064 (17.1%) |
| Texas | 847 (13.9%) | 188 (12.2%) | 126 (23%) | 1,161 (14.6) % |
| Total | 3,033 (18%) | 565 (18.6%) | 470 (29.4%) | 4,068 |

*Sources:* Census of 1860 Manufacturing Schedules, newspapers, county directories, journals, and the R. G. Dun Credit Reports.

*General note:* Figures in parentheses are the percentage of firms of the given ownership type missed by the census marshals.

Overall, as Table 2.8 shows, the distribution by ownership type for all manufacturing firms comes close to matching, proportionally, the breakdown of the census displayed in Table 2.5. This suggests that the organization of concerns in the region followed a pattern. Most firms

TABLE 2.8. Distribution of firms by ownership type, 1860, from all sources

| | Individual | Partnership | Company | Total |
|---|---|---|---|---|
| Alabama | 1,327 (72%) | 246 (13.3%) | 270 (14.7%) | 1,843 |
| Mississippi | 859 (80.7%) | 131 (12.3%) | 74 (7%) | 1,064 |
| Texas | 847 (73%) | 188 (16.2%) | 126 (10.8%) | 1,161 |
| Total | 3,033 (74.5%) | 565 (13.9%) | 470 (11.6%) | 4,068 |

*Sources:* Census of 1860 Manufacturing Schedules, newspapers, county directories, journals, and the R. G. Dun Credit Reports.

*General note:* Figures in parentheses represent the percentages of the total firms from all sources.

were owned by individuals and were founded to produce for their local areas. This was a function that could be performed by one owner who hired a few hands, such as Adam C. King's small tannery and saddler in Houston County, Texas.[40] King's concern was able to serve the needs of the local area for leather goods, with most of the work being done by his own labor. But larger firms did exist, and these manufacturers used the advantages provided by transportation and raw materials to form larger and more complex concerns. The large number of partnerships and companies, making up 25 percent of all firms in the Gulf South, shows that industry was developing and expanding.

The companies engaged in manufacturing in the Gulf South were distributed throughout the region, but tended to be concentrated along railroads lines and in areas where raw materials were readily available. Map 2.4 plots the distribution of companies in Alabama, Mississippi, and Texas. This map also delineates the areas off the main transportation routes that had no companies. But almost any area with raw materials or access to transportation and markets supported at least one manufacturing company. Many of these concerns, such as Pratt's factory, which built some of the best cotton gins in the nation, took advantage of the resources in their local areas to produce goods demanded by southerners. Alfred A. Jenney followed Pratt's example, taking advantage of iron deposits in Alabama, when he established a very large and profit-

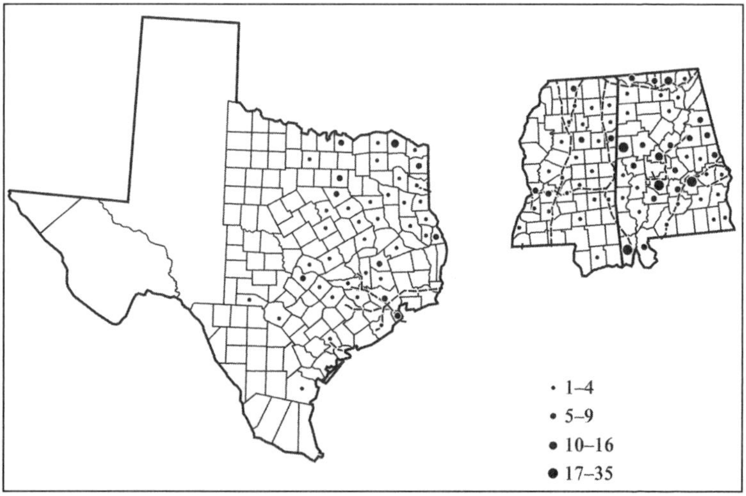


MAP 2.4. Numbers and locations of companies from all sources in 1860.
*Sources:* Census of 1860 Manufacturing Schedules, newspapers, county directories, journals, and the R. G. Dun Credit Reports.

able foundry and iron works in Montgomery. Jenney was not as lucky as Pratt, though. During the war, federal raiders burned his establishment to the ground.[41] Other firms used local cotton to feed textile mills, while iron foundries, such as the Selma Iron Works and the Alabama Iron Manufacturing Company, took advantage of nearby iron and coal deposits to turn out a range of iron products.[42] The Planters Factory in Autauga County, Alabama, spun and wove locally grown cotton into thread and cloth, and it had the "reputation of dg a gd & safe bus [*sic*]."[43]

The companies missed by the census marshals were located, for the most part, in urban areas and along railroad routes, as shown by Map 2.5. The location of companies in urban areas such as Vicksburg, Mobile, Montgomery, or Natchez is understandable. As stated earlier, concerns in these areas benefited from the availability of transportation lines, access to raw materials, and the existence of complementary firms, all of which spurred growth. For example, George F. Plant and Company of Selma, Alabama, was able to build a well-respected tinware and stove firm not only because of the "good habits and character" of the

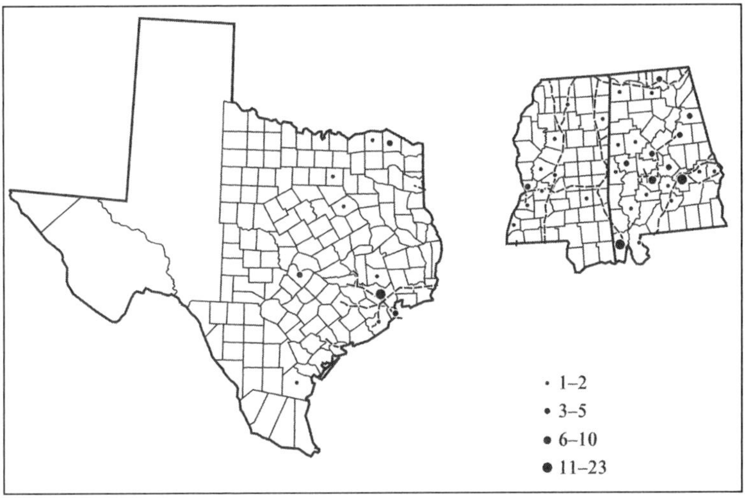


MAP 2.5. Numbers and locations of companies not listed in the Census of 1860.

*Sources:* Newspapers, county directories, journals, and the R. G. Dun Credit Reports.

men involved in the company, but also because of the urban character of its local markets.[44] Somehow, though, the census marshals missed this firm. It is interesting that any concerns, let alone companies, were missed in urban areas. Unfortunately, the reason for their omission may never be known, but incompetence and laziness seem to be the most likely explanations.

Another organizational type that existed in the Gulf South was state ownership of a manufacturing operation. The primary examples of such enterprises were the region's state penitentiaries, and, of course, the census recorded them. Prisoners were another kind of unfree labor of which southerners took advantage, and state prisons were some of the largest industrial enterprises in the region. The Mississippi State Penitentiary, for example, was a major and growing concern. As early as 1846, its superintendent, Benjamin G. Weir, advertised in local newspapers that the prison was selling "horse and ox wagons, carts, drays, carryalls, buggies, carriages, sulkies, spinning wheels, reels, cooper's ware, chairs, cribs, washstands, wardrobes, safes, plows, boots, and harness."[45] By 1860, the prison turned out thousands of dollars of products each month from its cotton factory, woodshop, shoe shop, and smithy and purchased cotton from as far away as New Orleans.[46] The Alabama State Penitentiary was also an important industrial concern. An advertisement in the March 21, 1860, issue of the *Southern Messenger* informed readers that the prison factory sold a variety of products, including sashes, doors, blinds, russet brogans, wagons, carts, and threshing machines.[47] Finally, the Texas Penitentiary, which opened its factory in October 1849, was running one hundred looms and producing a great amount of osnaburgs and woolens by 1860.[48] Plantation owners from the local area in Walker County supplied the factory with cotton and bought the firm's finished products.[49] These prison factories were not small firms focused on one product; they were, instead, very large and diversified undertakings that produced many different items.[50]

Most manufacturing establishments were, of course, not companies or prison enterprises, but were, instead, privately owned firms. What then do we really know about their owners? Managing a successful concern required a range of skills and a sharp mind. Understanding more about these owners will help us to understand better the development of industry in the region. The manufacturing schedules of the census provide no information about owners beyond their names. The Dun reports, though, provide a glimpse into the men and women who owned firms in the Gulf South. For example, the Dun report on Bexar County, Texas, listed a boot and shoe manufacturer, M. Eisman. He was described in January 1860 as "young and industrious," and doing a "fine trade," even though, according to Olmsted, Eisman would have never seen a book.[51] Moreover, Dun judged Eisman to be worthy of credit by the northern investors who ordered the company's report. Robert Clark, a carriage manufacturer in Adams County, Mississippi, owned, according to the Dun report on him, a "valuable manufactory employing some 12 or 15 workmen," and was worthy of northern support.[52] Of course, not all of the owners listed in the Dun reports were good credit risks. One report described a nephew of the great southern industrialist Daniel Pratt as always being behind in his payments and noted that his creditors had a hard time getting repaid. But, the credit reporter believed that his uncle

TABLE 2.9. Place of birth of firm owners listed in Dun reports

| | |
|---|---|
| South | 87 |
| North | 34 |
| Europe | 32 |
| Miscellaneous[a] | 2 |
| Total[b] | 155 |

*Sources:* R.G. Dun Reports and the 1860 Population Census Schedules.

[a] Miscellaneous includes birthplaces listed as Canada West and Born At Sea.

[b] Two owners had no birthplace listed.

might still make good his debts.[53] Along the same lines, J. Franklin Kerr owned a gunsmithy in Jackson who was not very well thought of before the war, and Dun reported in 1863 that he was "not worth anything, not good, deserted from Rebel Army."[54]

Curiously, while the manufacturing census missed many industrial concerns, owners of some of these missing firms nevertheless appeared in the population and slave census schedules. Cross-referencing the names of the owners of the 334 firms found in the Dun reports with the names in the population and slave census schedules, returned 157 owners of concerns for whom census information exists. One piece of information recovered was birthplace. Finding out where an owner of a concern was born can tell us to what degree southern industrial development was home-grown. As Table 2.9 shows, industrialists in the Gulf South were born across the region, the country, and the world, with one man even listing his place of birth as "At Sea."[55]

Contrary to what Olmsted asserted, the majority of these entrepreneurs were southern-born. Moreover, most of the European- and northern-born owners were craftsmen such as jewelers, watchmakers, tinsmiths, and silversmiths. Many southern-born owners, though, devoted themselves to heavier industry: foundries, carriage and wagon factories, mills, and similar enterprises. Many of the southern-born owners were from the Gulf South. Some areas of these states had, by 1860, only recently opened to settlement; this was especially true of Texas. Thus, a number of owners came from other southern states, mostly Virginia and the Carolinas.[56] Industrial development in the Gulf South, especially heavy industry, was therefore very much driven by firms owned and operated by native-born Southerners.

The population census schedules also list the occupation for each person interviewed by census marshals. Position in southern society was based partly on occupation, with planters at the top. But many southerners wore numerous hats. Thus, how owners reported their profession in the schedules says a great deal about the position of industry in the antebellum Gulf South. Most southern firm owners listed their occupation as that of an operator of an industrial concern such as a mechanic, millwright, carriage manufacturer, boot or shoe maker, harness maker, and others covering the wide range of industrial work carried on in the region. For example, according to Dun, S. C. Tanner, who owned a major lumber mill and was an influential man in Dallas County, Alabama, does not appear in the manufacturing census but was listed in the population census as being in the lumber trade.[57]

Sixteen industrialists listed their occupation in the population schedules as something unrelated to their manufacturing concerns. These men, who owned large amounts of real and personal estate, including significant numbers of slaves, listed their occupations as farmer or planter. Owning a plantation, or being a farmer, had greater cachet than owning an industrial concern, so status-conscious men strived to reach this level. More important, however, this planter investment in manufacturing suggests the transfer of capital from agriculture to industry. Close students of antebellum southern manufacturing have tended to minimize the importance of this transfer because, so the thinking goes, planters had "a general inability or unwillingness to transfer resources out of agriculture."[58] But, it should not be surprising that planters would diversify their interests. As the *Trinity Advocate* editorialized: "Each planter will improve his condition by producing everything which he consumes, and the community would be an hundred fold enriched by the establishment of manufacturing industry in close contiguity to the cotton fields, not only producing at home the fabrics we consume, but exporting the manufactured article instead of the raw material."[59]

Also, planters and large farmers had the capital to invest in, and sustain, industrial firms.[60] Planters, then, based on this evidence, played an important role in southern industry by investing in manufacturing concerns when they saw they could be profitable.

Owners of manufacturing firms possessed widely varied amounts of both personal and real estate to draw upon for their industrial endeavors. In the census, personal estate was anything that could be moved or carried off, while real estate was, of course, land and buildings. The owner of a manufacturing concern would have had a large personal estate because the census usually included the products of the firm in the total. The mean value of the personal estate of the men who were missed by the census was $15,216; their average real estate holding was $7,358. These amounts were equivalent, respectively, to personal and real estates of $440,000 and $213,000 today.[61] The size of such estates made their owners men of considerable wealth. Personal and real estates were important to the reporters who contributed to the Dun evaluations, when it was available, because such information could be used to determine creditworthiness. For example, J. C. McGuire, a foundry owner in Mobile, was reported as "doing well, owns real estate and slaves, [and was] good for contracts."[62] Another owner, J. C. Harris of Carroll County, Mississippi, was a "very industrious and economical man, worth at least $100000."[63] Many of these manufacturers were men of substance who had the capital resources needed to run successful firms.

Many of the owners of these industrial concerns also owned slaves, something that lay outside Olmsted's conception of the possible. Olmsted said many times in his book that owning slaves caused slave owners to degenerate, and that they therefore could never own modern industrial concerns.[64] This feeling was held by many people in both the North and the South at the time. Bateman and Weiss said much the same thing, asserting that slave owners ignored investment opportunities and avoided risk whenever possible.[65] The evidence supports neither Olmsted nor Bateman and Weiss. One-third of the business owners who were the subjects of Dun reports owned at least one slave. The typical industrial entrepreneur listed in the Dun reports owned twelve slaves. There is no way to know whether slaves held by owners of manufacturing firms labored in those concerns, and the Dun reports are of little help in providing an answer because they only mention slaves as collateral for credit. For example, the credit report on Isaac Young listed him as a successful carriage maker in Franklin County, Alabama, and noted that he owned slaves as part of his personal property.[66] The report, however, made no mention of what labor the slaves performed. But slaves worked in many industrial concerns in the South, and it would not be surprising if the slave owners used slave labor in their manufacturing operations.[67]

Olmsted offered a picture of the antebellum South based on very little hard evidence and considerable bias. Firms were located all over the region, and existed in larger numbers than previously thought. Moreover, there were few areas which were not penetrated by industrial concerns. Southerners were comfortable with industry being a part of their society. In addition, the data presented here paint a very different picture of the average antebellum Gulf South manufacturer. Owners lived and worked in sparsely settled semi-frontier areas, as well as in large urban centers. The average southern manufactory owner had been born in the region, and well over half had been born in one of the states studied here. He owned sufficient personal property and real estate to enable him to found his firm, operate it, and turn a profit. Moreover, there was a one in three chance that he was also a substantial slave owner. These industrialists were esteemed by the other members of their communities and were men of significant wealth and enterprise. As substantial as many of these owners were, we might well expect that the marshals would have listed their firms in the census. The inclusion in the census of these firms and their owners would have contributed to a more complete and more accurate view of the industrial base of the South on the eve of the Civil War. Their omission has distorted the views of both contemporaries and historians alike, and has greatly affected our understanding of the southern landscape.

# 3

## DIGGING FOR A FOUNDATION

### Resources and Raw Materials

One of the greatest challenges facing industrialists in the Gulf South was pulling together the resources needed for development. As the *Daily Confederation* of Montgomery, Alabama pointed out in an editorial about the region in February 1859, "Outside of Agriculture and Commerce the great mass of our people require for their employment, cotton, iron, leather and coal, none of which, save iron and leather, and these to a very limited extant, have we here."[1] A lack of such natural resources, and a weak transportation system to move resources around, were cited as reasons for the backwardness of southern manufacturing.[2] But the South did possess more of the resources needed for industrialization than casual observers perceived. While cotton dominated the southern landscape, "the Southern states, even the cotton states, together possessed population and resources sufficient to enable them to take their place among the nations of the earth."[3] What was both on and under the landscape of the Gulf South would be a major factor in the growth of manufacturing in the region.

Availability of the natural resources necessary for southern industrial development was, of course, a function of the region's geography, and their supply, even if far behind that in the North, did not hinder early industrial development. Those large fields of cotton, common across the region, played a vital role in the growth of southern industry, supplying raw material, capital, and often during off-seasons, labor. The assertion made by historian Harold Woodman that "the South was hamstrung by its climate, topography, natural resources, [and] location with respect to the North and to Europe," is overstated.[4] An accurate assessment of the industrialization of Alabama, Mississippi, and Texas must rest on an understanding of the foundation upon which it was built: the natural resources available to the average southern entrepreneur. As H. P. Chapman and J. F. Battle asserted, capitalists in the Gulf South had the capacity to develop manufacturing: "It is the land for the husbandman, for the merchant and manufacturer; for the hunter, for the lumberman, for the tourist."[5] While they wrote this statement after the war, it rings true for the antebellum period too.

The Gulf South's endowment of natural resources played an important role in manufacturing. While resources could be, and often were, imported from other regions, indigenous resources also facilitated the establishment of new manufacturing concerns. Local iron, coal, cotton, and other materials cut the cost of manufactures and potentially made southern firms more competitive with those outside the South. The Gulf South possessed those resources in abundance, but the technology of the time and the knowledge of what was under the ground limited what people were able to obtain, a circumstance that was hardly peculiar to the South.[6] Of all the South's resources, land was of course the most important, especially acreage planted in cotton.

Cotton was king in the South and was the region's signal economic asset.[7] Map 3.1 illustrates the extent of cotton production in the region. Manufacturing in the region always ran second to cotton production, but running second does not mean that industry was insignificant. Moreover, cotton stimulated the development of manufacturing. Henry Hughes, an important southern writer of the day, explained that British industry 75–80 percent of its cotton from the South and that southern cotton also supplied the needs of northern textile manufacturers along with the South's own mills.[8] Cotton production was profitable and, by 1860, "taken as a whole the cotton interest was never in a more prosperous condition."[9] As demand for cotton increased, the profits from growing cotton rose, and farmers increased their acreage of this "white gold."[10]

The industrial revolution that first swept Great Britain and Northern Europe, then the North, and then the South, drove the expansion

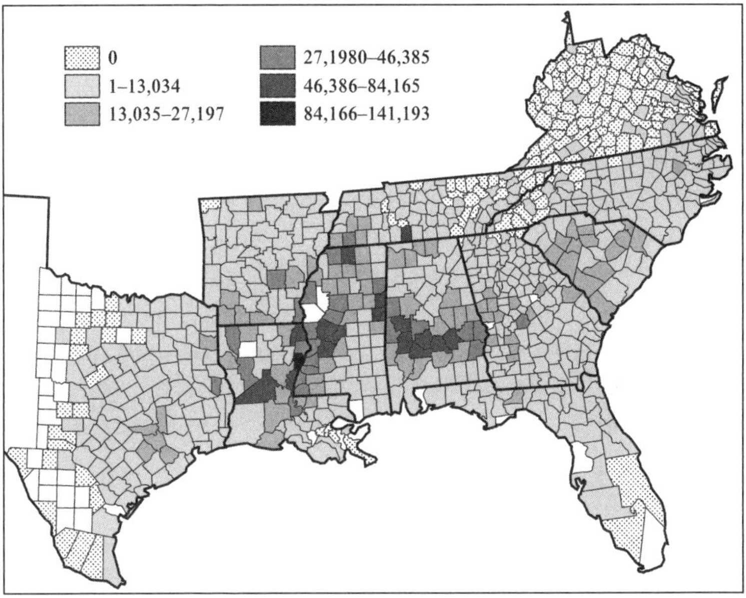


MAP 3.1. Cotton production in the Cotton Belt (bales).
*Source:* Census of 1860, Agriculture.

of cotton production as "agriculture was more and more called upon to produce what was necessary to the development of industry."[11] Moreover, wool was being shipped from Texas to Alabama to support regional development, as was cotton.[12] Rapid expansion of textile production, both woolens and cotton, drove much of the industrialization of Great Britain, as well as that of the northeastern United States, particularly in New England. Robert Russel explained the importance of cotton:

> The South produced an immense surplus for export of great staples, particularly cotton, which had become necessities for millions of people the world over, supported a large part of the commerce and trade of the world, constituted the raw materials for factories in England and America employing millions of capital and hundreds of thousands of hands, and furnished the basis for American credit in Europe.[13]

Cotton generated a great deal of money for southerners, much of which they reinvested in more land and slaves to grow more cotton.[14] But not all of the profits went back into cotton production; some became capital for other investments, such as manufacturing concerns.

Large-scale cotton production was possible because the Gulf South was one of the richest agricultural areas in the United States. Known as the Black Belt, or the Cotton Belt, it was an area intensively farmed by cotton planters. The combination of fertile river valleys and a congenial climate created an expanse of fertile agricultural land through the middle of the region that turned it into a major cotton-producing and manufacturing area.[15] The number of slaves increased to meet the labor needs of the area as white southerners moved west, filling in the land from Alabama to the Texas frontier.[16] When looking for a reason to explain the failure of the South to industrialize, many scholars point to the comparative natural advantage that climate and physical geography provided to the region. J. D. B. De Bow's explanation was that the region's good soil and cheap land drew people to the area in large numbers.[17] Thus, cotton agriculture created a way of life for the South, especially the Gulf South, and southerners capitalized on what nature had provided and grew as much cotton as possible.[18] But as shown earlier, industrial concerns existed and flourished in the same belt that produced the region's cotton.

Adequate sources of energy were also important for the development of industry in the Gulf South. While water was used wherever possible, other forms of power were needed, especially in the iron industry and for railroads. This power, by the 1850s, would come from steam engines, and those engines would need fuel. In the first half of the nineteenth century most power came from the burning of wood. Forests, which covered most of the Gulf South, were a major source of fuel in the form of chopped wood or charcoal.[19] Most fuel consumption across the entire nation was used not for industrial purposes but for home heating or cooking and "only about one-tenth of the total fuel supply was converted into mechanical energy."[20] This use of fuel wood was beginning to make significant reductions to the timber of the South, but before the war, wood was still readily available for use by industry.[21] Most wood used for industry was converted into charcoal because it was a superior source of

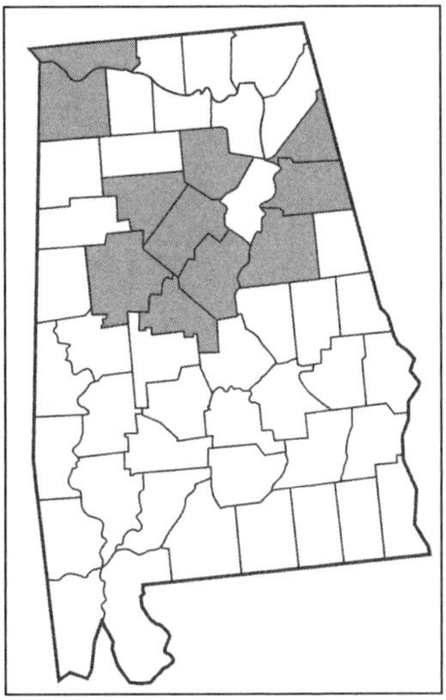

MAP 3.2. Coal-producing counties in Alabama before the war.
*Source:* Ethel Armes, *The Story of Iron and Coal in Alabama.*

energy. Railroads and steamboats still used most of the fuel wood, but the iron industry consumed large amounts of wood to make the 70–75 million bushels of charcoal that it used each year before the Civil War.[22] Charcoal production was widespread, and small local production supported manufacturing efforts in the Gulf South.

Coal was also available, but it was just beginning to be used for industrial purposes.[23] It was a better fuel than wood or charcoal because it provided more energy per unit of weight. Coal mining began in Pennsylvania, but fields spread all the way south into Alabama and helped to spur industrial development by making iron cheaper and easier to produce.[24] Large-scale coal mining in the South did not begin until after the Civil War, but some was used before. Alabama was the most important coal-producing state in the Gulf South, especially the northern part.[25] Map 3.2 shows all of the counties that produced coal in the state in 1860. Coal was very important to Alabama, as well as the rest of the Gulf South, for industrial development. In 1849, De Bow explained the state of coal mining in Alabama: "there were about 200 persons engaged in the coal trade of the state; and as only three beds are worked underground, the rest of the coal raised is taken from the bed of the river, and streams."[26] Production had only just begun in the state when De Bow wrote, but it would continue to grow throughout the antebellum period.

Many Alabama counties exported coal, and coal fields advertised in northern newspapers for experienced miners to manage and work at these concerns as they expanded their operations. For example, the Alabama Coal Mining Company in Shelby County hired a man from Philadelphia in 1854 to manage its fields, and "sent from fifty to a hundred boatloads of coal a year down to Wetumpka, Montgomery, and Mobile until the outbreak of the Civil War."[27] These Shelby County mines were the first underground mines in Alabama.[28] Shelby became the center of industrial development in antebellum Alabama because of its location in the middle of the Alabama mineral belt, where coal had been mined since 1830.[29] The large bituminous coal vein running through Shelby began near the Black Warrior River around Tuscaloosa and spread into Georgia and Mississippi, running forty miles wide and sixty-seven miles long in Shelby County.[30] By the eve of the war over half of the iron produced in the United States was produced using coal as a fuel, and Alabama coal went to furnaces around the region and country to spur this development.[31]

Of course, one of the most important resources for the development of manufacturing before the war was iron ore. In the South it came in many varieties: hematite, brown ore, magnetite, and iron carbonate.[32] Iron ore was mined, or at least gathered on the surface, from the earliest days of settlement, and iron foundries became commonplace parts of the southern landscape. The Gulf South took advantage of some significant sources of iron in Alabama as deposits were found in many places in the northern and central parts of the state.[33] Map 3.3 shows where iron ore was gathered in Alabama. One of the largest deposits was a vein of brown hematite ore near the Coosa River that encouraged the development of production in the area.[34] The first blast furnace to use this ore was in Franklin County and began operations in 1818. Called the Cedar Creek Furnace, it consumed surface deposits of ore and charcoal made from local cedar.[35]

The other major iron area in the state developed near Talladega,

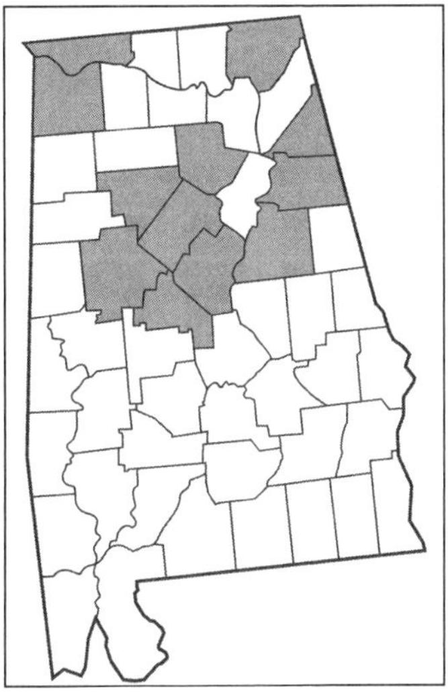

MAP 3.3. Iron ore–producing counties in Alabama before the war.
*Source:* Ethel Armes, *The Story of Iron and Coal in Alabama.*

where the Talladega Iron Works, founded six miles east of the town, smelted local brown hematite ore.[36] Brown hematite ore was also found in Cherokee, Benton, Shelby, Bibb, and Franklin Counties.[37] Three other furnaces also operated in Alabama: the Round Mountain Furnace, the Polkville Furnace, and the Shelby Furnace.[38] All three of these furnaces used charcoal, rather than the local coal deposits, and steam engines to power their blasts and produced a combined output of 1,495 tons of pig iron in 1856.[39] In another example, the Alfred A. Jenney and Co. Foundry and Iron Works of Montgomery County, Alabama used these local supplies and was "doing well and [has] considerable R.E. [Real Estate], a very extensive establishment."[40] Mining ore was often a family affair, and "the women and children shoveled out the ore and piled it on kilns of timber, where they roasted it to make it crumble. It was then carted to a forge, and they were paid for it by the load."[41] Moving south, Skates and Company, of Mobile, was "one of the safest concerns in the city," and used the coal and iron supplies of the state.[42] Thus, local development was driven by local resources.

Coal and iron were hardly Alabama's only raw materials. Alabama, according to De Bow, had "surplus productions [of] cotton, lumber, staves, turpentine, [and] coal."[43] The area near Bucksville produced red ochre, used to make paint. Lead ore was mined in Benton and Clark Counties, manganese was taken from Benton County, and limestone and marble deposits were available in many parts of the state, especially along the Cahawba River.[44] Much of the state's marble went to Mobile, where stonecutters shaped it "into everything from church altars to tombstones."[45] One of the firms that used this marble was Turner and Stackhouse, which was considered the top firm of its kind in the city and stayed in business well after the war.[46] Southerners were willing to invest capital in industrial ventures, just as they were willing to invest in the expansion of cotton production, as long as the necessary raw materials were available to allow development and a market for their goods.[47] Alabama had the raw materials to spur manufacturing investment and the market to consume any production.

Alabama's cotton, land, and other resources such as coal and iron combined to make it the most developed of the three states discussed here. Other states in the Gulf South did not have comparable endowments of raw materials. Yet, as John Hebron Moore has noted, Mississippi in 1860 "unquestionably possessed the essential elements for developing a balanced agricultural and industrial economy."[48] The state grew a great deal of cotton before the war, and the state's textile mills consumed some of the crop and possessed the potential to use more. Mississippi did not have an abundance of coal or iron, but people in the state still needed iron goods, and small producers arose to fill local needs, importing iron and coal as needed from neighboring states like Alabama. Such local demand helped to spur small-scale industrialization such as smithies and foundries that developed into larger concerns to serve nearby markets. Thus, while Mississippi's economy in 1860 was still overwhelmingly agricultural, some industrialization had already gotten under way. W. J. Heart ran a cotton factory in Tishomingo County, J. H. Buchanan ran a wagon maker in Tippah, and James Hinson ran a sawmill in Amite County was "considered safe being a prudent, economical and indus man."[49] Of course, these are just a few firms that were making use of the resources available in their local areas. Cotton could also drive industry, and Mississippi grew tremendous amounts.

The editor of the *Jackson Daily News* on March 14, 1860 argued that southerners needed to take advantage of what the Gulf South supplied in abundance: "An Opportunity for Southern Enterprise—we would not offer the following in a spirit of disparagement or derision, but only with the hope that the evil may ere long be corrected. Out of four million bales of cotton raised last year, only about one hundred thousand of them (one-fortieth part) were manufactured into cloth, in all the slave-holding States.[50]

In 1860, much of Texas was still a frontier region. Although some areas had been settled for decades, most were still being opened for settlement. Texans, then, were still discovering and developing their state's natural resources. De Bow's work is the best record we have of the resources used by Texans, including the great variety of mines in the state: silver from the San Saba mines and along the Bedais River, gold in Atoyac, iron ore scattered all over the state, bituminous coal near the Trinity and Upper Brazos rivers, and lime throughout North Texas.[51] Moreover, as many Texas towns were located along trade routes, they were able to bring in needed materials from distant sources. For example, a newspaper in Austin ran advertisements for the sale in town of copper from a mine in Arizona.[52] These readily obtainable raw materials encouraged industrial development. Manufacturers developed and served local markets that would otherwise have had difficulty getting goods from distant parts of the Union. So, while some believe that "antebellum Texas, surrounded by cotton fields and forests, imported cotton cloth and paper," the evidence does not support this.[53] Even with its small base, industry developed. Alexander McGowan built a successful factory in Houston, Bosque County had a steam mill owned by Ward Keeler, and while he was "boisterous, blustering, [and] inclined to dissipation," Major Jars Billups ran a cotton gin manufacturer in Mound Prairie, Texas.[54] Moreover, Texas supported some large firms, such as John Munchison's cotton spinning concern in Palestine, Texas that was "worth at least $50m."[55] Thus, even on the frontier, industry grew to meet local needs.

Many firms used these readily available natural resources. For example, there were many wool factories in Texas because the state had good land for running sheep. One company built a large factory three miles outside of San Antonio to take advantage of the abundant supply of raw wool and produce woolens for the area.[56] Of course, cotton spurred the founding and development of many concerns in the Gulf South. There were, for example, multiple firms in the Huntsville, Alabama, area that used locally grown cotton to produce cotton textiles "which, for quality and durability, would compare with goods made in the manufacturing towns of the North."[57] The Florence Factory, in Florence, Alabama, had forty-six looms and made 80,000 yards of cloth per week using locally grown cotton.[58] Moreover, firms like Daniel Pratt's produced machinery and other items, such as bale ties, that made cotton production easier. The Shelby Iron Company, of Shelby County, Alabama, took advantage of materials, including $2 worth of ore, $10 worth of charcoal, and $0.75 worth of limestone to produce one ton of iron in 1860.[59] From gins, to bale ties, to many other items, southern industrial firms took advantage of the materials available in the region to produce goods that people needed.

Thus, the value of raw materials used in industry is important. The Gulf South possessed substantial supplies of raw materials. Map 3.4 shows the value of raw materials used by firms listed in the census. The location of readily available raw materials influenced entrepreneurs' decisions about where to establish their manufacturing plants. Of course, the map of raw material values from the census firms tells only part of the story. When the estimates of the missing firms' raw materials are added to the census values, the picture changes, as Maps 3.5 and 3.6 illustrate. These maps show a range estimate, from low to high, of the value of raw materials used by Gulf South firms to manufacture their products. While it is impossible to determine the exact amount of raw materials used in antebellum Gulf South manufactories, concerns in the region, as the map shows, used large amounts of raw materials, at least some of which were locally produced. Moreover, locally available materials gave these firms a considerable advantage because they lowered costs.

"A Mississippi Planter," writing in *De Bow's Review*, explained that "there is no region on earth which can make and deliver coarse and

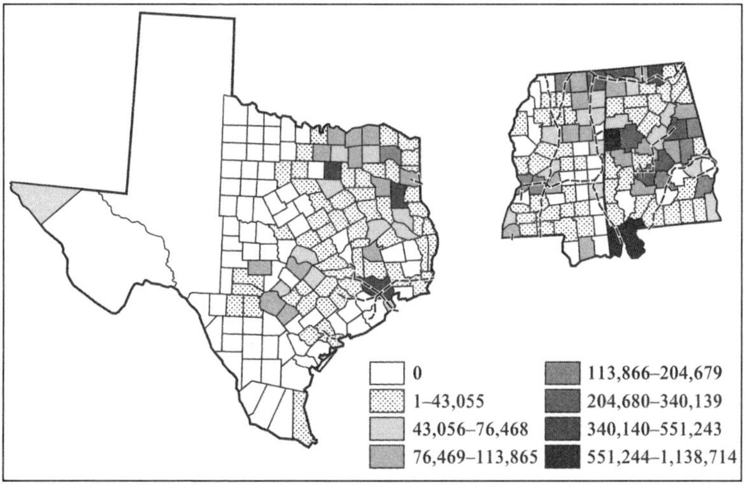


MAP 3.4. Raw materials costs listed in the Census of 1860 (dollars).

*Source:* Census of 1860 Manufacturing Schedules.

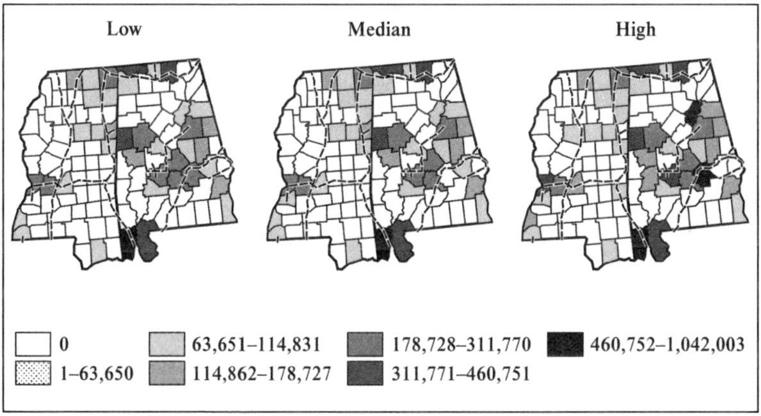


MAP 3.5. Estimates of raw materials purchased by all firms in 1860 for Alabama and Mississippi (dollars).

*Source:* Census of 1860 Manufacturing Schedules, newspapers, county directories, journals, and the R. G. Dun Credit Reports.

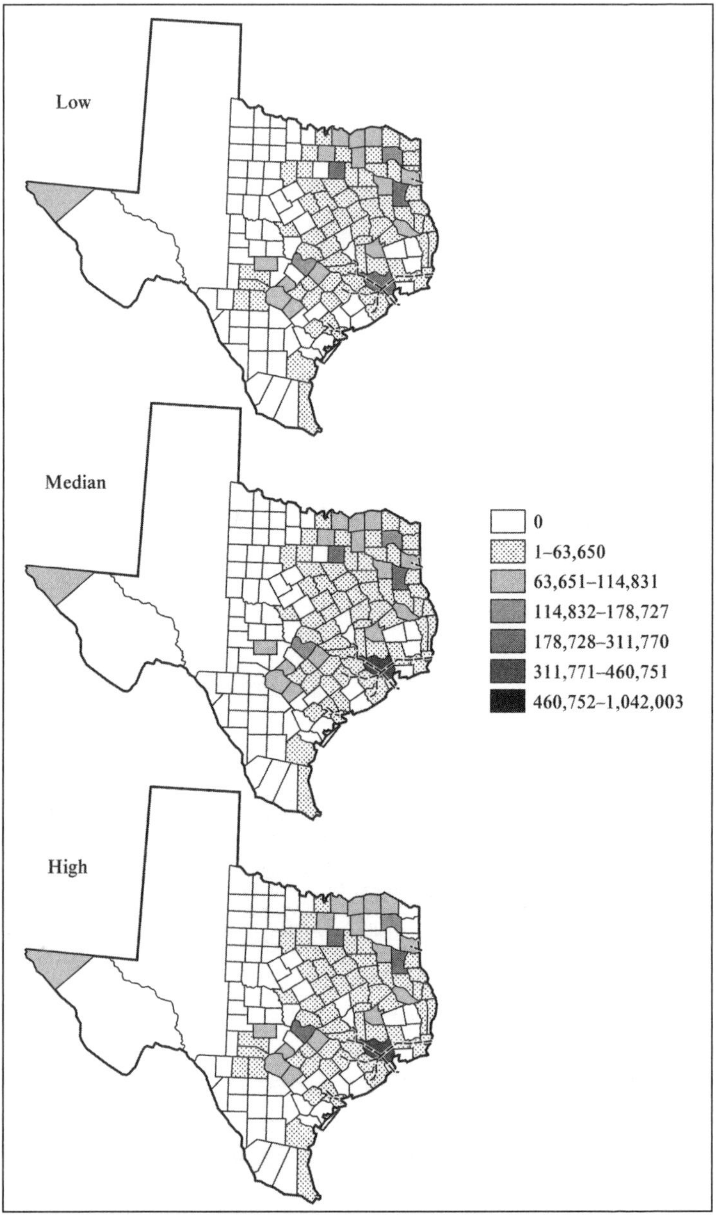


MAP 3.6. Raw materials purchased by all firms in 1860 for Texas.

*Sources:* Census of 1860 Manufacturing Schedules, newspapers, county directories, journals, and the R. G. Dun Credit Reports.

TABLE 3.1. Value of raw materials used by industrial firms in the Gulf South in 1860 for census and noncensus firms[a]

| | Census firms | Lower bound estimate | Mean | Upper bound estimate |
|---|---|---|---|---|
| Alabama | $5,597,848 | $5,817,559 (3.92%) | $6,151,698 (9.89%) | $7,229,698 (29.15%) |
| Mississippi | $2,502,866 | $2,580,785 (3.11%) | $2,700,566 (7.90%) | $3,092,666 (23.56%) |
| Texas | $3,421,006 | $3,502,676 (2.39%) | $3,626,956 (6.02%) | $4,028,906 (17.77%) |
| Total | $11,521,720 | $11,901,019 (3.29%) | $12,479,220 (8.31%) | $14,351,270 (24.56%) |

[a] See Appendix C, available at drmichaelfrawley.com, for a breakdown of this information at the country level.

*Sources:* Census of 1860 Manufacturing Schedules, newspapers, county directories, journals, and the R. G. Dun Credit Reports.

*General note:* Figures in parentheses are percentages above the value of raw materials used given by the census.

medium cottons and threads as cheaply as the South."[60] The *Trinity Advocate*, of Palestine, Texas, urged southerners to produce the textiles that they needed for themselves and export any extra that they could produce.[61] The editor of the *Southern Business Directory and General Commercial Advertiser* also thought that the region possessed excellent sources of raw materials. This guide praised Montgomery, Alabama, because "its iron, wood and other manufactories, are large, and creditable for so young a city."[62] If cotton agriculture had a natural advantage in the region, then any industry that either made use of this cotton, or could help with the production of cotton, would also have an advantage in the Gulf South. Overall, the estimate of the costs of raw materials was somewhere between 3.29 percent and 24.56 percent higher than what the census reported. Most likely, the actual number would be between the mean estimated value of 8.31 percent and the high value (see Table 3.1).[63]

Daniel Pratt, the quintessential example of a southern industrialist, proved the importance of local sources of raw materials with his Prattville factories. Pratt, a Whig who supported industrial development in the South, used locally sourced materials whenever possible for his firms.[64] He believed that "Alabama possessed the raw materials, labor and businessmen needed to increase its manufacturing, but her legislature had not enacted the proper legislation to encourage industry."[65] Pratt hoped that taxes could be lowered on manufactories to help promote development. He also pushed for other kinds of state support such as improvements to Alabama's transportation infrastructure, especially railroads, along with other internal improvements.[66] But Pratt was not all talk; he did what he could to support development himself by purchasing his raw materials from all over Alabama and the rest of the South. Pratt used 40 tons of shafting per year that he purchased from a firm in Etowah, Georgia; he got 150 tons of pig iron from Shelby County, Alabama; all of the lime and coal that Prattville used came from local sources; also, Pratt used 1,200 bales of Alabama cotton.[67] Moreover, the Prattville factories used 120,000 pounds of wool from Nueces County, Texas.[68] Pratt, a transplanted northerner, took to heart living in and supporting the South and its manufacturing efforts and used locally produced materials whenever possible to aid the region's development.

As Pratt and his imitators showed, the South was well situated to provide for itself. It had the climate to grow what was needed to feed its population and supply industry with raw materials. Although writing a few years after the war, H. P. Chapman nevertheless captured what the late antebellum South was like:

> Southern factories possess the advantages of proximity to the cotton fields, and a climate whose mildness insures them against these interlopers to work, which, in severe winters, are often causes of inconvenience and loss to Northern mills. Other advantages over the North are cheaper land, cheaper building material, fuel and labor, and longer working hours. Nearness to the cotton fields means not only a saving in cost of transportation of the raw material and a reduction to the minimum of inevitable

> loss in weight by handling, but it means also a better selection and lower prices. Southern mills can buy their cotton direct and save the profits and changes which the Northern mills must pay to brokers and middle-men.[69]

Yet as far as many were concerned, southerners ignored all of these natural advantages. According to a Mississippi planter, "the South sits immovable, and is content to derive her food and clothing from regions thousands of miles away."[70] But, that perception was wrong. The South was manufacturing for itself with its own resources.

# 4

## CREATING A MARKET

### Transportation in the Gulf South

One of the reasons that we can address the Gulf South as a region, rather than just a collection of states, is the transportation arteries that knit the area together into a coherent whole. Moreover, the tremendous growth in railroads in the decade leading up to the Civil War shows the connection between transportation and manufacturing that swept the Gulf South, pushing forward the region's economy and industrial development. Railroads, canals, and roads were not scattered haphazardly across the landscape, but were instead located where needed to support agriculture, commerce, and industry.[1] The South then was on a path to modernity, contrary to the widely held opinion about slave-based society at the time. As Richard Brown points out, "Historians frequently associate the modern era with dramatic technological advances in communication, transportation, and production as well as with the creation of the nation-state."[2] If we appraise the South against this standard of what constitutes a modern society, we see that the South does in fact measure up. De Bow saw a bright future for the South when he wrote in 1852 that "having constructed a system of railroads netting every section of our territory, the South and West will naturally resort to manufacturing which is our second great remedy for the evils which present [*sic*] shows and the future foreshadows."[3]

Railroads were the high technology of the day, and many felt that building them marked a modern society. The Gulf South was as modern as any other part of the nation, or the world for that matter. Of course, railroads were not the only form of transportation available in the region; rivers and roads also helped to meet the area's needs.

Economic development of any kind required infrastructure, especially a transportation network, as few towns enjoyed local access to all of the resources needed for industrialization. The usefulness of these internal improvements cannot be overstated: "literally fixed to the ground, roads, canals, and other internal improvements were capable of altering political and economic geography: such was their express purpose."[4] Interregional connection proliferated as canals, steamboats, and railroads permitted greater movement of people and gave entrepreneurs who wished to start manufacturing concerns access to the materials needed for their businesses, markets for their goods, and connections to credit to help with both. People in the Gulf South were just as affected by transportation developments as anywhere else in the nation and, as the transportation improved, the region shrank. New Orleans was the region's major metropolitan center, and those living in rural areas of Mississippi and Alabama "spoke of going 'to town' as if New Orleans was only a mile distant."[5] John C. Calhoun, the great southern booster, saw the importance of internal improvements, stating, "let us then . . . bind the Republic together with a perfect system of roads and canals. Let us conquer space."[6]

Rivers dominated transportation in the Gulf South, and as usual, Alabama led the way. Rivers served many of the state's needs, and railroads, when they developed, would first connect outlying areas to the river system. Rivers thus steered Alabama's development and broke the state down into six geographical regions based mostly on rivers: the Tennessee Valley, the hill region, the Alabama and Tombigbee river valleys, the Coosa River valley, the Black Belt, and the coastal plain.[7] Moreover, Alabama's river systems split the state into two large sections, a northern part oriented toward Tennessee and a southern part drawn to the markets along the Gulf of Mexico.[8]

River transportation and industry went hand in hand. One of the most important cities in Alabama, and the most developed industrially, was Mobile. It was the state's major port on the Gulf and, through the Mobile River, was connected to a river system consisting of the Tombigbee, Black Warrior, Cahaba, Coosa, and Tallapoosa Rivers. These rivers gave Mobile access to a large hinterland market for its goods and in turn gave hinterland manufacturers sources of raw materials and semi-finished goods.[9] For example, Turner and Stackhouse used the river to move marble to Mobile to turn into finished goods.[10] J. F. Jewett's steam lumber mill most likely also benefited from the water transport near the city.[11] Northern Alabama also benefited from its rivers because "the Tennessee valley was admirably suited, by virtue of its vast water power, for the introduction of manufactures."[12] Many of the state's rivers received some improvements before the war, funded for the most part by the federal government, as rivalries between sections of Alabama precluded state-supported improvements.[13] Franklin County, in the Tennessee Valley, had a major sawmill owned by James Throckmorton and a tannery owned by Norman and Wheeler; both could benefit from water-based avenues of trade.[14]

Mississippi also had industrial potential thanks to its transportation geography, with the Mississippi River especially vital to the state's development. The river allowed access to distant markets for the state's products and allowed Mississippians to import finished goods, technology, and materials, all of which encouraged and augmented the state's industrial development. Historians have often considered rivers to be conduits through which wealth flowed out of the South. But, in the case of the Gulf South, and Mississippi especially, there was a bidirectional flow that allowed development to flourish and served purposes beyond that of transportation. As was true of the other coastal states, Mississippi had several rivers that ran far into its interior. Most of these rivers eventually came to the fall line, the furthest point to which boats could travel upstream. This line became an important location for industrial development because the water power from the falls could drive a variety of manufacturing works.[15] Although Mississippi lacked extensive sources of raw materials, it had a strong river system that could nevertheless support industrial development. For example, Natchez, Mississippi greatly benefited from its location on the Mississippi River, and firms such as David Gunning's cabinet shop, George Dickerman's carriage shop, and A. R. Tyler's wagon manufacturing all drew on the prosperity the river brought.[16]

Texas, the third Gulf South state studied here, is the most geographically diverse. As Ray Stephens and William M. Holmes explain, "'Nowhere but in Texas' is an apt statement to describe the diversity that ranges from seashore to mountains, from swamps to deserts, from subtropical lands to wind-swept plains, from pine forests to short-grass country, with a variety of plant and animal life unparalleled elsewhere."[17] Despite this great diversity, antebellum Texas followed the pattern established in the rest of the South; as settlers moved west from places like Alabama and Mississippi, they brought with them their traditional way of life, one based on cotton and slave labor.[18] And, as with Alabama and Mississippi, industry followed. Texans made the same use of their rivers, such as the Red and the Rio Grande, that the residents of other Gulf South states made of theirs, planting cotton in the river valleys and using the water for power and transportation.[19] This pattern was especially pronounced in the two most developed regions of Texas—East Texas and the Houston-Galveston area—which were quickly becoming like the rest of the antebellum South.[20] Many small manufacturing centers developed throughout these regions to meet local demand for goods because transportation from other states was expensive.[21] Houston, as stated, benefited from its geographic location. Thos. Zimmerman built cotton presses to serve the area.[22] Paul Bremmond was building the Houston & Texas Central Railroad, and Alexander McGowan's foundry also took advantage of their geographic locations in Houston to become prosperous.[23]

Beyond natural routes of movement, the first transportation improvements to be built in any area were roads and turnpikes. In Mississippi, road building got under way almost as soon as settlers arrived, but few roads existed in the eastern part of the state, primarily because there were no large population centers to which to connect. By contrast, all of the roads in the western half of the state connected to New Orleans or Natchez, the major cities of the region, going through smaller cities and towns, such as Jackson, Monticello, Columbus, and Madisonville.[24] Firms such as John H. Bobb Sr's brickmaking concern, George Smith's foundry, and Bob Tappin's ironworks, as "large profitable businesss," took advantage of the roads built in their local areas to bring in materials and send out finished products.[25] Centers of trade developed where roads came together and met with water transport to places such as those listed before and also Memphis, Jackson, Columbus, Vicksburg, and Mobile.[26] Roads in Alabama followed the same pattern as in Mississippi, connecting hinterlands to major centers like Mobile and Montgomery.[27] These roads allowed a "good prudent sober and reliable man" such as Ralph Williams to run a profitable tin works in the state capital.[28]

Roads in frontier Texas were more important than in Mississippi and Alabama because of the state's size and its late settlement. Roads were the only form of transportation available in most areas, yet "most roads were little more than tracks through the woods and across the prairies, likely to be ankle-deep in dust in the summer and even deeper in mud during the spring and fall."[29] Carts were the major form of transportation, moving most products and materials around the state at a rate of almost ten cents per mile for heavy items.[30] The most important antebellum road was the El Paso Road. Split into upper and lower sections, it connected San Antonio with El Paso, a major trade center, and then went on to California.[31] In East Texas, roads ran to the coast at Galveston, Houston, or Indianola. Then, passengers and freight traveled, using the Southern Steamship Line to New Orleans.[32] These roads brought in raw materials from distant places, supplying Texans with the means to start industrial concerns. Thus, Marshall and Brother were doing a good business in tin and stoves and Soloman Rice produced highly valued saddles and harnesses, both in San Antonio, benefiting from the trade networks developed based on the region's needs.[33]

Railroads helped drive industrial development in the South by expanding trade networks and the demand from the railroads themselves for manufactured goods (see Table 4.1). Railroads were major undertakings, and the investments needed for land, track, locomotives, rolling stock, and labor to build one went far beyond that required for most other projects. There were two main kinds of railroad development. Exploitive development took advantage of avenues of trade that were already in use and was undertaken mostly by private companies for a quick return on investment. Developmental railroad construction, the second form, was not instantly profitable and was supported mostly by

TABLE 4.1. Gulf South railroad mileage

| State | Railroad mileage in 1860 |
|---|---|
| Alabama | 743.16 |
| Mississippi | 872.39 |
| Texas | 306.00 |

*Source:* U.S. Census Compilation, Schedule E, 230.

the state.[34] Only large companies or governments could find a way to get that funding, especially long-term loans for the development needed by the Gulf South.[35] John Larson asserts that "in the South, private capitalists habitually favored land and slaves over industry and commerce, so public officials pushed state investment in trunk-line railroads they hoped would be augmented by private branch lines."[36] This assertion is somewhat overdrawn. Southerners did invest in things other than slaves, but at their beginning southern railroads were an unfamiliar investment that southern investors approached warily.

But once the utility of railroads was proven, a "mania" developed in the Gulf South, as it did in much of the rest of the country, beginning in the 1830s and 1840s.[37] Public money was spent on these improvements from the very beginning. Consequently the Gulf South went deeply into debt to fund railroads in order to remain competitive with other states. The Panic of 1837 drove more of the funding from the public to private sector, however, as "lawmakers everywhere turned to corporations as buffers between the people's demand for transportation improvement and the state's responsibility for borrowing money or doing the work."[38] For example, by 1847, after which the state of Alabama stopped borrowing money to build railroads, the state had spent $204,998 on internal improvements, such as canals, roads, and railroads. Mississippi, in sharp contrast, spent only $46,500.[39] Thus, much of the public money for improvements came from the federal government after this point, not the states themselves, and was insignificant compared to what was required to develop the transportation services needed. All of this did not discourage people in the region from trying to create a transportation infrastructure, but it did cause promoters to move to the private sector for capital, with many state-owned works passing into the hands of private investors in the decade before the war.[40]

All of these problems aside, men in Montgomery, Jackson, and Austin saw how lucrative undertakings like the Pennsylvania Railroad were and wanted to encourage that kind of development in their own territory. State governments helped out when they could with money and land grants, but it took a combination of federal, state, municipal, county, and private funding to build.[41] Railroads in this period always were risky undertakings, though. Thus, the railroad boom left most of the Gulf South buried even further in debt by 1851 as depression and bad choices left these states on the hook for rail lines that were never completed.[42] Even with all of these problems, 57 percent of the money needed to build southern railroads came from the public sector, compared to the northern average of 25–30 percent.[43] This reliance on public funding was due in part to the fact that the South's manufacturing sector, while undergoing considerable growth, did not yet have quite the level of sophistication needed to create large private companies like the Pennsylvania Railroad. In 1842, the North and the South had the same railroad mileage, but another depression, in which many southern railroads went bankrupt, stunted development until the end of the antebellum period and put the South almost ten years behind the North. Railroad construction, even through all of this, continued unabated until the outbreak of the war, and "the region had about as much road per capita as the country as a whole."[44] So, in the decade leading up to the war, the South as a whole made tremendous gains.[45]

Southern railroads were built for a specific purpose and served this purpose well. They were not built to support a nation trying to fight a major continental war; they were built to connect the various parts of the South with outside markets, bringing in needed goods and sending out the South's products, building up its economy, particularly its industry.[46] Rail lines then ran from interior areas to water transportation, or connected two major market centers.[47] They were not built to connect the Gulf South to Virginia, even though, by the end of the antebellum period, rail lines had become so interconnected that this travel was possible.[48] Many of the rail lines ran north to south, from the Border South to areas such as the Gulf South, bringing manufactured goods in and taking out staple products.[49] This is the traditional view of U. B. Phillips again, but in this case Phillips was at least partially correct in his understanding of how goods flowed in and out of the South.[50] What he and others missed was how the interregional traffic into and out of the South spurred the development of southern internal markets, especially by 1860. Southerners, as they produced more for themselves, greatly changed these market flows and helped prepare, unwittingly, for the disruption of traditional market connections and for breaking the control of southern wealth by merchants in northern cites.[51]

In following the example of northern development, southerners used methods of railroad building and management that the North had been perfecting for years, as the "South, in terms of railroads, took the same path to modernization as the North, except for one critical difference—slave labor."[52] The South built up a modern, industrial enterprise, using slave labor, showing thereby that slavery and modern development could go hand in hand.[53] This push for a modern industrialized economy resulted in the South building more miles of track than the North in the 1850s.[54] While this edge was due to the fact that the North really did not need as many new lines as the South, it does show that the South was industrializing. Railroad development was so intense that "in the five years just prior to the Civil War . . . the section made rapid progress towards bringing the quality of its rails back up to national standards. Given another decade of peace the South might have succeeded."[55] It was not just the networks created by the railroads that drove industrial expansion; it was also everything needed by a railroad to operate that helped drive manufacturing development, as "every large southern railroad built maintenance shops to repair locomotives and cars. Some even constructed their own freight cars, box cars, platform cars, wheel cars, and second-class passenger cars."[56]

Every state of the Gulf South participated in the railroad boom. As one would expect, Alabama was the most developed of the three states discussed here. Map 4.1 shows the location and extent of railroads in the state. Because of the debt Alabama was under when the boom began,

MAP 4.1. Alabama railroads in 1860.
*Source:* National Historical Geographic Information System, https://www.nhgis.org/.

from bad investments in canals and early railroad ventures, the state had problems directly supporting railroad development. Most tax money in the decade leading up to the war was needed to pay down the public debt.[57] Most of the public funding for railroads in Alabama came from land grants and bond sales, as "legislation had proceeded not by sudden and radical measures differing from all precedent, but by small beginnings which gradually prepared the public mind for the more elaborate schemes which were to follow."[58] These corporations did make many southerners nervous, though. There was a fear that they took power away from the people and made their money through no productive efforts, and thus getting acts of incorporation proved difficult at times. But railroad investors pushed ahead and Alabama began to get the roads it needed.[59]

In the 1850s many railroads in the state received land grants, including the Mobile & Ohio; the Alabama & Florida; the Selma, Rome, & Dalton; the Alabama & Chattanooga; the South & North Alabama; and the Mobile & Girard.[60] Not all of these railroads would be completed, or even started for that matter, but the state willingly supported any chance at getting tracks laid. Moreover, Alabamians even went outside the state for support, asking at the 1852 Southern Commercial Convention, held in New Orleans, for investment in the Mobile & Ohio railroad.[61] Like railroads around the rest of the nation and around the world, Alabama railroads helped spur industrial development. Hence a brief review of the Alabama rail network is important to our understanding of Gulf South industrial development.

The center of the Alabama railroad network was Mobile, and, as Alabama's only seaport, it served as the state's connection to the rest of the United States and the world. A great deal of traffic went into and out of Mobile. Industry quickly developed in the city, and the need to be able to move goods into the interior of the state became very important, not just for the economic development of Mobile, but for the entire state and region. The major rail line into the city was the Mobile and Ohio Railroad, which connected the city with the Ohio River and gave it access to western markets, bringing staple crops into the city and creating a market in which Mobile manufacturers sold their goods.[62] This railroad was founded in 1857, funded by $300,000 from the city government of Mobile, but not completed until 1861 when it reached Cairo, Illinois, although it began carrying traffic in sections as soon as possible.[63] It also received indirect federal funding through an 1850 act that gave federal land to states that in turn gave it to railroad companies to defray construction costs.[64] This was not the only line to run out of the city, as the Mobile & Cedar Point Railroad, running twenty-eight miles, was also there.[65] Milton Brown was its president, and, in February 1861, Dun reported that the road was "finished to Corinth, Tennessee, pay no dividends yet or debt until they choose, think the road will yet pay, Certificates of stock sold at Auction @ 33 cts on$ [*sic*]."[66] Thus Mobile, because of its geography and its transportation connections, grew into a major industrial center.

In addition to the Mobile railroads, Alabama boasted other lines that were "pressed by the people with a zeal and activity that are the guarantees of the highest and most brilliant success."[67] Many people in the state saw the importance of railroads to economic development. Railroads were the future, and few wanted to be left behind. So, Alabamians bought into the railroad craze in full force. In his work on industry in the South, De Bow lists four other major railroads in Alabama: the Montgomery & West Point; the Alabama & Tennessee; the Tuscumbia, Courtland, & Decatur; and the Memphis & Charleston.[68] The Montgomery & West Point actually appeared in the Dun Reports and was reputed as "eminently solvent," and even after the war, in February 1866, was "good but slow."[69] Moreover, Arnold Seale was running the Union Railroad in Montgomery and "was rich and able to pay all contracts," and like the Montgomery & West Point, was still in business after the war.[70] In 1860, the Alabama & Tennessee Railroad was "in better condition than ever before, the legislature has loaned it $225000 and land grants by Congress of near 300,000 acres, add much to the strength of this corporation."[71] From these beginning railroads grew across the state at an amazing rate. The Wetumpka Railroad was built to connect the Tennessee River with the Alabama River at Wetumpka, Alabama, which was the furthest steamboats could use the Alabama River before hitting the fall line, extending the reach of the natural waterways of the state.[72] The Montgomery & West Point Railroad, an eighty-seven-mile-long rail line, which was built to connect the Alabama railroad system with Georgia, increased the markets available to people in each state and drew them closer together.[73] The Selma & Cahawba Railroad was built as a branch of the Pensacola & Montgomery Railroad to pull central Alabama into the transportation network of the South, and to allow the growing city of Selma access to developing markets in Florida.[74] Cahawba, because of its location, became a rail juncture, and the Cahawba & Marion Railroad further extended and integrated Alabama railroads, reaching Marion in 1857.[75] The Selma & Tennessee Railroad was the closest that Alabama would come to a major north/south connection before the war, while the Tuscumbia, Courtland, & Decatur Railroad, running about forty-four miles, became another link with Georgia.[76]

The Montgomery Railroad, originally chartered in 1832, was an important line for the state and was built with mostly slave labor.[77] This was not unusual. Slaves were a ready source of labor, and planters were more than willing to lend or hire out their spare hands for railroad construction, especially if it ran near their plantations. Overall, even with cheap labor available, railroads were very expensive undertakings. For

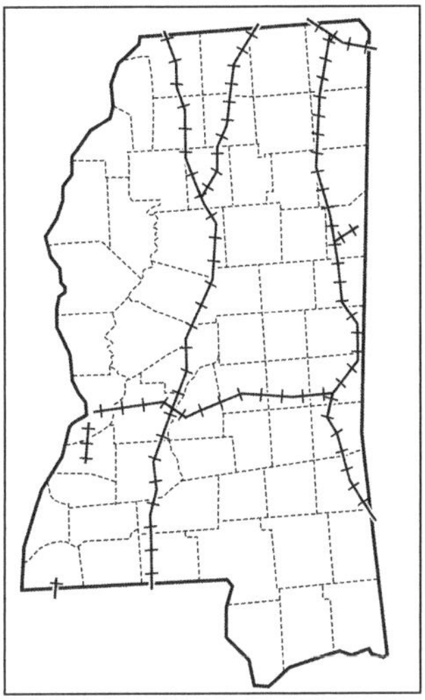

MAP 4.2. Mississippi railroads in 1860.
*Source:* National Historical Geographic Information System, https://www.nhgis.org/.

example, the Alabama, Florida, & Georgia Railroad, which ran from Pensacola, Florida to Montgomery, cost $5,500 per mile to build, and the total cost of the road, including track, buildings, and other expenses came to $2,500,000.[78] Thus, railroads were not individual undertakings, a large amount of money and many people needed to be brought together and organized. This organization bled into other parts of Alabama's society, such as manufacturing.

Altogether, Alabama had 743 miles of railroad in 1860, with a great deal more under construction.[79] Alabama had more than enough miles of rail line to be able to meet its needs to move products and resources around the state. Moreover, railroad construction in the state created a boom in industry to support these new transportation networks.[80] Also, the northern and southern parts of the state needed railroads to tie them together into one working whole.[81] The railroads not only knitted the region and the country together, they brought together states and spurred people into keeping up with modern development. As the maps of industrial concerns in chapter 2 shows, industrial development and railroads went hand in hand.

Mississippi also played a major role in the development of the Gulf

South rail network. These lines are shown in Map 4.2. Mississippians felt "that railroads signaled economic independence since they provided access to markets," and "viewed railroads as another sign of their autonomy."[82] Much of Mississippi's railroad development was brought on by New Orleans and Mobile merchants attempting to capture the Mississippi market.[83] In Mississippi, as in Alabama and much of the rest of the South, the role of railroads was to tie together hinterlands with market centers.[84] This was borne out by the industry found in the Dun Reports and the Census. But because of bank failures and other economic problems, a familiar refrain, the credit of the Mississippi state government was not well suited to support widespread railroad development.[85]

Other sources of funding were available, however. For example, in March 1860, the *Jackson Daily News* reported that all of the bonds for the newly planned Vicksburg and Shreveport Railroad had been sold in the city and that "A safe investment like these securities offer, at 80c. for 8 percent bonds, never remain long on our market, because there is usually a large surplus of capital here watching such opportunities."[86] Dun lists Fanin Grant and Company as the leases of the Vicksburg and Shreveport and found it "no doubt is good for contracts."[87] Thus, the public paid for building the roads, and a local company turned it into a productive concern. Also, Mississippi, like many other states, looked not just for internal sources of capital for their new lines, they looked outside the state also. Mississippians at the 1852 New Orleans Commercial Convention asked, as Alabama had, for funding for the New Orleans, Jackson, & Nashville Road; the New Orleans, Holly Springs, & Ohio Road; and the Vicksburg & Jackson Road.[88] At the time of the 1852 Commercial Convention there were five railroads in operation in the state: the Raymond, the St. Francisville & Woodville, the Vicksburg & Brandon, the Mobile & Ohio, and the Memphis & Charleston.[89] But Mississippi needed more as far as De Bow and many others were concerned, as "Mississippi can as yet boast of but few works on internal improvement."[90] The most important line in the state during the antebellum period was the railroad between Jackson, the state capital, and Vicksburg, the most important trading center in the state with access to the Mississippi River.[91] Vicksburg held a place in Mississippi much as Mobile did for Alabama.

By 1860 there were many railroads in operation, connecting most of the state's plantation regions with market centers and linking the state to rail networks in other states. The Mississippi Railroad ran from Natchez to Canton, through Gallatin and Jackson for a total length of 150 miles connecting inland areas with market centers.[92] The Springfield & Liberty Railroad ran thirty miles through Amite County to bring plantation products to market.[93] The Vicksburg & Clinton went between its namesake cities and was planned to be expanded as far as Jackson in the future.[94] There were also many smaller lines. The Grand Gulf & Port Gibson was only a little over seven miles long, while the Jackson & Brandon ran for fourteen miles, connecting outlying areas with Jackson.[95] Overall, when the first shot was fired in the war, Mississippi had about 872 miles of operating track.[96] This network served the needs of the state, connecting inland areas to established water routes, moving goods cheaply and reliably, all of which was needed for manufacturing development. Moreover, railroads were an important undertaking that brought together people such as the members of the board of directors of the Gulf & Ship Island Railroad Company (see Table 4.2). The men listed here were leaders of their communities who saw how bringing a railroad to an area could benefit the people of Mississippi. They worked to bring this railroad into being, and the local population recognized and supported it. As this table suggests, many parts of Mississippi participated in the development of the state's railroads. When taken with the evidence from Dun, we can see that cotton, while important, was not the only economic engine driving Mississippi before the war.

Texas experienced a large railroad boom in the 1850s, in large part because of the drive for new cotton lands. Texas had some of the best, and cheapest, cotton lands left in the South, and needed some form of reliable transportation to exploit them.[97] In 1853, in the aftermath of the Mexican-American War, Texas only had twenty miles of track. Less than a decade later, in 1860, the state had built 306 miles of railroad (see Map 4.3).[98] Texas was by far the largest state in the Union and arguably had the greatest need for railroads to push it from being a frontier area into

TABLE 4.2. Board of Directors of the Gulf and Ship Island Company

| Name | County | Name | County |
|---|---|---|---|
| Cornelius McLaurin (Pres.) | Jackson | Walter Goodman | Marshall |
| Joseph McAfee | Rankin County | Samuel White | Hancock |
| M. J. Mackie | Madison | T. J. Blackwell | Smith |
| Joel E. Welborne | Jones | Porter J. Myers | Perry |
| Dan'l McLaurin | Covington | F. Pope | Covington |
| L. B. Walker | Simpson | L. Lulienne (Sec. of Board) | Jackson |
| W. R. Tegarden | Harrison | | |

*Source: Jackson Daily News*, March 13, 1860.

the mainstream of the American economy. The construction of railroads did not even begin in Texas until 1852, much later than any other state in the South, even though charters had been granted for many roads before that time.[99] But even with the drive to open new cotton lands, railroads brought industry to the state in the decade leading to secession.

The first railroad opened in the state was the Buffalo Bayou, Brazos, & Colorado Railroad in 1853.[100] But from the beginning, Houston served as the railroad hub of the entire state because "Houston businessmen were particularly adept at securing railroad transportation and by 1861 rail line stretched from Houston up to Washington and Brazos counties and down into Brazoria County."[101] Railroads were important to manufacturing in Texas to expand and develop markets and industry over such vast distances. Before the war, though, no railroad line crossed the borders of the state; all of them either connected with rivers or to the coast.[102] Although the growth in mileage in the decade leading up to the war was fantastic, it really did not begin to reach all of Texas. De Bow called for more development in the state and attempted to get its railroads tied in to the rest of the South, but this did not occur before the war as he had hoped.[103] By late 1859, there were eight major railroads

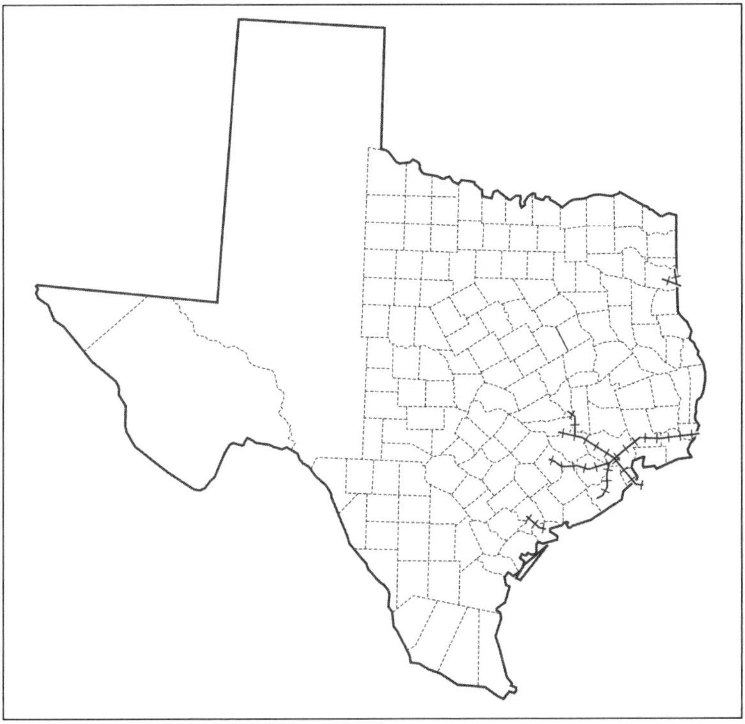

MAP 4.3. Texas railroads in 1860.

*Source:* National Historical Geographic Information System, https://www.nhgis.org/.

operating in Texas: the Galveston, Houston, & Henderson; the Buffalo Bayou, Brazos, & Colorado; the Houston Tap & Brazoria; the Houston & Texas Central; the Washington County Line; the San Antonio & Mexican Gulf; the Southern Pacific; and the New Orleans & Texas.[104] The state supported this development the best it could and offered land grants to railroads along with state-backed loans.[105] Paul Bremmond was the contractor hired to build the Houston & Texas Central. Dun reported in July 1859 that "the road is being pushed ahead first class, some 60 miles finished, and its prospects are excellent."[106] Some smaller lines were also recorded by Dun; for example, Major Williams was listed as the engineer running the Harrisburgh Railroad in Harris County, "but know nothing of this responsibility."[107] On the eve of the war a group of Galveston businessmen founded the Houston, Trinity, & Tyler Railroad, "on the cash basis, principal directors are first bus men in Galveston [*sic*]."[108] While the road did not succeed, the drive was there to build more lines. Moreover, Dun discussed a railroad contractor in Trinity County named C. C. Coppedge. While he was not listed as being associated with any specific country, he did know the business well.[109] So, Texas had the drive and expertise to develop its rail network. Luckily, the one thing that Texas, and the rest of the Gulf South, had was the labor to build and maintain any railroads they constructed.

In the antebellum South, slavery and railroads went hand in hand. Many southerners believed that "the railroad ensured slavery's and the South's future."[110] This was not a universal view. Slavery was sometimes perceived, especially by people outside of the South, as backwards. Railroads were cutting-edge technology. Supposedly, then, a slave society should not be able to support railroad building internally. But as James Ward explains: "A closer look at the development of antebellum railroads in the South indicates that a rural slave owning society was not inherently incapable of financing and constructing a quality rail system."[111] Now this is not to say that southerners themselves were able to build everything needed to run a railroad, including track, cars, and other necessities. They had to go outside the region for some of the material that they needed, especially at the beginning of railroad development.[112] But over time, many major southern railroads began building their own cars, and made use of slave labor to do so. In 1860, at least 14,600 slaves worked on southern railroads, with many more unrecorded.[113] Some railroad companies owned their own slave workforce, while almost all hired slave labor as needed. Because of this, "the use of slave labor was nearly universal on antebellum railroads in the South."[114] Of course, slaves that could be used for railroads could also be used for industry.

Slave labor for railroad construction had advantages over free labor for antebellum southern entrepreneurs wanting to make the South more modern and economically competitive. First, slaves were widely available throughout the region. Second, slaves were a guaranteed workforce that once trained would be on the job permanently. A third factor was the cost of slave labor versus free. For example, a white railroad carpenter in Charlotte, North Carolina demanded a wage of $40 a month, a black carpenter on the same line would only need room and board of about $20; a white foreman had to be paid $35 a month, while a black foreman only required $15 in room and board.[115] While the initial cost of buying a slave has to be factored in, over time, slave workers more than paid for themselves when labor cost, training, and control are taken into account. R. G. Morris, Esq. reported in 1854 that "slaves belonging to a company can excavate earth for less than half—can excavate rock for about one-fourth—and can construct culverts, bridges, abutments, locks, dams, &c. at about one-seventh that the same kind of work will cost contractors."[116] Edward G. Parker, the treasurer of the Charleston & Savannah Railroad, hired a slave named Caesar from a Rev. L. H. Cavnish of Aiken, South Carolina for seventeen days of work for $9.80.[117] While the type of work Caesar did is not listed, this receipt shows that railroad companies used slave labor. For the South, slaves were good workers for both skilled and unskilled labor, and the use of slaves on railroads was widespread throughout the region.[118]

As steam and rail replaced horse and cart, industrial development swept the Gulf South. Citizens of Alabama, Mississippi, and Texas pushed infrastructure projects forward, and the region had the resources to make development possible. While cotton and slaves still dominated the landscape, these other projects were also driving forces in changing and expanding the markets of the region. Moreover, Gulf South residents recognized the importance of these projects and reported on them far and wide. Between the resources and transportation available to Gulf South entrepreneurs, the industry that existed in the region should not be surprising, and it was not surprising to the inhabitants of these states. The men who worked on and founded these infrastructure concerns were seen as strong and important members of their communities, respected and celebrated, not marginalized and ignored. Of course, now that it has been established that there were more industrial concerns in the region than previously believed, and some attempt has been made to explain their existence, the potential scale of this development can be discussed.

# 5

## FACTORS OF INDUSTRIAL PRODUCTION

### Capital and Labor in the Gulf South

On January 11, 1860, the *New Orleans Bee* printed an editorial celebrating "the determination of Southern men to encourage their own home industry, in order to protect their rights and institutions."[1] There were, as we have seen, many southerners to be celebrated. These entrepreneurs were willing and able to build manufacturing concerns and worked to develop an industrial base in the Gulf South. But there is a great deal more to the creation of a successful concern than a willing owner, a good location, and the availability of resources and transportation. Other factors—availability of capital and raw labor—were essential to manufacturing, and the Gulf South had ample supplies of them. As the Dun reports show, southerners had money of their own to invest, and northerners were willing to extend them credit. These sources of capital, applied to the region's raw materials by the labor of its white and black workers, fueled the antebellum South's industrial development. The location of firms, their ownership, and their organizational forms provide the outlines of a picture of manufacturing in the Gulf South. The factors of production that this chapter discusses will provide definition to that picture.

As the number of manufacturing firms in the Gulf South increased, their supplies of the factors of production increased as well. Industrial boosters understood the importance of capital and labor and pushed entrepreneurs to apply these factors of production to new undertakings, urging: "Why not then embark a portion of your capital, or your labor, which is the same thing, in manufactures? It would be an experiment, it is true; but without experiments great results can never be obtained."[2]

The creation and operation of these firms began a transformation of the region. While many hoped this change would be for the better, some feared it would be for the worse. J. D. B. De Bow confronted this uncertainty:

> It is also said, that where manufacturing and commerce flourish, morals are corrupted and free institutions do not prosper. It is undoubtedly true, that when men congregate in cities and factories, the vices of our nature are more fully displayed, while the purist morals are fostered by rural life. But, on the other hand, the compensations of association are great. It develops genius, stimulates enterprise, and rewards every degree of merit.[3]

Probably, for every naysayer there was at least one booster, touting the benefits to be realized from industrialization.

Although information on capital, labor, and wages was listed in the manufacturing census schedules, such information was, for the most part, not available for firms missed by the census. Newspaper advertisements listed the location of such concerns, what they sold, and the cost of their products. Some even included an illustration or two. But they did not present any information about how many employees worked for the firm or their wages. The Dun reports had the same deficiencies. They included information on a firm's creditworthiness and sometimes on its personal property, real estate, and slave ownership, but the reporters rarely provided any information on capital investment or the wages that they paid their free workers. Contemporaneous local histories and city and county directories, which focused on political, military, and social events, also offered little in the way of such information. But it is possible to arrive at estimates of the capitalization and wage bills of firms by using the averages of each of those factors of production provided for firms enumerated in the census.[4]

Investors in the Gulf South had many different capital investment opportunities available to them. The traditional view of the southern economy holds that southerners invested primarily in land and slaves because of the high returns that could be made in cotton and other sta-

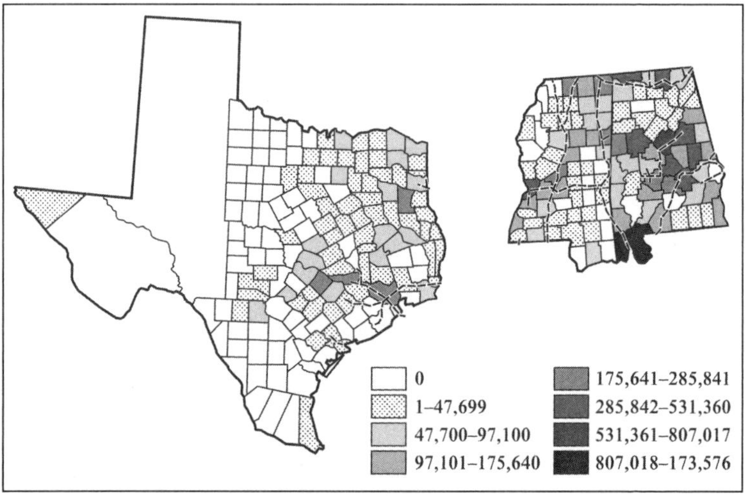


MAP 5.1. Capital investment of firms listed in the 1860 Census (dollars). *Source:* Census of 1860 Manufacturing Schedules.

ples. This characterization of antebellum southern investment practices somewhat overstates the case. Of course, many men in the region did buy land and slaves to engage in cotton production. But entrepreneurs invested capital in several types of business in the region, including "foreign and domestic commerce, city and town property, houses, canals, railroads, manufactures, banking, insurance, iron and coal mining, timber trade, steamboats, and shipping."[5] Industrial firms required capital to buy land or rent buildings, purchase machinery and raw materials, and meet other, miscellaneous expenses. The census schedules included a column in which marshals were to record the amount of capital invested in each firm. The results of the census's tabulation of capital invested in manufacturing are displayed in Map 5.1. Not surprisingly, the greatest concentrations of industrial capital were in the major urban centers of the Gulf South. But overall, investment in manufacturing, at least according to the census, was fairly widespread. Moreover, as the map shows, there was a belt of strong capital investment that ran through the middle of Alabama and Mississippi. This belt followed the railroad lines and also corresponded to counties with large amounts of cotton production, and, unsurprisingly, large numbers of slaves.[6] As chapter 3 explained, some of this capital came from cotton planters who diverted it from further agricultural investment and moved it into manufacturing enterprises in an attempt at diversification. A long line of writers, from Olmsted to Charles Beard to Bateman and Weiss, have asserted that economic diversification in the antebellum South was inhibited, even precluded, by the investment preferences and behavior of the planter class.[7] But that view does not stand up well in the face of new evidence presented here. As William Scarborough has demonstrated, planters were one of the largest sources of capital in the region, and any significant economic development would have required their support.[8]

The amount of capital investment in manufacturing in the Gulf South was considerably larger than the census reported. Maps 5.2 and 5.3 display the estimated capital investment for each county in Alabama, Mississippi, and Texas. These maps show a range of possible estimates of investment in the region, and it is clear that capital investment was

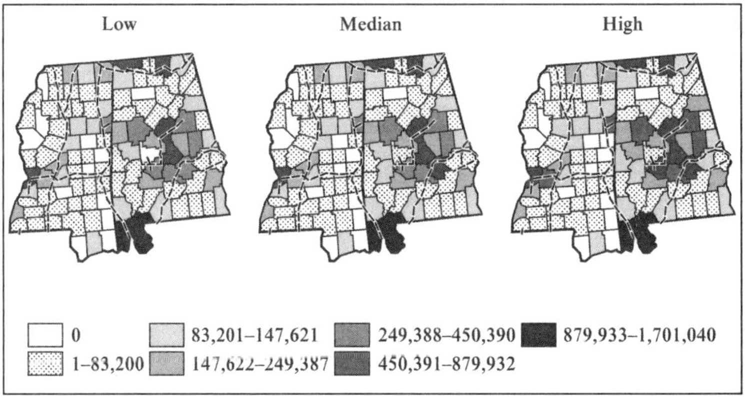


MAP 5.2. Estimated levels of capital investment in 1860 for firms found in all sources for Alabama and Mississippi.

*Sources:* Census of 1860 Manufacturing Schedules, newspapers, county directories, journals, and the R. G. Dun Credit Reports.

more widespread than the census reported and also significantly larger in those areas where it was geographically concentrated. The urban Gulf South had far more investment than the marshals found, and entrepreneurs put industrial capital to work in almost every part of the region. Table 5.1 displays estimates of the actual total amounts of industrial capital in the Gulf South.[9] These estimates suggest that capital investment in the region's manufacturing concerns in 1860 was between 3.40 percent and 21.47 percent greater than the census reported. Industrial boosters, entrepreneurs, and plantation owners were rational economic actors. People living and working in the Gulf South needed goods that local industrial concerns could supply, and the region offered many advantages to founders of manufacturing firms, such as transportation lines, readily accessible raw materials, and abundant supplies of labor. Consequently, men with capital saw the Gulf South as a fertile region for manufacturing investment, not just in the larger urban areas, but in more rural parts of these states as well.

Industrialization was centered on the use of machines to augment the labor of people. While most workmen in the Gulf South labored on the land, there was a small, but nevertheless significant, number of workers employed in manufacturing. Map 5.4 shows the concentrations of industrial workers in the Gulf South for firms listed in the census. These employees came mostly from the large group of lower-class whites that existed throughout the South. This class, according to some contemporaries and historians, opposed any kind of industrial labor, perhaps because of a cultural antipathy toward manual labor, concern over a loss of social standing, or the fear of change inherent in something as unsettling as moving from the farm to the factory.

Grady McWhiney claimed that southerners would not work in manufacturing because they "favored fighting rather than business and looked down on townspeople and tradesmen."[10] While most historians of the South do not subscribe to McWhiney's interpretation, many nevertheless accept the idea that southerners resisted giving up their rural ways of life because "to forsake the soil for the factory signaled the white's failure within traditional Southern economic and social channels."[11] John Carines, writing during the Civil War from his home in

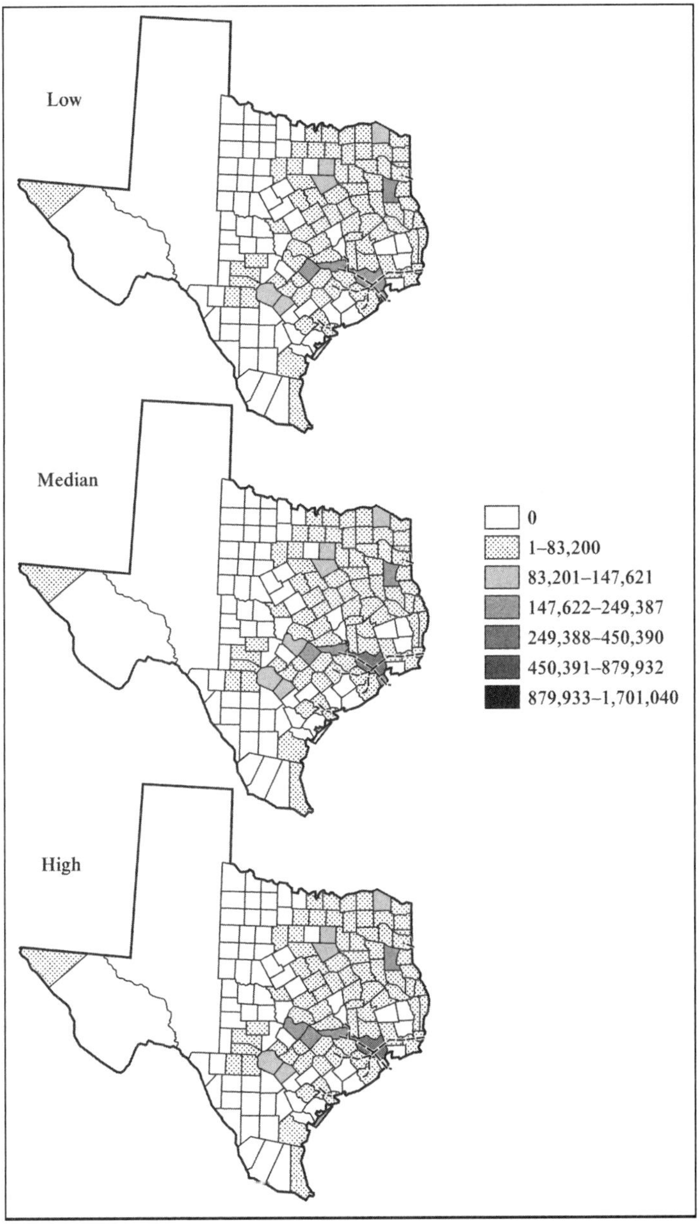


MAP 5.3. Estimated levels of capital investment in 1860 for firms found in all sources for Texas.

*Sources:* Census of 1860 Manufacturing Schedules, newspapers, county directories, journals, and the R. G. Dun Credit Reports.

TABLE 5.1. Range of possible capital investment in manufacturing concerns in 1860 for census and noncensus firms[a]

| | Census firms | Lower bound estimate | Mean | Upper bound estimate |
|---|---|---|---|---|
| Alabama | $9,382,593 | $9,709,809 (3.49%) | $10,215,898 (8.88%) | $11,464,593 (22.19%) |
| Mississippi | $3,658,468 | $3,772,286 (3.11%) | $3,940,858 (7.72%) | $4,368,468 (19.41%) |
| Texas | $3,502,014 | $3,622,631 (3.44%) | $3,806,609 (8.70%) | $4,261,014 (21.67%) |
| Total | $16,543,075 | $17,104,726 (3.40%) | $17,693,365 (8.59%) | $20,094,075 (21.47%) |

[a] See Appendix C, available at drmichaelfrawley.com, for lines of business and organization type data.

*Sources:* Census of 1860 Manufacturing Schedules, newspapers, county directories, journals, and the R. G. Dun Credit Reports.

*General note:* Figures in parentheses are percentages above the amount of capital investment given by the census.

Great Britain, attempted to explain what was transpiring in the United States. He asserted that lower-class white southerners were not good laborers because "the demoralization produced by the presence of a degraded class renders the white man at once an unwilling and inefficient laborer."[12] But the idea that the people of the Gulf South would not be industrial workers was incorrect, as Map 5.4 shows. Firms throughout the Gulf South employed white men and women, and between 1850 and 1860, a growing number of lower-class southern whites were giving up farm life for industrial labor.[13] Some in the region even saw manufacturing work as a good thing. Industrial employment, according to William Gregg, was a way to integrate people who lived on the margins into mainstream society and lift them "to the state of civilization that mills afforded them."[14]

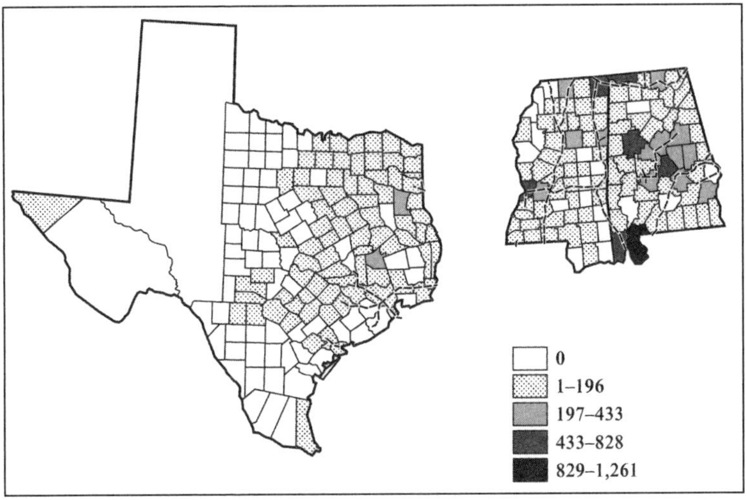


MAP 5.4. Industrial workers listed in the 1860 Census schedules.

*Source:* Census of 1860 Manufacturing Schedules.

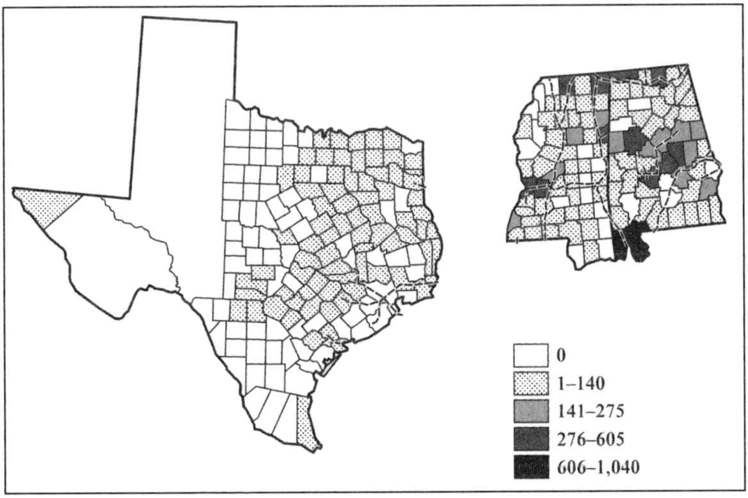


MAP 5.5. Male employees listed in the 1860 Census schedules.

*Source:* Census of 1860 Manufacturing Schedules.

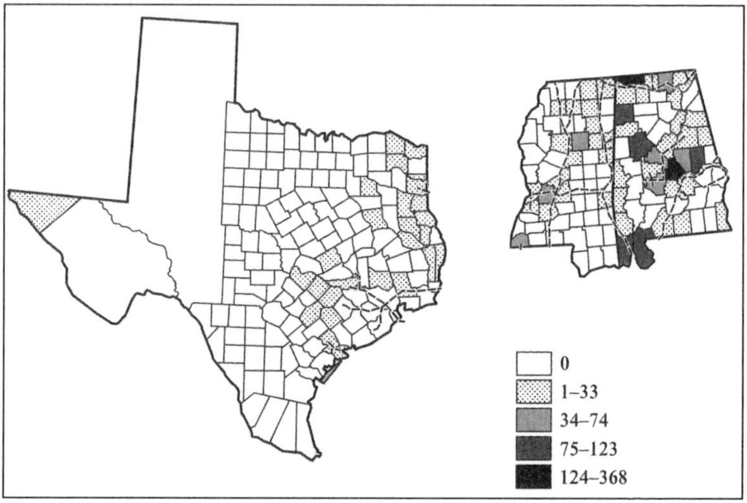


MAP 5.6. Female employees listed in the 1860 Census schedules.
*Source:* Census of 1860 Manufacturing Schedules.

There are some in the region who have argued that the problem of industry in the South was "ignorance and laziness on the part of those who *ought* to labor."[15] But industrial workers, both male and female, as Maps 5.5 and 5.6 display, were employed in most counties of the Gulf South. Industrial work became a part of life in the region, and learning that one's neighbor worked in a manufactory was, by 1860, likely to have been unsurprising. Moreover, as Maps 5.5 and 5.6 show, the largest concentrations of industrial workers, of either gender, were in the urban areas of the Gulf South.

Table 5.2 shows the distribution of employees by state and gender as recorded in the census. The marshals recorded 17,582 men and women employed in southern firms, or less than 1 percent of the total population.[16] But industry was just beginning in Alabama, Mississippi, and Texas. Moreover, it is important to note that these numbers do not contain any slaves who may have been part of the southern industrial labor force because the census schedules, except in one case, did not list slaves as workers.[17] The existence of these industrial workers had begun to

TABLE 5.2. Manufacturing employees listed in the 1860 Census schedules

| | Male employees | Female employees | Total |
|---|---|---|---|
| Alabama | 7,524 | 1,205 | 8,729 |
| Mississippi | 4,782 | 205 | 4,987 |
| Texas | 3,752 | 114 | 3,866 |
| Total | 16,058 | 1,524 | 17,582 |

*Source:* Census of 1860 Manufacturing Schedules.

change the Gulf South, however. Employees and owners both wanted a greater say in how the region was run as their numbers grew. This was seen by old guard, conservative political leaders as a threat because the clout of people tied to industry grew as their numbers increased.[18]

Men and women were not employed in equal numbers in the industrial concerns of the Gulf South. For a variety of reasons, many lines of business did not use women, while others found women to be much better workers than men. For example, foundries, which prized strength and stamina, shied away from hiring women, while textile firms, which did not have as much of a need for strength to run machines, hired many women. Thus, female workers were far more plentiful and widespread in Alabama where cotton textile manufacturing firms operated in greater numbers and were more developed. Even though most women worked in cotton, wool, and textile firms, as Table 5.3 indicates, they were also employed in many other lines of business. But of the 3,280 manufacturing firms listed in the 1860 census for the Gulf South, only 209, or 6.37 percent, employed women. Thus, women formed a small part of the southern industrial workforce, but one that was needed, or firms would not have hired any female employees at all. Also, as with other parts of the country, entire families were drawn into industrial firms as women and children found work in the same factories as their husbands and fathers.[19]

Of course, as the number of firms increased so, too, did the number of workers. Maps 5.7 and 5.8 display an estimate of the number of man-

TABLE 5.3. Lines of business that employed women and the number of employees recorded in the 1860 Census

| | | | |
|---|---|---|---|
| Baker | Blacksmith | Boots & shoes | Brickmaker |
| 1 | 1 | 8 | 52 |
| Cabinetmaker | Carpenter | Carriage & wagon | Charcoal |
| 2 | 2 | 1 | 2 |
| Coal | Confectioner | Cotton & wool | Cotton gins |
| 3 | 2 | 924 | 6 |
| Grist Mill | Hats | Leather | Lime |
| 20 | 10 | 6 | 15 |
| Lumber | Marble & stone | Millinery | Oysters |
| 117 | 1 | 5 | 3 |
| Pottery | Printer | Rope and bags | Saddle and harness |
| 4 | 5 | 5 | 1 |
| Salt | Sawmill | Textiles | Tobacco |
| 6 | 9 | 179 | 3 |
| Turpentine | | | |
| 131 | | | |

*Source:* Census of 1860 Manufacturing Schedules.

ufacturing employees at firms listed in all of the available sources. Manufacturing was just beginning in the region, and industrial workers still only made up about 1 percent of the population of the Gulf South, even after adding in the employees of firms missed by the census.[20] Table 5.4 shows an estimate of how many employees were hired by Gulf South firms. Based on this estimate, somewhere between 5.86 percent and 23.83 percent more manufacturing employees should be added to the 1860 census to get closer to the real number of people in the South who worked for industrial firms. Moreover, the number of missed employees is, based on the distribution of firms, closer to the middle value of 14.57 percent. The reason for this under-reporting was the lines of business that were missed by the census. Concerns such as textiles and milling,

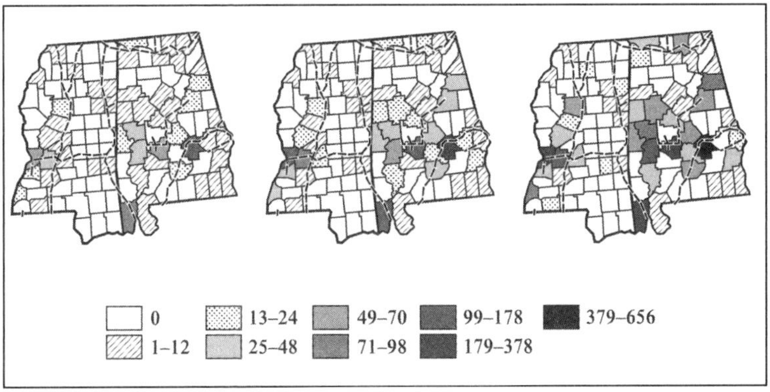


MAP 5.7. Estimates of manufacturing employees for industrial concerns not listed in the 1860 Census for Alabama and Mississippi.

*Sources:* Census of 1860 Manufacturing Schedules, newspapers, county directories, journals, and the R. G. Dun Credit Reports.

which made up 115 of the 788 concerns missed by the census marshals, hired more employees than other kinds of firms, increasing the number of missing workers.[21] As stated earlier, enslaved workers were not recorded as part of the manufacturing census. So, the true number of industrial workers was undoubtedly higher than estimated here.

Many southerners, then, did not have an anti-industry bias. Men and women in the region worked for southern firms and depended on them for their livelihood. Some of these workers came a great distance to work in the Gulf South. For example, Louis Ferdinand Alexander Hoffman was born in 1823 in Berlin and learned his trade at a machine and locomotive shop there. He immigrated to the United States in 1852 and ended up working in the Zimmerman and Reading Foundry in Vicksburg in 1860.[22] Local histories do not record any more information about Hoffman, but the free population schedule of the 1860 census lists him as a "Gun Smith" with real estate valued at $4,000, the equivalent of $116,000 today.[23] The foundry was capitalized at $130,000 and employed 125 workers, paying the highly skilled among them, such as Hoffman, accordingly.[24]

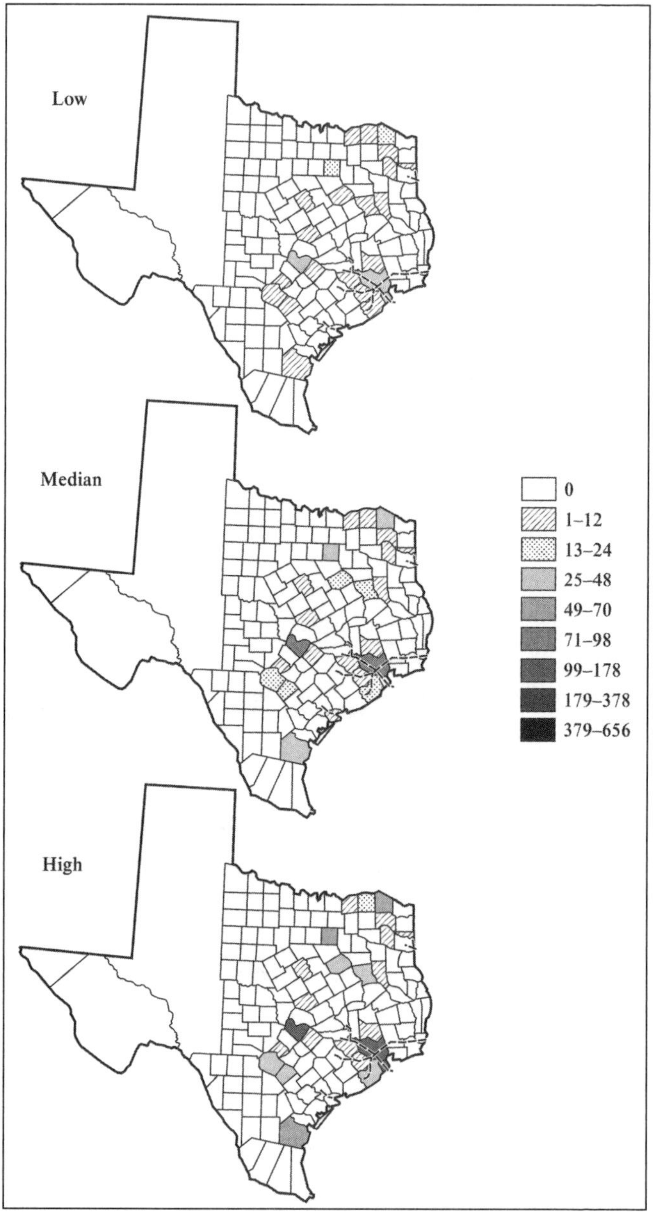


MAP 5.8. Estimates of manufacturing employees for industrial concerns not listed in the 1860 Census for Texas.

*Sources:* Census of 1860 Manufacturing Schedules, newspapers, county directories, journals, and the R. G. Dun Credit Reports.

TABLE 5.4. Estimates of employees for firms listed in all sources in 1860

| | Census firms | Lower bound estimate | Mean | Upper Bound estimate |
|---|---|---|---|---|
| Alabama | 8,729 | 9,323 (6.80%) | 10,443 (19.64%) | 11,151 (27.75%) |
| Mississippi | 4,987 | 5,203 (4.33%) | 5,403 (8.34%) | 5,855 (17.41%) |
| Texas | 3,866 | 4,087 (5.72%) | 4,297 (11.15%) | 4,766 (23.28%) |
| Total | 17,582 | 18,613 (5.86%) | 20,143 (14.57%) | 21,772 (23.83%) |

*Sources:* Census of 1860 Manufacturing Schedules, newspapers, county directories, journals, and the R. G. Dun Credit Reports.

These industrial workers, whether listed in the census or not, needed to be gathered in by entrepreneurs to work in their firms. To that end some manufacturers tried to found new urban areas from scratch based on the model created by the mills of Lowell, Massachusetts. Daniel Pratt was a prime example of this approach to industrialization, and he created a manufacturing town of 943 free people, centered on his concern.[25] Many contemporaries believed that these towns had a great advantage and "with a small, homogeneous population such villages were secure from the crime and social '-isms' which disrupted Northern urban life."[26] Places like Prattville, and nearby Autaugaville, which was centered on the Autaugaville Mill, were founded at the fall lines of rivers where they could get the power needed to run their firms and have access to transportation.[27] Again, the South was just following a tried and true pattern. These new towns attracted the workers that owners needed to fill factories and served as "the prototype of ante-bellum Alabama industrial enterprise."[28]

To be able to live, industrial workers needed to be paid. Thus, wages were another important factor of production. Employees needed to earn not just enough to live, but enough to be willing to give up their traditional, agricultural way of life and work at a manufacturing concern. This wage is known as the transfer wage and, according to research done by Carville Earle, was higher in the South than in other parts of the nation because of the existence of slavery and the high value of cotton.[29] Many southerners resisted performing what they saw to be slave labor in a factory and would have to be paid enough to overcome this very strong and important bias. Cotton agriculture also drew off its share of labor from the workforce. Moreover, labor markets did not compete on an equal footing with one another. Labor did not move from place to place as needed because of the limitations of communication and transportation in 1860. The real competition for labor was not between various urban areas, but between rural and urban areas.[30] Thus, Vicksburg and Natchez did not compete, for the most part, with one another for the available labor in the market; Vicksburg and Natchez industrialists competed with agriculturalists in their hinterlands for whatever labor was available. Once the shift from agricultural to industrial work had begun, though, it was only a matter of time before employees became dependent on their manufacturing wages. Over time, many members of a family were drawn in to industrial work, including wives and children.[31]

Industrial workers made enough to support themselves and their families. Based on the 1860 census schedules, the average male manufacturing employee earned a monthly wage of $30.51 while female workers were paid $10.47 per month. These wages varied by type of firm and location. For example, the Census Compendium for 1860 placed the average wage for an employee in a southern textile mill at $145.41 per year.[32] But this was just an average wage, and people working in specific concerns made vastly different amounts. Male employees at Pratt's factory in Prattville were paid $37 a month, while a smaller firm in Bibb County, Alabama, only paid $13 a month.[33] Thus, location and concern size mattered in determining the wage rate. Moreover, the census does not have any records about the term of employment for these workers. This is something that Olmsted came across in his travels. In Mississippi, a local man explained to him that unskilled laborers were paid from fifty cents to one dollar a day if hired by the day, eight dollars a month if hired for that term, and these workmen were never hired by

TABLE 5.5. Annual wages for firms listed in the 1860 census and an estimate range for firms from all sources

| | Census firms | Lower bound estimate | Mean | Upper bound estimate |
|---|---|---|---|---|
| Alabama | $2,132,940 | $2,936,172 (37.66%) | $3,201,060 (50.08%) | $3,747,900 (75.72%) |
| Mississippi | $1,618,320 | $1,850,400 (14.34%) | $1,924,920 (18.95%) | $2,072,040 (28.04%) |
| Texas | $1,161,756 | $1,431,844 (23.14%) | $1,516,336 (30.41%) | $1,676,596 (44.19%) |
| Total | $4,913,016 | $6,218,416 (26.57%) | $6,642,316 (35.20%) | $7,496,536 (52.59%) |

*Sources:* Census of 1860 Manufacturing Schedules, newspapers, county directories, journals, and the R. G. Dun Credit Reports.

*General note:* Figures in parentheses are percentages above the amount of wages given by the census.

the year.[34] This fits with the idea that industry was beginning its development in many parts of the Gulf South as people were just starting to make the transition from agricultural work to industrial labor.

At first, many workers sought factory jobs during slack times in the fields. Over time workers came to see steady wages as a good thing and spent more and more time working in industrial concerns, helping to create growing urban areas in the region.[35] Table 5.5 shows the wages that firms in the census annually paid to their workers along with estimates of what the wage bill looked like when firms not listed in the census are included. As this table illustrates, wages varied greatly from state to state. Also, there is no proof that the wage bill for the census concerns, on which the estimates for the firms missed by the marshals is based, is accurate. The census marshals recorded wages as the total paid to employees monthly. There is no indication that workers were hired for an entire year, so wage costs could be lower than what was listed in the census compendium. But if we assume year-round employment, as the census did, 26.57 to 52.59 percent more in wages should be added to the census totals.

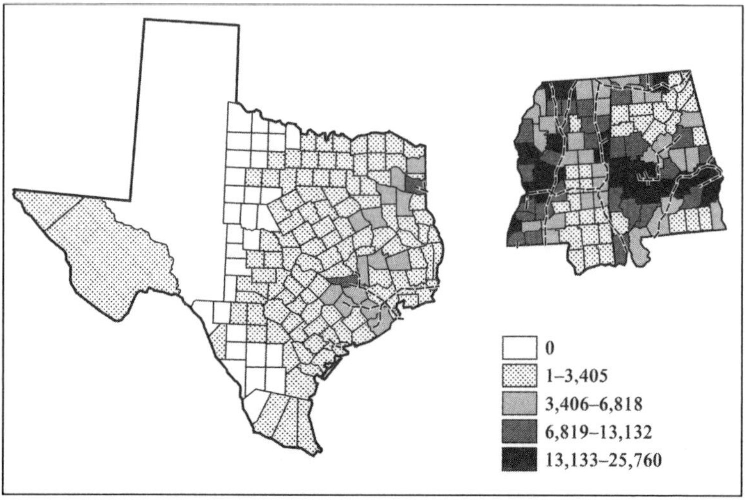


MAP 5.9. Slave population in Alabama, Mississippi, and Texas in 1860.
*Source:* Census of 1860 Manufacturing Schedules.

Not all workers in the South were paid wages. Slavery was an important part of southern life and, of course, this system of labor would be important to industrial development in the region. As Carville Earle and Ronald Hoffman so succinctly explain, "the halting steps toward manufacturing in the 1850s were aimed not at inducing white labor to the factories but at adapting slave labor to the factory system."[36] Even Karl Marx saw the importance of slavery in economic development as "the veiled slavery of the wage-workers in Europe needed, for its pedestal, slavery pure and simple in the new world."[37] As Map 5.9 displays, there were slaves in every single settled county in the Gulf South.[38]

The slave population was especially dense in many parts of Alabama and Mississippi. These areas made up the wide cotton belt that stretched through the region and created a great deal of the wealth in these states. As discussed earlier, this belt corresponds with the counties that earlier maps showed as having large amounts of industrial investment. Thus, we can assume that some of the money made through slave-based cotton agriculture was being transferred into manufacturing.

Even though slave labor made many southerners rich, there were still problems with the system. Owners lost money anytime a slave sat idle. Slaves could not be fired or laid off; they had to be cared for until death.[39] Moreover, agricultural slavery had limits, as many southerners saw. As William Harper explained in 1838, "When the demand for agricultural labour shall be fully supplied, then of course the labour of slaves will be directed to other employments and enterprises."[40] De Bow also believed that slave labor would have to be turned to pursuits other than agriculture because the amount of new land to be opened to cotton agriculture was dwindling and "in this way the slave labor of the south will, instead of contributing to the wealth of the north, as it has heretofore done, become the successful competition of northern white labor in those departments of industry of which the north has in times past enjoyed a monopoly."[41] Thus, if slavery was confined to where it existed in 1860, at some point in the future the slave population would be so large that other uses for their labor would have to be found. As De Bow again argued: "The 'slave states,' so called, have the black lines drawn about them. There will soon be no more Mississippi lands to clear, no more cotton fields to subdue, and unless some means be devised of getting rid of the negro increase, the time must come—and sooner or later it will come—when there will be an excess in these states of black people."[42]

While some people in both the North and the South felt that slaves were not intelligent enough to be able to perform industrial tasks, a writer in an Augusta newspaper felt that they would make good industrial workers: "The African has an aptitude for endurance, and at the south will succeed in many of the laborious operations where others would fail. For manufacturing in the hot and lower latitudes, they are peculiarly qualified; and the time is approaching when they will be sought as the operators most to be preferred and depended on."[43]

Of course, industrial firm owners did not need to be told that slaves would make good manufacturing employees. Entrepreneurs wanted their concerns to make money and used enslaved labor anytime it was profitable. Once a slave was trained to perform industrial jobs their skills could not be lost, they could not quit or go on strike, take a day off, or make any demands on their employers.[44] Slaves could also be used as a source of capital by their owners. As part of an industrialist's personal property, slaves could be moved around the region and were also easy to sell. This meant that along with being laborers, enslaved workers could also be used as collateral for loans and "slaves represented a huge store of highly liquid wealth."[45] Industrial concern owners could enter the credit market and use slaves as a way to get money for new machines and materials. This is why the Dun reports were so concerned with slave property.[46] Slaves then served as both labor and capital for antebellum southern industry.

Industrial firm owners and southern industrial boosters put a great deal of effort into persuading planters to transfer slaves from agricultural to manufacturing endeavors. Cities like Birmingham, which developed into an important postwar industrial center, were "planned by prewar agricultural capitalists as . . . industrial center[s] where surplus slaves could be profitably utilized in staffing blast furnaces and rolling mills."[47] Slaves filled this role well and profitably across the South. Col. James Wesson used slaves to operate many parts of his firm, the Mississippi Manufacturing Company in Choctaw County, Mississippi, including the steam engine and other dangerous and "very dusty" parts of his factory, even though the majority of his employees were white.[48] When Wesson used slaves to perform this kind of labor, he was very pleased to discover that they "were equal to the task."[49] William Gregg employed slaves in his factories because of the many advantages they provided: they could be put to work at a younger age than white workers, they needed no education, and they could not strike. Moreover, they could not quit, so there were no worries that as soon as a person was trained to do their job, they would pack up and leave.[50] One of the largest industrial enterprises in the antebellum South, the Tredegar Iron Works in Richmond, Virginia, also employed a large number of slave laborers.[51] Thus, industrial slave labor was important in the region and, perhaps, should have been more so, as De Bow explained: "Wherever negro labor has been applied, it has been with great success. Of the 700,000 negros, whose labor has added nothing to the wealth we had ten years ago, could 100,000 be diverted to the construction of railroads, the South might open several thousand miles every year, and would have the same means of ironing them that she has now from her other resources."[52]

Pratt also used slaves in his factories, not because they were always better workers, but to fight against the growth of organized labor in Prattville and to be able to make sure his workforce stayed after he trained them.[53] Moreover, slaves worked on almost every railroad line in the South, with more than 14,600 employed by 1860.[54] These slaves performed every task possible from clearing rights of way, to laying track, to building and maintaining rolling stock.[55] It seems that enslaved labor could be turned to any task and owners could expect them to perform it well. Thus, slaves were a well-known commodity in the southern labor market, and manufacturing firm owners used them if the opportunity presented itself either through industrial firm operators looking for labor, planters looking for work for their slaves, or even through slaves looking for work themselves.

John P. Parker, a slave in antebellum Mobile, is a good example of an enslaved laborer used for industrial work. Parker convinced a widow to buy him and allow him to hire himself out. He earned money for his owner and, through overwork, money to buy his own freedom.[56] Parker described his hiring situation, writing: "A new foundry was starting. They needed molders and I applied for a job and got it at once. The next morning I was around as soon as the doors were opened, once more alert and hopeful. The first week I lived in that shop. Early and late I was at my bench."[57] Enslaved workers had constantly to prove themselves so that they could keep these sought-after positions. As Parker explained, "long before other workmen were around in the morning, I was hard at work over my molds."[58] Moreover, slaves changed jobs to ones that had better working conditions or that paid for work by the piece, so that the harder they worked the more they made.[59] But these were still slaves, and they had to get their owners' permission to work for any business that wanted to hire them. Enslaved workers would negotiate with an employer, then return to their owner, explain the deal, and get permission to work. Slaves even bid against each other to get better deals for themselves to be able to work for businesses that would treat them well and pay them as much as possible. Owners would generally

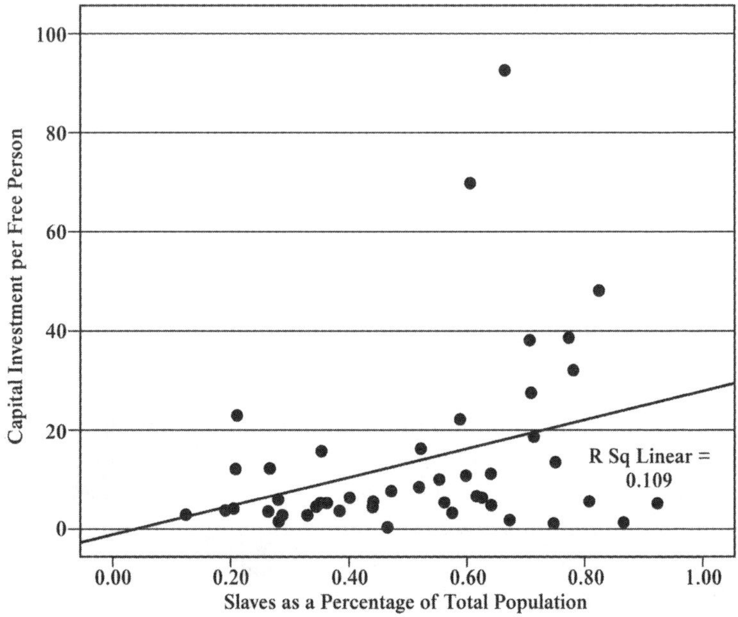


United States Bureau of the Census, *Eighth Census of the United States: 1860, Manufacturers* (Washington: US Government Pricing Office, 1865), 285–94.

listen to their slaves about where they could earn the most money for both of them and would then give them permission to work for that business. Many southerners, though, were afraid that allowing slaves control over their own time, in the way that Parker did, weakened the entire slave system.[60] Nevertheless, the labor of enslaved workers was needed by manufacturing firms.[61] No matter the feelings of some people about slave use in industry, they were a very important part of the development of manufacturing in the antebellum Gulf South.[62]

To see if slavery held back manufacturing investment we need to follow the money, and we can use Mississippi as a case study. While this is ground that many historians have gone over, the validity of Woodman's idea that "available capital was not used for industrialization and diversification simply because it could be more profitably used in agricultural production" can shed some light on the place of industry in a slave society.[63] Reviewing the investment patterns in a state like Mississippi by looking at the county level census returns and looking for patterns can refute Woodman's statement. These records contain the amount of capital invested in manufacturing and the free and slave population for each county. By dividing the amount of capital invested into the free population, we can get per capita investment per free person for each county. We can then take that statistic and cross-reference it with the total percentage of the county's population that was enslaved and determine if capital investment per free person was higher in areas with a large slave population.

Each mark on the graph above represents a county in Mississippi. As it shows, the amount of capital invested per free person increased as the amount of slaves as a percentage of the total population increased. This seems to go against the common idea that slavery in some way stifled manufacturing. As this was a frontier area that was still developing, the amount of money shown is not an enormous sum, but this graph does show that there is a connection between capital investment and slavery, a positive correlation.[64] Some may question the use of only free people as part of the per capita statistic, but when the main comparisons that are done with the South are free labor areas, this tends to be the best way to create a statistic that is meaningful in all areas.[65]

But that does not mean that we cannot look at per capita investment for the total population. As the second graph shows, when the total population, both slave and free, are figured into per capita investment, the trend, while not as pronounced, still holds. So, the statistics show that investment took place, including in areas that had large enslaved populations. This makes a great deal of sense, contrary to popular opinion among historians. Slave owners, especially large slave owners, had the capital to invest. The poor small farmer who did not own a slave would not have that capital, so they would not invest, and thus the areas that they lived in with other people like themselves would not have a great deal of capital investment. This is capitalism pure and simple. The people with the money invested in whatever made them a profit. As Scarborough writes, "I submit that capitalism is simply an economic system

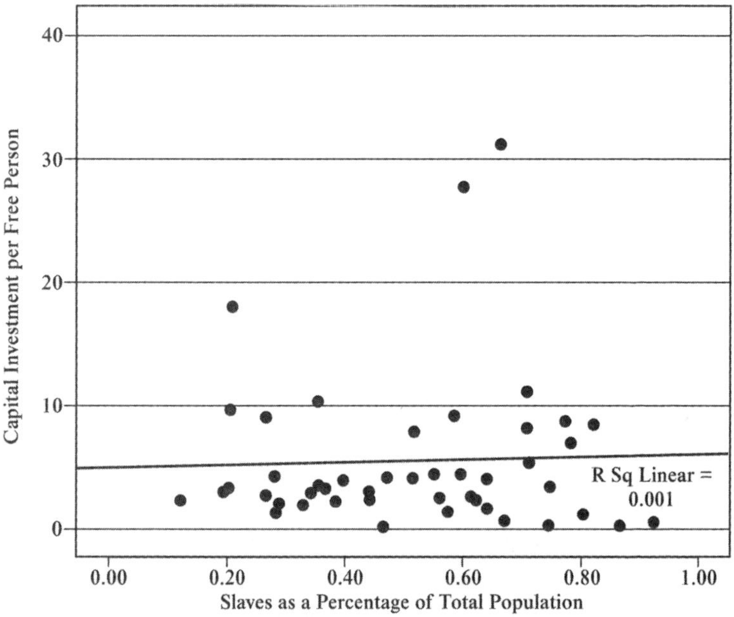


United States Bureau of the Census, *Eighth Census of the United States: 1860, Manufacturers*, 285–94.

in which individuals invest capital, from whatever source and by whatever labor system derived, with the hope and expectation of generating additional capital."[66] While some historians, such as Douglas Egerton, have argued that the South was really not a capitalist area, Scarborough's definition rings more true and the census data seem to uphold his definition.[67]

The existence of slavery did not create a barrier to investing capital. The areas that show the greatest investment would also have been the areas where, according to Phillips, we should see the least. Investors, it seems, were not just plowing their capital back into land and slaves; they saw manufacturing as a good investment for their money. Southerners, as the data show, had no problem investing in manufacturing. Even in a frontier state like Mississippi, where the opportunity to find manufacturing to invest in would be harder, there was still a great deal invested. But these statistics function on a macro level and only show how investment worked overall in each individual county. More data that support these conclusions can be found if we focus closer on the individuals doing the investing.

The *Manufacturing Census Schedules for Mississippi* provides a tremendous amount of data about the manufacturers who set up shop in the state. The data here was derived from these schedules, filled out by individual census takers in their home counties. Each schedule gives the name of the owner, the type of manufacturer, the amount of capital invested, raw materials used, labor information, and finally the value of their output. The elements of the census that are most important to this discussion are the names of the owners and the capital invested. By taking the names of the owners of the manufacturing establishments and cross-referencing them with the population census and the slave census, we can determine how many of these businessmen were also slave owners. This will show whether slave owners directly invested in manufacturing and will also deal a blow to the idea that slavery was a detriment to developing manufacturing. Problems exist with the census data itself. Some of the pages of the census are unreadable, as they have faded over time. Also some of the owners could not be found in the population census to verify their information. Because of this, some manufacturers have been left out of the data shown in the following chart. But enough remain to be able to draw some conclusions based on the evidence.

As can be seen from the data presented in the graph above, a large number of the manufacturers in Mississippi were slave owners. Out of a total of 296 manufacturers, 155 owned slaves. These men had no problem with investing their surplus capital in manufacturing rather than in more slaves. This shows that Scarborough's ideas on capitalism were correct, not just for large slave owners, but for small slave owners with much less available to invest. Again, slavery does not seem to have held back the development of manufacturing in Mississippi. While most of these establishments are very small, they represent the beginning of an industrial base, and were on par with the development in other areas. As Edward Pessen points out, "At mid-century industrial workers in the

South as in the North worked primarily in small shops and households rather than in factories."[68] Referring back to Taylor's view on industrial development, this was just the natural first step, especially for a frontier area like Mississippi. It is impossible to determine from this data how these slaves were used, whether they did their labor in household occupations, in the manufacturing concern, or for something else altogether. But, in reality, this does not matter. This data shows without a doubt that slave owners invested their available capital in manufacturing and turned a profit while doing it. This data runs counter to Phillips's idea that "when profits actually accrued there was nothing available as a rule more tempting than slaves as investments."[69] The people with money invested in manufacturing, and those people owned slaves.

Stanley Lebergott, in his book *The Americans*, wrote, "Manufacturing expanded on a broad front from the mid-1820s to 1860—textile firms, tanneries, iron forges, chemical and glass works. But it is well to keep in mind that the nation's comparative advantage still lay in agriculture."[70] Moreover, Tennessee governor Aaron Brown, at the 1852 New Orleans Southern Commercial Convention, said "manufacturing was an attractive addition to the South's economy, but not a replacement for the agrarian mode."[71] Brown and Lebergott were right; industry was not a replacement but, as the maps presented in this chapter show, it could be a complement that perhaps, given time, would develop into a partner of cash crop agriculture. Many southerners were not opposed to modernization; they merely wished to follow their own road.[72] As De Bow wrote: "Cotton, wool, and iron may be regarded as the three great staples of the southwest. But there is so close a relation between these and many other branches of manufacturers, that the establishment of any one or more of them upon an extensive scale would draw after them others."[73]

Firms could, and did, use the resources of the region to drive the development of industry in the Gulf South, as this review of the factors of production has shown. We now have a more accurate picture of what manufacturing in the region really looked like. There were not only firms and owners in many parts of the Gulf South; there was also a great deal of capital invested in these concerns. Manufacturers purchased raw materials in sufficient quantities to turn out products needed by the region. Moreover, industrialists found free workers for their firms in Alabama, Mississippi, and Texas and paid them enough to induce them to give up agricultural work. Slaves augmented the supply of free labor for the region's manufacturing firms. Manufacturers in the Gulf South wielded a substantial labor force, considerable capital investment, and readily available raw materials to produce a large and varied array of goods for other industrial producers, farms and plantations, and individual consumers. As the next chapter will make clear, the scale of this production was considerably greater than contemporaries thought, and historians believe, was the case.

# 6

## MANUFACTURING IN THE GULF SOUTH

### Production and Scale

In the May 19, 1858, issue of the Montgomery, Alabama *Daily Confederation*, the paper's editor celebrated the South's agrarian character:

> That the North does our trading and manufacturing mostly is true, and we are willing that they should. Ours is an agricultural people, and God grant that we may continue so. We never want to see it otherwise. It is the freest, happiest, most independent, and with us the most powerful condition on earth. We never want to become a section of shop-keepers, or a hive of manufacturers.[1]

This was the traditional view of the South held by many people before the war. Southerners worked the land; they did not work in factories. Moreover, according to this editorial, the people of the region were happy about their agricultural way of life and had little interest in industrial development. William Gregg, who ran a large manufacturing enterprise in South Carolina, bemoaned the fact that the region functioned in the fashion described in the *Daily Confederation* and wrote in exasperation about how cotton left plantations in the South, went into northern factories to be turned into cloth and clothing, and then returned to southern plantation for purchase at an inflated price.[2] Notwithstanding such commonly held views, however, entrepreneurs in the antebellum Gulf South were developing the beginnings of a "hive" and were manufacturing a broad range of products, from clothing to saddles to iron products to agricultural equipment, for consumption by the people of the region. The southerners who purchased industrial wares realized the importance of these business owners and their concerns to their communities.

The tangible effect of industry on society was, of course, the goods that it produced. A "Mr. Marshall," in an article published in *De Bow's Review,* understood how important manufacturing production was for the South and argued that the region needed to "manufacture at home—the actual necessities—such as farming implements, clothing, and shoeing."[3] Manufacturers' hopes for profits depended for realization on the existence of vigorous and growing markets. Industrialists in the Gulf South therefore took every opportunity to showcase their wares. For example, in October 1860, the people of Navarro County, Texas, hosted the "First Annual Fair of the Navarro County Agricultural and Mechanical Association," the highlight of which was a competition of domestically manufactured goods.[4] Thus, even on a frontier—Navarro County was on the far western part of settled Texas—people recognized the importance of industrial production and celebrated the availability of locally manufactured goods. Moreover, as this book has explained, owners used local newspapers to promote their concerns' wares.

There are many examples of manufacturers opening firms and producing goods needed in their local areas. The Spangler family of Mississippi, made up of siblings Joseph, Seraphine, and Hubert, founded firms in several parts of the state. Joseph built a cotton factory on the banks of the Pearl River, Seraphine built saw mills in Rankin and Madison Counties, and Hubert founded a blind and sash firm in Jackson.[5] All of these enterprises, according to family history, produced goods sold in local markets and did very well until they were burned during the Civil War. John Alexander Klein, who was born in Virginia, moved to Vicksburg in 1836 and opened a jeweler's shop. With the money that he made from this business he opened several sawmills in and around the city, most of which, again, were destroyed during the war.[6] The products of his mills helped to build and expand Vicksburg and were very important to the people of the area. What was true of Vicksburg was also true of other communities, large and small, in which industrialists and manufacturers lived and worked. Thus, while capital, labor, and materials were important, the production of a firm really integrated industry into a community.

The 1860 census reported the dollar value of production for each manufacturing firm. As was explained earlier, the census only reported such firms that produced goods worth at least $500. This output value was not differentiated into the various items a firm produced. For example, a carriage and wagon manufacturer may have produced a variety of different carriages, wagons, and carts, and may also have produced related items such as wheels and other replacement parts. The census does not break down the value of industrial production to reflect how many of each of these items were produced; the returns only show a total value for all of the output of a concern. Thus, we cannot know exactly how many carriages or wagons a firm was able to build in 1860.

Map 6.1 displays the value of production listed in the census for firms in the Gulf South. As the map shows, there were manufacturing concerns that operated in many parts of the region. But there were still counties, according to the census, that had no industrial activity at all, and many urban areas, such as Natchez, Montgomery, Vicksburg, and Mobile, had little manufacturing output despite their size and importance. Moreover, as the map illustrates, counties that had railroad lines running through them had a larger amount of production, whereas in general, areas further away from rail transport had lower amounts. Railroads were built in the antebellum Gulf South as "vehicles of trade" to serve the backcountry and connect it with urban areas.[7] Thus, it is no surprise that many of the counties that had no production listed were off the major lines of transportation.

Table 6.1 provides the value of production recorded by the census for firms in Alabama, Mississippi, and Texas. Taken together, the map and the table indicate that the Gulf South did possess some considerable concentrations of industrial production. Moreover, some places in the region were becoming known for certain products. For example, Alabama was the largest cotton gin–producing state in the country, with sixteen different manufacturers listed in the 1860 census, thanks to Daniel Pratt and others who attempted to compete with him.[8] Also, Alabama was becoming known for its iron production and had a large

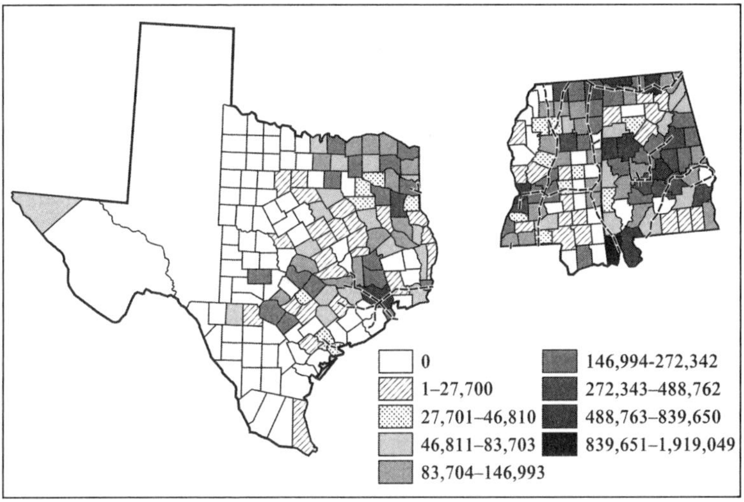


MAP 6.1. Value of production for firms listed in the 1860 Census (dollars).
*Source:* Census of 1860 Manufacturing Schedules.

number of firms that the marshals recorded in the manufacturing census schedules.[9] Most of the iron-producing concerns in Alabama were founded in the 1850s and, by 1860, were producing more than enough iron for local needs and had begun to export their products, especially to other Gulf South states.[10] Some lines of business were more important than others in the region, especially concerns that worked in the primary processing of raw materials. According to the census, mills, both lumber and grist, produced the greatest value of output in the region with a total of $11,291,779 in 1860, which was 47.6 percent of the total value of output for Alabama, Mississippi, and Texas.[11] Cotton and wool textile factories were also large producers according to the census. Textile concerns accounted for $2,074,741 of output. The only other lines of business to produce over one million dollars were carriage and wagon makers, with a total output of $1,211,193, and foundries, which turned out $1,242,247 of goods. Overall, the census records fifty-eight different kinds of concerns that produced at least $500 worth of products in 1860. Thus, according to the census alone, manufacturing was develop-

TABLE 6.1. Value of production for all firms listed in the 1860 census[a]

| | Value of production | Share of total regional production |
|---|---|---|
| Alabama | $10,454,762 | 44% |
| Mississippi | $6,345,862 | 27% |
| Texas | $6,927,015 | 29% |
| Total | $23,727,639 | 100% |

[a] For a breakdown of the value of production, see Appendix C—Data, available at drmichaelfrawley.com.

*Source:* Census of 1860 Manufacturing Schedules.

ing in the Gulf South and industrial production was reaching a level in some industries to adequately supply needs outside of firms' local areas. Moreover, some industries and concerns, such as Pratt's gin factory, attracted national attention.

Of course, as earlier chapters have established, the census was not a complete listing of all of the firms that operated in Alabama, Mississippi, and Texas in 1860. Firms missed by the census in each state produced goods, the value of which ought to be added to the reported census totals to yield a more accurate determination of the Gulf South's production capacity. Maps 6.2 and 6.3 show estimates of the production of all firms located in the region. As with capital and raw materials, estimates have to be made of the value of production based on what similar firms in the census listed for their output. Once this was done, a range of output levels was created of what all firms in the Gulf South could have potentially produced. When these estimates are represented geographically, as in Maps 6.2 and 6.3, we can see that there was a greater value of production in the Gulf South than previously believed.

More counties were involved in industrial work, and many areas had a larger output than the census recorded. The census missed many types of firms, the largest number having been eighty-seven boot and shoe manufacturers. Marshals also missed eighty-one carriage and wagon makers and sixty-six mill operators. It was interesting that these types of

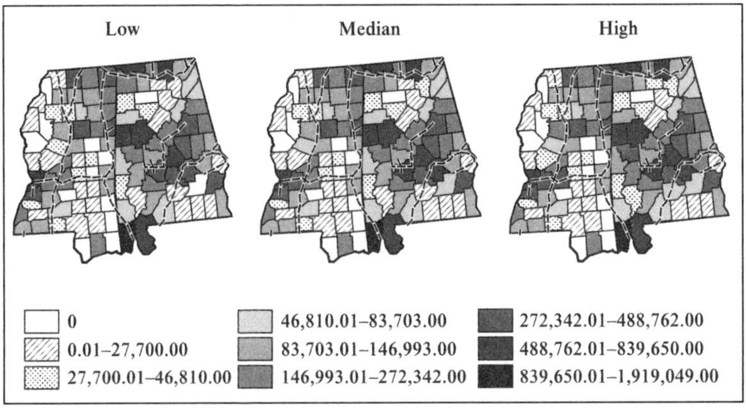


MAP 6.2. Range of estimates for the value of production for all firms in Alabama and Mississippi in 1860 (dollars).

*Sources:* Census of 1860 Manufacturing Schedules, newspapers, county directories, journals, and the R. G. Dun Credit Reports.

concerns were the most often missed. While boot and shoemakers may not have needed large physical plants to operate profitably, such was not true of mills and carriage and wagon works. The considerable floor space and grounds of these enterprises should have been very hard to overlook. Moreover, these firms produced considerable quantities and values of output. The average boot and shoe concern turned out $2,946 of product in 1860, while carriage firms produced $4,923; mill output was $9,532.[12]

Table 6.2 shows the estimated value of production for firms listed in all sources in the Gulf South in 1860. The level of underreporting for the region was 2.37 to 14.84 percent, which means that at least a half a million dollars of production was missed. In today's money this comes out to at least $16,200,000 in unreported output.[13] This was a significant amount of industrial production that went unrecorded by the marshals. Alabama had the greatest amount of missed production because the state had the most firms unrecorded by the census takers, and these concerns were in lines of business that generally had greater amounts of

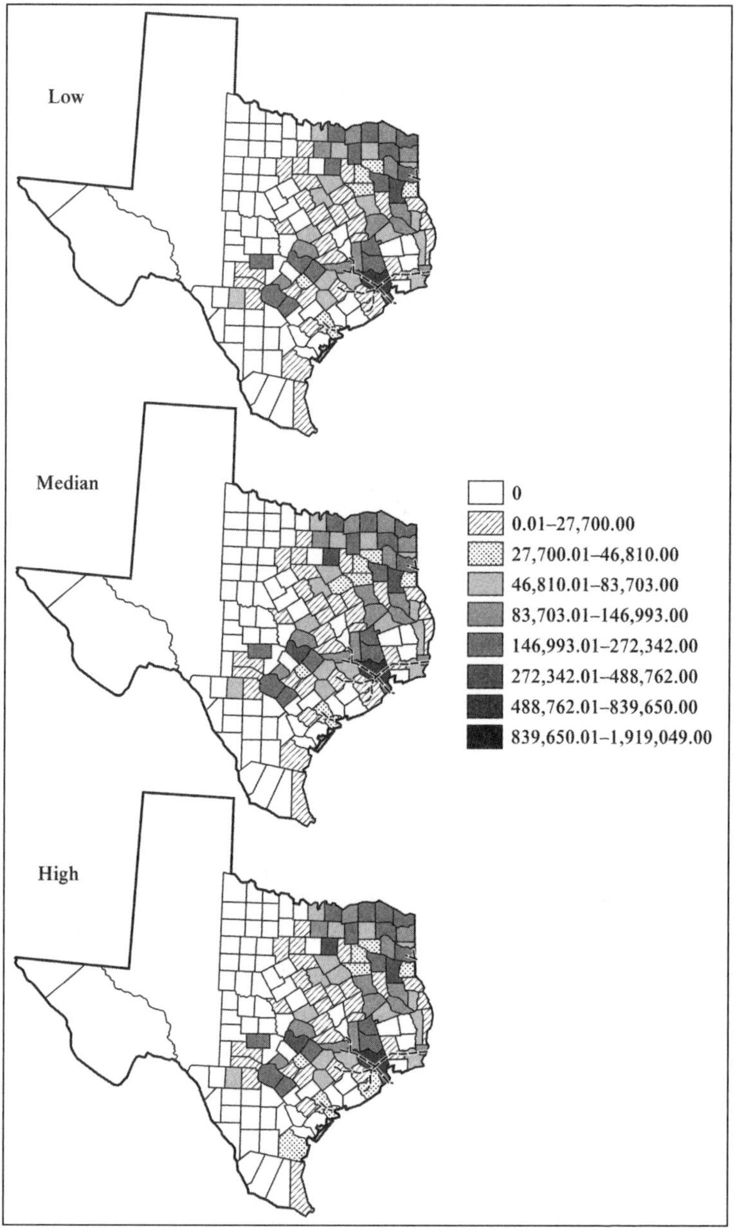


MAP 6.3. Range of estimates for the value of production for all firms in Texas in 1860.

*Sources:* Census of 1860 Manufacturing Schedules, newspapers, county directories, journals, and the R. G. Dun Credit Reports.

TABLE 6.2. Value of production for concerns listed in the census and estimations for firms listed in all sources in Alabama, Mississippi, and Texas in 1860 (percentage of underreporting)[a]

| | Census | Low | Median | High |
|---|---|---|---|---|
| Alabama | $10,454,762 | $10,781,971 (3.13%) | $11,288,067 (7.97%) | $12,531,762 (19.87%) |
| Mississippi | $6,345,862 | $6,459,682 (1.79%) | $6,628,242 (4.45%) | $7,049,862 (11.09%) |
| Texas | $6,927,015 | $7,047,627 (1.74%) | $7,232,210 (4.41%) | $7,668,015 (10.70%) |
| Total | $23,727,639 | $24,289,280 (2.37%) | $25,148,519 (5.99%) | $27,249,639 (14.84%) |

[a] See Appendix C, available at drmichaelfrawley.com, for a breakdown of production by line of business and organization type.

*Source:* Census of 1860 Manufacturing Schedules, newspapers, county directories, journals, and the R. G. Dun Credit Reports.

*General note:* The value provided in parentheses is the percentage over the census totals of the estimated amount.

output. For example, concerns that produced blinds, sashes, and doors and foundries had larger than average production values.[14] In Mississippi the census marshals missed one blind, sash, and door firm and four foundries. Marshals missed two blind, sash, and door enterprises and three foundries in Texas. Ten blind, sash, and door manufactories and fifteen foundries were missed in Alabama.

The large number of missing firms in Alabama is not surprising; the state had a more developed transportation network and more raw materials than Mississippi or Texas, which allowed it to create and develop a larger number of firms. Moreover, of the concerns missed in Alabama, many were of more complex organizational types, such as partnerships and companies, while most of the firms missed in Texas and Mississippi were individually owned.[15] While the value of production in Mississippi and that in Texas were almost equal, as Table 6.3 shows, Texas had a

TABLE 6.3. Per capita output derived from the 1860 census for Alabama, Mississippi, and Texas

| | Population | Value of production | Per capita output |
|---|---|---|---|
| Alabama | 964,201 | $10,454,762 | $10.84 |
| Mississippi | 791,305 | $6,345,862 | $8.02 |
| Texas | 604, 215 | $6,927,015 | $11.46 |
| Total | 2,359,721 | $23,727,639 | $10.06 |

*Source:* Census of 1860 Manufacturing and Population Schedules.

higher per capita output because of its lower population. In general, though, per capita output was relatively equal throughout the region.

When compared with Map 6.1, the production for concerns listed in the census, we can see through Table 6.2 and Maps 6.2 and 6.3 that production was, as stated earlier, more widespread and deeper in the region than the census recorded. Moreover, concerns missed by the census were producing goods that people in their local areas were willing to purchase while also providing owners with the potential to grow and expand. For example, John Sciple was a sawmill owner in Macon, Mississippi. This mill produced goods for the town and, according to the Dun reports, Sciple was industrious and good for any amount of credit that a subscriber to the reports would be willing to extend.[16] E. R. Johnson, a shoemaker in Vicksburg, Mississippi, had a listing in Dun similar to that of Sciple and was "responsible for any amount he would venture to ask for."[17] Thus, Sciple and Johnson made products that the local area needed, and, if they wanted to expand, other people in their communities thought they would be good risks to which to extend credit. While it is true that "of population, of internal improvements, of manufactures, and of all artificial wealth the North held much the larger share," the Gulf South was more industrially developed than anyone at the time, or any time after, has really understood.[18]

Maps 6.4 and 6.5 show the amounts of estimated production for just the firms missed by the census marshals. These maps illustrate that the areas where one would expect to have large amounts of industrial development, the urban centers of the Gulf South, also had the most value of production not listed in the census. As discussed earlier, the fact that so much output was missed by census marshals in urban areas was surprising. What was not surprising was that so much industry existed in the larger towns and cities of the region. The urban South was important to industrial development and the people who lived in these cities "showed . . . heightened levels of excitement about future progress."[19] But this view was based on the census returns alone. As Maps 6.4 and 6.5 show, there was much more to be excited about in the Gulf South, as some counties potentially had over a half a million dollars' worth of missed production.

Counties off of the major transportation routes did have some missed production, but, as Maps 6.4 and 6.5 show, the estimates of the unrecorded output in these counties was not as large as in the cities of Alabama, Mississippi, and Texas. The firms in areas outside the Gulf South's urban areas were more likely to be smaller individually owned concerns, while those in cities were more likely to be larger partnerships and companies. But when these smaller amounts of missed production are combined, they too reach significant amounts. Some of these unrecorded concerns were in large cotton-producing counties, which shows that agriculture and industrial development were not antithetical to each other. Moreover, as stated in chapter 2, they may have even supported one another, especially in outlying areas where access to capital and credit was harder for an industrial entrepreneur to obtain. Manufactory owners founded firms wherever in the Gulf South their products were needed and turned a profit especially if the owner wanted their business to succeed. Producing for a local market was less risky for an entrepreneur.[20] As they were a part of the local community, credit reporters were also familiar with what was going on in a given area, saw the need for these firms, and recorded them in their reports.[21]

An in-depth look at the production of firms missing from the census in the Gulf South's urban areas can tell us more about industrial output and development in the region. The cities of the Gulf South, like

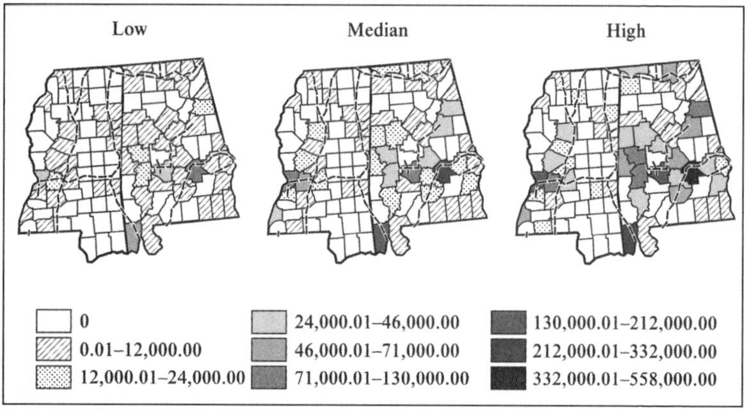


MAP 6.4. Estimates of the value of production for firms not listed in the 1860 Census for Alabama and Mississippi (dollars).

*Sources:* Census of 1860 Manufacturing Schedules, newspapers, county directories, journals, and the R. G. Dun Credit Reports.

those elsewhere, performed a variety of essential commercial functions, including providing services as importation hubs and distribution centers.[22] But, industry was developing in these urban areas, as well. Mobile and Montgomery in Alabama and Natchez and Vicksburg in Mississippi all had many firms that the census marshals failed to record. Even without the production value of those missing firms, these cities, and their surrounding counties, supported a considerable amount of manufacturing. Mobile, for example, was the center of the leading industrial area in Alabama based on the census records alone.[23] But, census marshals missed a great deal of manufacturing output in Mobile. Table 6.4 shows the value of production for all four of these cities as recorded in the census, as well as estimates of the likely output of all firms listed in the available sources for these urban areas. These four cities had higher levels of production underreporting than any other regions in Alabama and Mississippi, as shown when you compare Table 6.4 with Table 6.2. Montgomery, Alabama, which received Olmsted's praise for being a "pleasant" town with "prosperous and energetic" people, was massively

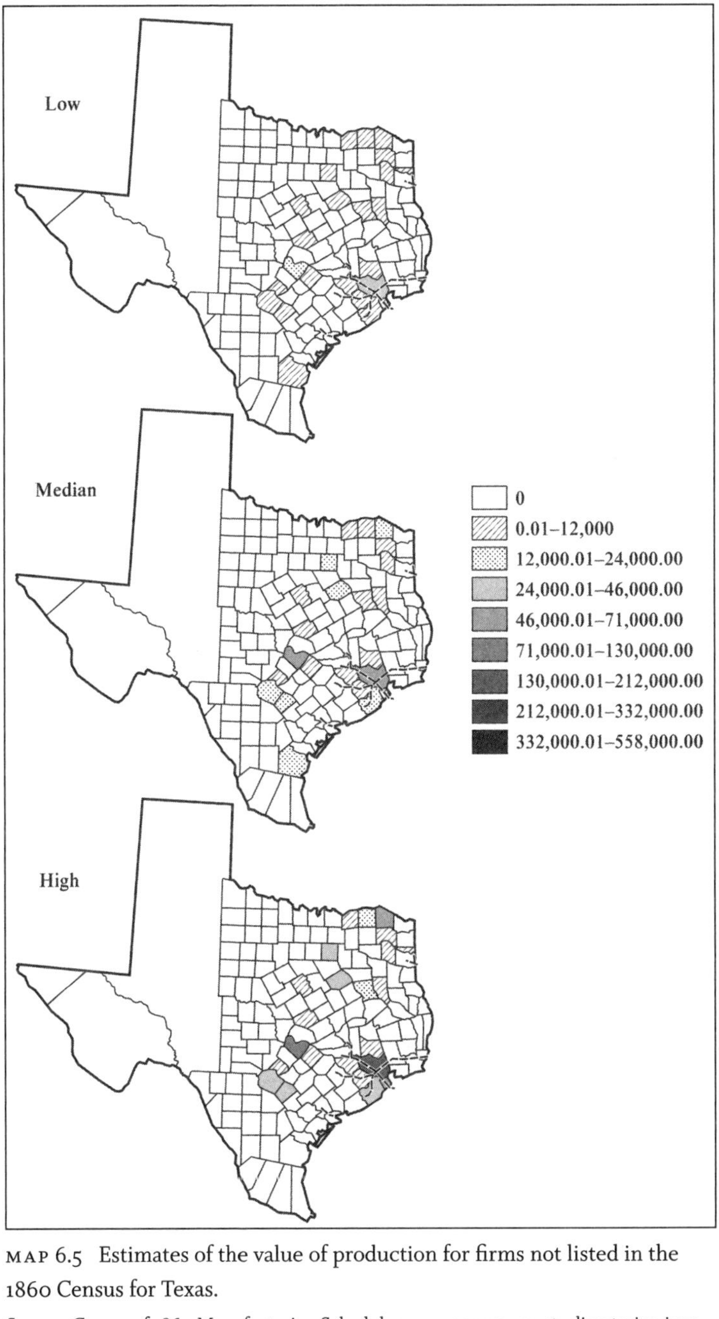


MAP 6.5 Estimates of the value of production for firms not listed in the 1860 Census for Texas.

*Sources:* Census of 1860 Manufacturing Schedules, newspapers, county directories, journals, and the R. G. Dun Credit Reports.

TABLE 6.4. Value of production for firms listed in the census and estimated value of production for firms listed in all sources for four cities in the Gulf South in 1860

| | Census | Low estimate | Median estimate | High estimate |
|---|---|---|---|---|
| Mobile | $1,587,049 | $1,638,816 (3.26%) | $1,720,284 (8.40%) | $1,919,049 (20.92%) |
| Montgomery | $281,650 | $369,885 (31.32%) | $505,515 (79.48%) | $839,650 (198.12%) |
| Natchez | $236,000 | $247,539 (4.89%) | $264,610 (12.12%) | $307,000 (30.08%) |
| Vicksburg | $646,300 | $675,919 (4.58%) | $719,065 (11.26%) | $828,300 (28.16%) |

*Sources:* Census of 1860 Manufacturing Schedules, newspapers, county directories, journals, and the R. G. Dun Credit Reports.

*General note:* The value provided in parentheses is the percentage over the census totals of the estimated amount.

underrepresented in the census.[24] In a state capital, one would expect the work of the census marshals to be more thorough.

Although it was surprising that the marshals did not record all of the production of concerns in cities such as Montgomery, it was not surprising that these areas had many firms in them. In cities, all of the ingredients for industrial development came together and production grew accordingly. Manufacturing endeavors in these cities had access to transportation to bring in raw materials and ship out finished products. Moreover, complementary concerns were also located here, which spurred growth. Thus, the foundries and mills in these urban areas supplied needed materials to other firms, keeping the cost of production lower for businesses like furniture makers or wagon factories.[25] In Mobile, Bowen and Gillman was a cabinet concern that was "quite wealthy and doing a good business," and was "good beyond a doubt," and their products were well thought of in the city.[26] This firm, missed by the census, most likely took advantage of the iron and lumber that other firms in the city produced. By 1860, a shift occurred in Mobile from imported goods to the use of local industrial products. The large number of industrial firms in the city, both recorded and unrecorded in the census, most likely sold at least some of their goods locally. These concerns produced for the market, and the most easily accessible was in the local area.[27] Also, manufacturing was seen as important enough to tax as a source of revenue, and Mobile started to tax manufacturing machinery in 1857.[28] Other cities also had large amounts of production missed by the census that earned the respect of their local areas based on the goods they produced. A. R. Tyler, a wagon and carriage maker in Natchez, Mississippi, turned out good products and was considered "safe" by the community at large.[29] A foundry owned by Ben Tappan in Vicksburg was a "large profitable business" that produced products used by many other firms in the city.[30] These are just a few examples of manufacturers the marshals missed, which made these urban areas more important industrial centers than the census has led us to believe.

There are other ways to put the value of manufacturing production into perspective. One way is to examine the wholesale prices of specific commodities and then to determine how many units of each commodity were produced. For example, R. A. Baker and Company, a firm in Baldwin County, Alabama, was "extensively engaged in the turpentine business of large means and property."[31] Census marshals missed this important concern. Because no census record exists, we cannot know the value of its production. But for a firm of this type, the estimated value of its production was somewhere between $2,500 and $16,000.[32] Because the Dun credit reporter characterized the firm as large and having a lot of property, we may assume that the concern's scale of production was closer to the higher end of this range. Next we can divide the lower and upper bounds of the value of the firm's output by the price per gallon. The wholesale price of turpentine in 1860 was just over 42 cents per gallon.[33] Thus, R. A. Baker and Company produced between 5,910 and 37,825 gallons of turpentine. In today's dollars the value of the firm's output ranged somewhere between $72,000 and $462,000.[34] Another fairly large firm missed by the census was H. Mayer and Company, a grist mill in Austin, Texas, and again, because it was not listed in the census, we can only estimate the value of its production.[35] Based on H. Mayer and Company's line of business, the concern most likely produced between $2,995 and $12,500.[36] The wholesale price of a 196-pound barrel of flour was $5.19.[37] Using that figure, we may estimate that H. Mayer and Company produced between 577 and 2,408 barrels of flour (or 113,092 to 471,968 pounds) in 1860. When converted into today's money, this output would be worth somewhere between $86,600 and $361,000.[38] Of course, as noted earlier, none of this production was recorded in the census.

Beyond looking at just the value of production and what this output actually meant in finished products, we may also use other approaches to appraise a firm's activities. A particularly useful measure of a manufacturer's operation was the ratio of its output to its capital investment. By looking at this ratio we can see how much output each dollar of capital represented. Investors in Alabama, Mississippi, and Texas wanted to get a return on any capital that they put forward and, to the extent that they could, they pressed their equipment to produce the largest output possible.[39] Table 6.5 shows the ratio of capital to output for firms listed in the census by organizational form. As this table illustrates, as the organizational complexity increases, the capitalization of the firm also increases. Tables 6.6, 6.7, and 6.8 show estimates of the ratio of output to capital for concerns found in all sources based on organizational form. The addition of the firms missed by the census marshals increases the ratio of capital to output, and, just as with the census concerns alone, as the organization of a firm became more complex, the level of its capitalization also grew. No matter how a business was organized, an industrial entrepreneur could expect to get $1.28–$1.61 worth of output for every dollar of capital invested in a manufactory. These figures do not, of course, apply to every industry. Rather, this is the ratio of output to capital for the entire industrial sector. There were industries with higher, and others with lower, rates. Table 6.9 shows the average output to capital ratio for agricultural implement firms. For this high-technology line of business we can see that partnerships had a much higher amount of capital and output per firm than individually owned concerns did, while companies were considerably larger than partnerships.[40] Tables 6.10

TABLE 6.5. Average capital, output, and ratio of output to capital for firms listed in the census by organizational form

| Firms owned by | Number of firms | Average $ of capital per firm | Average $ of output per firm | Average ratio of output to capital |
|---|---|---|---|---|
| Individual | 2,488 | 3,661 | 5,661 | 1.55 |
| Partnership | 460 | 5,970 | 8,127 | 1.36 |
| Company | 332 | 14,124 | 17,782 | 1.26 |

*Source:* Census of 1860 Manufacturing Schedules.

TABLE 6.6. Estimates of average capital, output, and ratio of output to capital for the 3,033 individually owned firms listed in all sources

| | Low estimate | Median estimate | High estimate |
|---|---|---|---|
| Average $ of capital per firm | 3,093 | 3,218 | 3,542 |
| Average $ of output per firm | 4,856 | 5,084 | 5,687 |
| Average ratio of output to capital | 1.57 | 1.58 | 1.61 |

*Sources:* Census of 1860 Manufacturing Schedules, newspapers, county directories, journals, and the R. G. Dun Credit Reports.

and 6.11 show that this holds true for firms that used a median level of technology, boot and shoe firms, and also for a low-technology industry like lumber mills. Moreover, the lower-technology, primary-processing lumber firms had a much larger ratio of output to capital than the higher-technology agricultural implement and boot and shoe firms.[41]

An example of a specific firm illustrates this point. J. O. and D. L. Young were "both honest and upright industrious men," who owned a successful tanning, shoe, and harness-making firm in Carrollton, Mississippi.[42] A reporter for the R. G. Dun Company recorded that the firm

TABLE 6.7. Estimates of average capital, output, and ratio of output to capital for the 565 concerns owned by partnerships listed in all sources

| | Low estimate | Median estimate | High estimate |
|---|---|---|---|
| Average $ of capital per firm | 5,030 | 5,251 | 5,790 |
| Average $ of output per firm | 6,989 | 7,368 | 8,475 |
| Average ratio of output to capital | 1.39 | 1.40 | 1.46 |

*Source:* Census of 1860 Manufacturing Schedules, newspapers, county directories, journals, and the R. G. Dun Credit Reports.

TABLE 6.8. Estimates of average capital, output, and ratio of output to capital for the 470 companies listed in all sources

| | Low estimate | Median estimate | High estimate |
|---|---|---|---|
| Average $ of capital per firm | 10,389 | 11,139 | 12,914 |
| Average $ of output per firm | 13,295 | 14,616 | 17,259 |
| Average ratio of output to capital | 1.28 | 1.31 | 1.34 |

*Sources:* Census of 1860 Manufacturing Schedules, newspapers, county directories, journals, and the R. G. Dun Credit Reports.

produced $6,000 to $8,000 worth of products in a year.[43] Based on the estimate calculated from the census for capital investment in a concern such as the Youngs' in 1860, the ratio of output to capital for this firm was between $2.31 and $3.08, which was much higher than that of an average firm listed in the census. This firm, and its significant production, was somehow overlooked by the census marshals. Of course, receiving two to three dollars in production for every dollar invested

TABLE 6.9. Average capital, output, and ratio of output to capital for agricultural implement firms listed in the census

| Firms owned by | Number of firms | Average $ of capital per firm | Average $ of output per firm | Average ratio of output to capital |
|---|---|---|---|---|
| Individual | 16 | 3,573 | 3,735 | 1.05 |
| Partnership | 1 | 5,100 | 6,750 | 1.32[a] |
| Company | 5 | 10,800 | 9,818 | 0.91 |

[a] The values listed in Table 6.9 for capital, output, and ratio of output to capital for agricultural implements concerns owned by partnerships are not an average. There was only one firm of that type listed in the census, and thus the values in the table are for that one concern.

*Source:* Census of 1860 Manufacturing Schedules.

TABLE 6.10. Average capital, output, and ratio of output to capital for boot and shoe concerns listed in the census

| Firms owned by | Number of firms | Average $ of capital per firm | Average $ of output per firm | Average ratio of output to capital |
|---|---|---|---|---|
| Individual | 173 | 1,343 | 2,801 | 2.09 |
| Partnership | 22 | 2,593 | 3,972 | 1.53 |
| Company | 19 | 1,525 | 3,088 | 2.02 |

*Source:* Census of 1860 Manufacturing Schedules.

does not mean that a company was profitable. There were many other costs associated with doing business beyond capital investment. But historians determined that people with capital in the South could earn a good return on manufacturing investments in the region, something that these output-to-capital ratios seem to uphold.[44] As William Scarborough pointed out, "Some used the capital generated by their agricultural

TABLE 6.11. Average capital, output, and ratio of output to capital for lumber firms listed in the census

| Firms owned by | Number of firms | Average $ of capital per firm | Average $ of output per firm | Average ratio of output to capital |
|---|---|---|---|---|
| Individual | 447 | 5,762 | 7,879 | 1.37 |
| Partnership | 106 | 5,501 | 9,334 | 1.70 |
| Company | 79 | 7,519 | 10,940 | 1.45 |

*Source:* Census of 1860 Manufacturing Schedules.

enterprises to purchase additional land and slaves, but others developed extremely diversified economic portfolios."[45]

Output per worker is another way to look at industrial production. By dividing the number of workers a firm employed into the value of its output for the year, we can determine the output per worker. This ratio showed how productive a worker was in the Gulf South. Efficiency is the mark of a modern, industrial society, and output per worker is one measure of this.[46] Moreover, as chapter 5 explained, there were many people in the antebellum United States who did not think that lower-class southern whites made good industrial workers.[47] But others, such as the editor of the *Independent Monitor*, felt that "there was a large population of a class whose means of support are very uncertain . . . [whose] labor at cheap rates can always be commended."[48] Cheap, of course, does not necessarily mean that workers were good at their jobs. Seeing how productive labor was, by determining output per worker, could help to put to rest the idea of a southern workforce that did not perform well. Based on the census returns, an average industrial worker in the antebellum Gulf South produced $1,353.62 worth of industrial products in 1860.[49] Chart 6.1 displays comparable values for Gulf South firms missed by the census according to type of organization. As one would expect, there were some gains on a per-worker basis as the size and complexity of industrial concerns grew, that is, companies generally produced somewhat

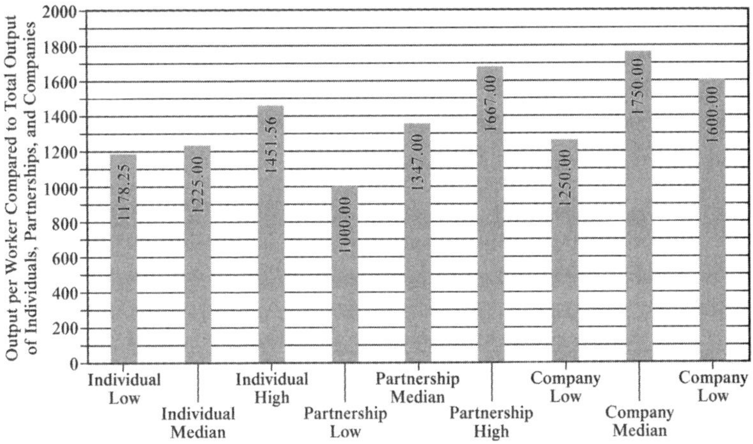


more per worker than did individually owned firms or partnerships.[50] Moreover, for the United States as a whole in 1860, the average value of production per worker was $1,426.70. Comparing this figure to the ones in Chart 6.1 shows that the Gulf South was right in line with the rest of the nation.[51]

George Fitzhugh wrote before the outbreak of the Civil War, in *Sociology for the South*, that there was a "tendency of modern improvements in locomotion and intercommunication, which naturally rob the extremities to enrich the centers of Power and Trade."[52] Perhaps this was happening. As the maps in this chapter show, industrial production was concentrated in the cities of the Gulf South. Railroads promoted the development of markets and provided connections to distant sources of raw materials. The growth of urban economic and industrial centers was, though, notwithstanding Fitzhugh's misgivings, not a bad thing. Development of this kind allowed Southerners to obtain locally the manufactured goods they needed rather than having to spend extra money to import them. Moreover, industrial firms in the Gulf South produced a considerable volume and variety of goods and did so at rates in line with the rest of the nation. De Bow argued in support of just such development: "It is strenuously contended that the introduction of manufacturers in the South would undermine our free-trade principles, and destroy the last hope of the great agricultural interest. It is susceptible of demonstration, that the consequences would necessarily be precisely the reverse."[53]

De Bow was right. Cotton production was extremely high in 1860, yet a large number of manufacturing concerns, larger than contemporaries in 1860 and historians writing since then thought, operated without any detrimental effects on the cotton economy.[54]

# EPILOGUE

## Manufacturing a War

Bateman and Weiss, in their work on antebellum southern industry, explain that "the traditional interpretation depicts the South, even during the late antebellum era, as an agrarian-commercial export economy almost totally devoid of any manufacturing."[1] Thus, the South has generally been seen as having had little industrial development because of the region's dependence on slavery, a way of life that did not embrace change, and a worldview that looked backward rather than forward. Antebellum southerners, though, were more modern on the eve of the war than even they may have understood. Some in the region, such as De Bow, Pratt, and Gregg, pushed for further manufacturing development and felt that the South needed to "inaugurate its own industrial revolution."[2] These men struggled to attract investment to the region, get more manufacturing firms founded, and gain broader public support.[3] By 1860, with the development that had taken place, "the South as a whole—was as much a land of villages and towns as of planters, slaves, and yeoman farmers."[4] There was more manufacturing in the Gulf South than the census marshals recorded. Moreover, the region, if left to its own devices, with no major disruption to its society, would likely have continued to create and expand its already considerable number of industrial concerns.

Most historians agree that at the outbreak of the Civil War, the South, when compared with most nations in 1860, was well developed industrially. Fogel and Engerman determined that the states that made up the Confederacy ranked fifth in the world in cotton manufacturing and eighth in the world in iron production on the eve of the war.[5] Moreover, this would-be nation had the world's fourth-highest per capita income in 1860.[6] As Gavin Wright argued, the "South was not one of the truly impoverished or backwards economies of its day."[7] The region was, as he determined, fifteenth on a world scale economically and fell in with other "middling" nations, such as Spain, Austria, Norway, and Portugal.[8] Engerman agreed, writing that "the image of a backward, low-income economy is certainly not the appropriate one for the antebellum South."[9] These assertions were based on the census records. As we have seen, the actual amount of industry in the region, once the firms missed by the census are added to the census totals, was considerably greater.

But then the war came and industry in the region was put to the test. The Civil War was an industrial war. It would not just be southern men marching off into combat; southern industrial firms, owners, and employees were also called upon to play their parts.[10] Winfield Scott's Anaconda Plan, something many northerners scoffed at, became the strategy by which the Union forces ultimately fought and won the war. The implementation of this plan increasingly cut the South off from the outside world and forced the Confederacy to rely almost wholly on what could be produced within its territory. Thus, the war pushed southern industry to its limits.[11]

Before any shots were fired, secession caused economic disruptions. *The Panola Star,* of Panola, Mississippi, on the eve of secession, warned its readers to use up all of their banknotes from South Carolina, Georgia, and Tennessee because there was no way of knowing what was going to happen next.[12] As we now know, what happened next was four long years of grinding war. Industry in the region was not built to fight this kind of war. Entrepreneurs had founded manufacturing firms in the Gulf South to turn a profit by catering to local markets, and hopefully, in the future, to grow and diversify. Although concerns could convert to war production, they were organized, even on the eve of the war, to meet the demands of a peacetime economy.[13] Grist mills and foundries were not established to feed the army or make equipment for troops. They were founded to make flour and iron goods for local consumption.

Thus, southerners marched off to war without many of the pieces of basic equipment that soldiers should possess. For example, in a letter to his wife, June, in December 1861, George Dobson, of Jackson, Mississippi, reported from his camp that there were not enough rifles for all of the new troops being enlisted.[14] This complaint was often repeated at the start of the war.

Upon the outbreak of fighting, most discussions of southern industry focused on shortages and breakdowns. These complaints confirmed what many believed, that manufacturing in the South was either almost nonexistent or quickly overwhelmed by wartime demands. But when the war broke out, there was more industry in the Gulf South than had been previously reported, and production was turned to the war effort. The additional industrial capacity discussed here may explain how the South was able to sustain its war effort for four years.[15] When the shooting began, many manufacturing firms in the Gulf South switched from the production of goods for southern consumers to items that the Confederacy needed to fight a war. The Confederate government sent purchasing agents throughout the region to find industrial goods for the army.[16] Soldiers frequently needed to replace their equipment, so industry had plenty of orders to fill. "Patriotism and profit," in the words of Mary DeCredico, now became driving forces in Gulf South manufacturing.[17]

Many firms in the Gulf South turned to war production. Mississippi, for example, had several major manufactories that helped to support the Confederate war effort. The A. B. Reading and Brother Foundry, in Vicksburg, produced three-inch rifled cannons for both the state of Mississippi and the Confederate government throughout much of the war. Of course, this was a new type of production for the firm, and there were problems. The *Vicksburg Whig* reported in May 1861 that one of the cannons produced by the concern exploded in testing and killed a bystander.[18] The Confederate government took much of the foundry's equipment during the war, and the business was in shambles by the end of the conflict.[19] The textile factory in Bankston, Mississippi, joined the war effort by manufacturing uniforms for the army which "greatly enhanced the economic importance" of the concern."[20] Thus, needs of the army altered the character and demand of the market. In order to survive and make a profit, firms needed to produce for that changed market.

In 1860, Alabama produced the most industrial goods in the Gulf South, so naturally there was war production in the state. Selma, Alabama, became a major Confederate industrial center, something that began before the war. In 1860, the census listed fifty-nine firms in Selma, while other primary sources added forty-two more to the total. These concerns were founded to take advantage of the natural resources, such as lumber, coal, and iron, which were available in the area. During the war a government arsenal was founded in the city because "the facilities here for the production of cartridges, saltpeter, powder, shot and shell, and for the assemblage of lumber, coal, and iron, were greater than at any other point existing in the South."[21] Of course, Mobile, Alabama's most important industrial city, also had concerns that changed over to wartime production. The Mobile Foundry, owned by Skaates & Company, for example, signed a contract to produce cannons for the government, along with artillery shells and mortars.[22] The Wright and Rice Foundry in Florence, Alabama, also produced cannons for the army.[23] Another arsenal was established in Montgomery, which made accoutrements and cartridges.[24] Thus, if the South was to survive, any firm that could produce goods needed to sustain the war effort was going to need to expand to its limits. Shoemakers, saddlers, ironworkers, and many other firms could no longer only be concerned with their local area; they needed to outfit men going to war as well. Thus, while these firms may not be considered by many as industrial, the needs of war forced expanded, industrialized production on almost all southern manufactory owners.

Of course, many industrial concerns did not survive the conflict, especially as Union troops entered the Gulf South on offensive operations. The textile mill in Bankston, Mississippi, was burned in 1864, and, without its economic engine, the town itself was abandoned soon after.[25] The Mississippi State Penitentiary Factory, which produced large amounts of material for the army, such as uniforms and other accoutrements, met its end on November 20, 1863, as was recorded in the inspection records of the factory: "Then, here came the Blamed Yankees under Tecump. Sherman—Blue bellies—and burned the penitentiary with fire [*sic*]."[26] The Alabama Iron Manufacturing Company was listed in the Dun reports in 1866 as "dissolved, their works were destroyed when the federal forces occupied Selma."[27] Destruction by enemy troops, though, was only one way that industrial firms stopped production during the conflict. As Harold Wilson explained, "after four years of deprivation and eighty-hour work weeks, many southern workers were in a poor physical state."[28] So, after fighting four years of war, a great deal of southern industry was either worn out or destroyed.

The credit reporters employed by R. G. Dun provide the first look we have at the war's effect on Gulf South industry. As earlier chapters explained, before the war, the Dun reporters recorded information about manufacturing firms in the Gulf South that the census marshals missed. These reporters saw that the region was more industrially developed than anyone really understood. Moreover, these reports showed no recognition that the war was on the horizon. As late as March of 1861 reports were being entered into the R. G. Dun Company's ledgers about the creditworthiness of southern firms even for states that had left the Union, such as Mississippi, Alabama, and Texas. In 1866, a year after the end of hostilities, information on firms began to be entered again for the Gulf South states. Some concerns did not survive the war. W. T. Gunter, a railroad contractor in Jackson County, Alabama, was listed in the Dun reports after the war as "Busted."[29] J. Franklin Kerr, a gunsmith in Hinds County, Mississippi, went out of business because of his wartime conduct. The reports recorded that Kerr was "not worth anything, not good, deserted from Rebel Army."[30] Kerr's entry was a rarity, though. There was actually very little mention of the war in these post-war updates beyond whether the firm survived the conflict and whether it was creditworthy.

By looking at the Dun reports, then, we can see which firms persisted through the conflict. Table E.1 shows the concerns listed in the Dun reports that survived the war. In 1866, 28.1 percent of the manufactories listed in the ledgers of Dun still existed. Map E.1 illustrates the location of the firms that made it through the conflict. The largest

TABLE E.1. Persistence of firms listed in the Dun Reports

| | Listed in Dun Reports for 1860 | Listed in Dun Reports after the Civil War |
|---|---|---|
| Alabama | 170 | 57 (33.5%) |
| Mississippi | 121 | 32 (26.4%) |
| Texas | 43 | 5 (11.6%) |
| Total | 334 | 94 (28.1%) |

*Source:* R. G. Dun Credit Reports.

*General note:* Percentages listed in parentheses represent the percentage of 1860 firms that were still in existence in 1866.

concentrations of concerns that made it through the war were in the urban areas of the Gulf South. But there were other scattered concerns that survived the conflict. For example, James Throckmorton, who owned a sawmill in Franklin County, Alabama, survived the war "very good" and thrived during Reconstruction.[31] As the table and the map illustrate, there were many concerns across the Gulf South with a story similar to Throckmorton's. Some counties in Alabama, Mississippi, and especially Texas were untouched by the conflict.[32] Contrary to popular belief, Union forces did not go out of their way in an attempt to burn everything in the region to the ground, and thus, many firms survived the war.[33]

Owners of industrial concerns founded before the war played a role in the war effort and even in postwar reconstruction. The Gulf South in 1860 was endowed with a great deal of human capital. Gulf South industrialists knew how to take advantage of the resources, transportation, and markets available to build successful concerns. Moreover, these manufacturers "helped lay the foundation of a later, eager acceptance of manufacturing and the city as parts of the way of life in the South. In the years before 1860 they were far-sighted."[34] Southerners invested in manufacturing as "a growing number of planters, farmers, and merchants in the Cotton South placed their limited capital and more bountiful rhetoric into new businesses and increased manufacturing."[35]

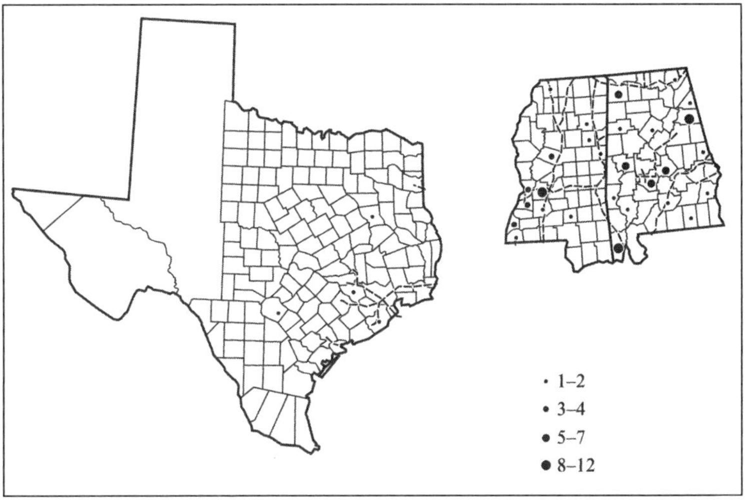


MAP E.1. Location of firms listed in the Dun reports that survived the war.
*Source:* R.G. Dun Credit Reports.

While a great deal of the Gulf South's industrial development was based on the creation of firms that processed primary materials, it was a beginning that could be used for further development.[36] Thus, in 1860, the industrial development of the South was great enough that perhaps we can point to the decade leading up to the war as the beginning of the "New" South.[37] Even if the owners of manufacturing concerns lost firms during the war, their entrepreneurial knowledge survived and could be drawn upon during Reconstruction.

The South was not as industrially developed as the North in 1860. Even including all of the missed firms rediscovered over the course of this study, the region suffers greatly in comparison. Hinton Helper went to great lengths in his antebellum work to show that while the South and the North were on an equal footing at the time of the American Revolution, by the time he wrote his work, the South had fallen far behind in manufacturing.[38] Bateman and Weiss, who found such a "deplorable scarcity" in southern industry, also agreed that the region did not compare with the North.[39] I will not attempt to dispute that idea here, as this is not a work of counterfactual history. Southern industry lagged far behind northern in 1860. The concerns missed by the census marshals, when added to the census totals, did not put the South on par with the North. Perhaps, though, comparisons between the two parts of the country should never have been made. As Engerman explains, "In comparing the South with the Northeast we often overlook the point that, however justified the comparison, it was the Northeast and not the South that was to be considered unusual in the mid-nineteenth-century world."[40] The regions were more alike, though, than one would expect. The North and South were similarly affected by modern developmental ideas because "in spite of their differences, every region was experiencing modernization. Modernization was a more pervasive, influential process in the North than it was in the South, but the differences were relative, not absolute."[41] The North was ahead, but the South was developing and, as the war showed, southern manufacturing helped to support the four-year war effort before it wore out and broke down.[42]

Industry in the antebellum South has been misunderstood for a long time. The census marshals, when compiling census information, missed almost 20 percent of the firms in Alabama, Mississippi, and Texas. This underreporting produced a distorted view of the region. The Gulf South was not as agrarian as its residents believed and historians have argued. The people and industries of these states were also not as dependent on imported goods as southerners feared and northerners hoped. Manufacturing was more geographically diffuse and locally intensive than the census showed, and more of the Gulf South was involved in industry than anyone realized. Moreover, slavery did not hold back the region and even was able to help with industrial development as both labor and capital.[43]

Bateman and Weiss, in their work on southern industry, explain: "Having considered these alternatives, specifically that of industrialization, we have found that the South could have done better than it did. Had there been more manufacturing investment, southern economic performance would have improved."[44] Bateman and Weiss were right that more investment would have helped economic performance. But there was more investment in the antebellum Gulf South then they knew about. There was investment missed by the census marshals, and thus Bateman and Weiss missed it because they based their work on the census alone. Conclusions based solely on the census records, then, such as Bateman and Weiss's, require revision based on what was not recorded. The Gulf South was an agrarian golconda. There were huge fields of cotton that stretched across the region, worked by slaves, which made their owners large amounts of money. But built upon the same landscape were industrial firms. Most people have constructed their views of an antebellum South with little manufacturing based on the concerns reported by the census. When the missed firms are accounted for, though, we can see a deeper belt of industry across the region. This belt corresponded to the railroad network and took advantage of the supplies of raw materials, capital, and labor that the Gulf South possessed. But even with the missed firms added in, the South was not a manufacturing juggernaut that could have won the war that erupted the next year. The Gulf South, though, was a region more industrialized and modern than suggested by the census. More to the point, the thinly industrialized South of Frederick Law Olmsted, and even that of Bateman and Weiss, almost certainly could not have sustained a four-year, increasingly grinding struggle for independence. The "deplorable scarcity" has largely rested on what really was a deplorable misunderstanding, one that this work attempts to correct.

# APPENDIX A

## SOURCES

As noted in chapter 2, this work rests on an extensive database of antebellum Gulf South industry. Evidence from a wide range of primary sources went into its construction, and the result is a complete, or as nearly complete as possible, list of all of the manufacturing concerns active in Alabama, Mississippi, and Texas in 1860. No one primary source listed all of the industrial firms in the region. Even the census, which scholars have supposed to be the most complete, missed a large number of concerns. As chapter 3 explained, the census left unrecorded almost 20 percent of the manufactories in Alabama, Mississippi, and Texas. Thus, the census can only be the starting point for any study of the manufacturing base of the antebellum Gulf South. Other sources, notably gazetteers, city and county directories, newspapers, periodicals, the R. G. Dun Credit Reports, and local histories, provide evidence to augment the listing of manufacturing firms in the census.

### THE FEDERAL CENSUS OF 1860

The first and most important listing of manufacturing firms in the Gulf South in 1860 was presented in that year's decennial census of the United States. The census record was, by far, the most comprehensive enumeration. Census marshals were hired all over the country and gathered information about the United States, including data about population, agriculture, and most importantly for this work, manufacturing. The census contained not just the names and owners of industrial firms, it also reported capital, output, raw materials used, number of male and female employees, and wages. No other source available for 1860 had this level of information. The census law that was passed by Congress and was sent out as the instructions to the marshals, told them how to gather the information that would make up the census and included an oath to do the best that they could to gather information to enumerate every last item in the census schedules. The manufacturing schedule instructions also discussed how to overcome any resistance of owners to providing data. It seems that, before any work began, Congress had anticipated that the marshals would have difficulty in gathering all of the information requested. As the instructions state:

> Should any one object on the ground of not wishing to expose the nature of his business, the Assistant Marshal should state that it is not desired to elicit any information which will be used or published as concerning the operations of any individual or concern. The primary facts are confidentially received, and will only be published in connexion with, and as a part of, a great body of similar facts, from which it will be impossible to abstract or distinguish those of an individual firm or corporations. Individual statements are necessary for the formation of aggregate results. If necessary you may state that examination of the returns is not permitted for any private purpose, nor does the Department allow access to them for other than public uses.[1]

The schedule had places for capital, materials, labor, and output. But just because information was entered onto the schedule, it does not mean that the data was readable or correct.

The completed schedules were forwarded to clerks who compiled state- and national-level statistics. The census supposedly had strict standards for the workers that they hired. As a Galveston, Texas, newspaper explained:

> The census board has become censorions [*sic*], in the matter of applicants for clerkships. A dispatch from Washington says that ten out of the twelve first examined were rejected for inability to pass the rigid examination to which they are subjected in math-

> ematics, &c., and among the rejected ones was a professor in a literary institution![2]

But the many errors in the census, at all levels of data entry, seem to belie the idea that census employees were held to rigorous standards. That the census incorporated errors, both of recording and omission, has been a circumstance that scholars have long recognized. A large part of these errors arose because of the difficulty of counting every person, farm, or industrial concern in the nation. J. D. B. De Bow, as superintendent of the 1850 census, saw some of these problems as "hundreds of important towns and cities . . . are not even distinguished on the returns from the body of the counties in which they are situated."[3]

As we have seen, the errors of omission in the 1860 census resulted in a decidedly distorted view of southern industry on the eve of the Civil War. Ronald Lewis perhaps explained these errors best, referring specifically to the 1860 census: "Census data do not provide much assistance . . . since they were collected haphazardly."[4] That is, we cannot know the quality and drive of the men sent out to gather census information. Thus, the census marshals left out or misreported any number of items addressed by the census schedules. In some counties there were more workers listed in the manufacturing census than people who, according to the population schedules, actually held these jobs, making one wonder where the mistakes were made and how they could have happened.[5] Moreover, some historians believe that wages and other labor costs were not correctly listed in the census because of "the high reported profits for small firms."[6] Also, a great deal of industrial production occurred on plantations in 1860. This industrial activity, such as sugar processing, milling (both saw and grist), iron work, and many other lines of business, should have been reported in the manufacturing census. But the marshals listed this production, when they recorded it at all, in the agricultural schedules. This practice made the South's industrial output in the census seem smaller than it was.[7] There were other problems associated with the census. Census takers in both the North and the South were very lax when counting and labeling places as towns and villages. These small places were important as trading centers and markets for industrial production "and historians who accept the labels at face value do so at their own peril."[8] For example, Gallatin, Mississippi, was a small town in the central part of the state. It was bypassed by the railroad and quickly began to lose population. Even so, there were still many people living there in 1860. The town and its people, though, were not listed in the census returns.[9] The omission of Gallatin from the 1860 census was, of course, not a unique occurrence, and many other communities shared Gallatin's misfortune. Marshals did not record this area because the railroads had bypassed it and, thus, it was harder to reach and easier to leave out. Unfortunately, even with all of these census-related problems, most historians who look at industry in 1860 continue to assume that the records are substantially correct and, accordingly, base their work on this information.[10]

## NEWSPAPERS AND JOURNALS

Periodicals from 1860 were another source of information about what industrial firms existed in the Gulf South. While the census had the stated goal of finding and listing all of the manufacturing concerns in the nation, newspapers and journals only published information about manufacturers that made the news or paid for an advertisement. Across the Gulf South, in almost every city and town, there was at least one local newspaper. While some of these papers have been lost over time, many from 1860 have survived. Journals, while fewer in number, circulated over wider geographical areas than did local papers. We may reasonably infer that firms that advertised in these journals sought customers in distant markets and that, correspondingly, such firms tended to be fairly large concerns.

Newspapers and journals carried many articles and editorials about industry. Moreover, the advertising sections of these publications, which ran for numerous pages in most issues, provided information about industrial firms. As stated in chapter 3, firms that advertised in newspapers and journals were most likely substantial ones because of the expense of running an advertisement. Thus, the census should have listed them. These sources, then, supplied information missing from the census of manufacturing in the Gulf South.

The front page of most newspapers in Alabama, Mississippi, and Texas had a column or two devoted to new advertisements. After running for a few weeks, these listings were then moved to the two to three pages of advertising that made up the end of the paper. As most papers consisted of only six to eight pages, these advertisements constituted a substantial amount of space in each issue. For most newspapers, the main advertisement section, at the end of the issue, did not change much from day to day or week to week. This made identifying new listings easier. Unfortunately, beyond the name of a firm, its location, a listing of what they sold, and perhaps a picture, these advertisements did not provide a great deal of information about individual firms or their proprietors. Owners did not tend to list capital investment, raw materials used, or labor information, when trying to find a market for their wares. Very few newspapers have complete runs available of every issue published in 1860, but most had enough issues to allow many missing firms to come to light. The bibliography of this dissertation contains the complete listing of the newspapers and journals used in this work. A majority of the firms not listed in the census were rediscovered in newspaper and journal advertisements.

## THE R. G. DUN CREDIT REPORTS

As one of the earliest credit reporting firms in the nation, the R. G. Dun Company compiled ledgers that provide valuable insight on southern industrial concerns. Born in Chillicothe, Ohio, R. G. Dun began working at age sixteen in a general merchandise store in his hometown.[11] Because most stores in this period extended credit to their customers, from the beginning of his work life, Dun learned how credit and credit markets worked. In 1841, Lewis Tappen founded the Mercantile Agency to write credit reports about firms in New York City.[12] Tappen hired a man named Benjamin Douglass, who was Dun's brother-in-law.[13] Douglass got Dun a job in the Agency. Dun worked with Tappen and Douglass to expand the scope of the firm and take their credit reports national.

In 1859, Dun bought the Mercantile Agency from Tappen and turned it into the premier credit reporting agency of its day.[14] By 1860, Dun's firm "dominated the southern credit-rating business and enjoyed a reputation in the South for accuracy and competence above that of any other credit-rating firm."[15] Tappen, and later Dun, used local attorneys as their unpaid credit reporters. The two men believed that locals knew their area the best and would be able to find out information that outsiders could not. As Tappen explained in a business circular he wrote in 1842, "the local agent . . . having his eye upon every trader of importance in his county, and noting it down, as it occurs, every circumstance affecting his credit, favorably or unfavorably, becomes better acquainted with his actual condition than any stranger can be."[16] Moreover, these local attorneys could make money on this arrangement as collectors for overdue bills on credit extended in their areas.[17]

When a business owner wanted to know about the creditworthiness of a firm, he would request a credit report from Dun. Then a local reporter would obtain information about the concern and send it back to the home office, where it was entered into ledgers organized by state and county. As new information came in on firms already listed in the reports, it was tacked onto the end of the existing entry. In this way, the Dun reports conveyed the perceptions of the standing of a firm in its community, how well-ordered the concern's business affairs were, whether it paid its bills on time, as well as other items that the reporters saw fit to include. The Dun reports, then, were a very valuable source for this work. While the reports did not contain much in the way of statistical data, such as capital or output values, the comments on firms' creditworthiness supply a great deal of insight into what local communities thought about the industrial concerns in their midst. Dun reporters were employed all over the Gulf South and reported to a mostly northern audience. The Dun reports also contained many firms that were missed by the census marshals, adding to the list of Gulf South concerns used in this work. Moreover, if an outsider wanted credit information on a firm, it leads one to believe that that concern was important and should have been listed in the census.

## LOCAL HISTORIES AND CITY AND COUNTY DIRECTORIES

Many people wrote histories about their local areas after the war as a form of boosterism for their cities. Other historians wrote about individual cities well after the fact. While these works were not specifically focused on industry in 1860, most begin their histories before the war and mention large firms owned by important people. While most of these firms were listed in the census, these works provide another local look at how people in the Gulf South viewed industrial development, while also contributing a few missed firms to add to the database of the region's manufacturing concerns. This was especially important for places like Vicksburg and Mobile because these areas did not have very many firms listed in the census for cities of their size and importance. Vicksburg had some of the most interesting histories written about it as the city tried to regain its prewar glory.[18]

City and county directories for 1860 were a valuable source of information about missing firms. Most directories began with a short history of the local area, similar to the boosterism found in local histories. These introductions explained all of the advantages to businesses that these cities provided to prospective entrepreneurs. Then, these directories went on to list all of the people living in the area and all of the businesses the cities or counties contained. By comparing these lists to the census, it was possible to uncover many missed firms. Moreover, the back of each directory was filled with advertisements that could be used to shed further light on southern manufacturing and to locate missed industrial concerns. Many directories were consulted for this work, including Marengo County, Alabama; Jackson, Mississippi; Montgomery, Alabama; Mobile, Alabama; Vicksburg, Mississippi; and general directories for the state of Texas and for all southern businesses. In the end, these two kinds of sources did not contain a large number of firms missed by the census marshals, but they did provide a valuable look at antebellum Gulf South industry.

# APPENDIX B

## METHODS

James De Bow explained the importance of statistics to his work:

> Statistics are far from being the barren array of figures ingeniously and laboriously combined into columns and tables, which many persons are apt to suppose them. They constitute rather the ledger of a nation, in which, like the merchant in his books, the citizen can read, at one view, all of the results of a year or of a period of years, as compared with other periods, and deduce the profit or the loss which has been made, in morals, education, wealth or power.[1]

As we have seen, statistics can be useful and should be a major part of any study of the industrial base of the antebellum Gulf South. So much has long been apparent. Anecdotal evidence cannot convey the extent and depth of manufacturing in the region. Moreover, while De Bow touted reliance on columns and tables of figures, today's technology allows us to use graphical representations, such as maps, to illustrate relationships at which De Bow's methods could only hint. Of course, because the time period studied here is 150 years in the past, not all of the information needed still exists or is listed in one place. Thus, some reconstruction was required to create the maps, charts, and tables presented here.

This book draws on a database of Gulf South industrial firms in operation in 1860. I constructed that database in the following manner. The first step was to record all of the industrial firms listed in the manufacturing census schedules, along with all of the information about them listed in the census, in a JMP database (a statistical program of the SAS corporation). Initially, the JMP database had entries abstracted from the manufacturing census schedules of the 1860 Census for state, county, firm name, owner, line of business, capital, raw material value, product values, male and female employees, and wages. This census information was the foundation upon which the rest of the database was built. Next, I added to the database all of the firms listed in newspaper and journal advertisements. At this point, two new fields were needed. The first of these was an origin field to note where a firm was first discovered. So, all of the firms found first in the census were listed as "schedule." If a firm was not recorded in the census but appeared in a newspaper advertisement, it was listed as such, and so on with each of the other sources used. The second additional field was actually a set of fields that noted all of the various sources in which a firm was listed. I then added to the database firms listed in the Dun reports. Finally, concerns located in all of the other sources, discussed in detail in Appendix A, were also added. In the end, the database became a listing of at least the name and location of every manufacturing concern that could be located for Alabama, Mississippi, and Texas. I could then use this database to determine how many firms were missed by the census and where they were located. Of course, for most of the firms missed by the census but found in other sources, data on capital, output, raw materials, or labor were also missing, which was a hurdle that had to be overcome.

With the JMP database complete, I then constructed a second, county-level database in Microsoft Excel. The first step in building this county-level database was to combine the JMP database with information on population, both free and slave, along with other fields that could later be used to create maps, such as one that showed which counties in the Gulf South had particular types of raw materials, for example, coal and iron. This second database was needed so that the information in the first database could be mapped using Geographic Information Systems (GIS) software. The level of the individual county was the lowest at which these data could be mapped. Once the Excel database listing the total number of firms and all available corresponding statistical data was complete, I geocoded this database so that I could match it to a GIS shapefile of counties in the Gulf South in 1860.[2] The Excel database was then saved in a Comma Separated Values (CSV) format so that it could be joined to the shapefile in ArcGIS, the GIS program used for this work. Once the two files were joined, I could then create maps of the data. But, before any map was possible, the problem of information missing from noncensus firms demanded attention.

The only source with extensive information about capital, raw materials, output, labor, and wages was, perversely enough, the 1860 Census. In order to have any idea about the factors of production and value of output of noncensus firms, I had to estimate what such concerns could have used, consumed, and produced based on the consumption and production figured for similar firms in the census. There were two ways to arrive at these estimates. The first was based on line of business or industry. For example, one could consider all of the grist mills listed in the census and, using JMP, calculate the dollar values of raw materials, capital investment, and wages, as well as the size of the workforce of the average firm in that industry. I computed just such averages for the largest 25 percent of firms, the smallest 25 percent of firms, and the middle 50 percent of firms in each industry. By creating this range, we can get some idea of the possible magnitude of the factors of production and output for noncensus firms. Most likely, because many such firms took the time and expense to advertise or were the subject of the Dun reports on their creditworthiness, these concerns were almost certainly similar to the larger firms enumerated by the census.

The second way to make these estimates was based on the organizational form of a firm, as discussed in chapter 2. The census schedules did not indicate whether a concern was an individual proprietorship, a partnership, or a company. But, based on the owners listed, the name of the firm, and its size, it was possible to determine how a given firm was organized. The same method described immediately above was used to estimate the highest, median, and lowest values of capital, raw materials, labor, wages, and output.[3] I calculated estimated values by using both methods, and the maps and tables are labeled accordingly to show which one was used. Of course, all of this work to create the two databases used here and to estimate values of the various factors of production was done to make possible the creation of appropriate maps.

The availability of data limits what we can glean from these kinds of sources. With the data that could be gathered, this work pushes to the limit what can be determined by estimation based on a source that is, as has been mentioned many times, not known for its completeness. So, some measures just cannot be reliably done with what is available at this time. Foremost, profitability is very hard to determine. There is really no way to know the full extent of the cost of operations for these firms. The census asks for data that could be used for this purpose, such as raw material and labor costs, but, it is so haphazardly gathered that we cannot even make reliable estimates as can be, and has been done in this work, for other factors of production. The costs of buildings, fuels, tools, machines, or even advertising are just not known to an extent that would allow an attempt at estimating profitability.[4] So, while we can see capital investment, and even estimate it, we cannot really determine, with the data available, whether investors put these funds to best use. Thus, while the data can help us determine efficiency of output, a measure of efficiency of investment will need new sources of data that researchers still are searching for today. Finally, this work tries to avoid the problems called out in other work, that of attempting to use incomplete data to draw conclusions. Where estimates have been made, they have been created based on information that is as solid as can be found for the time period, and, where the data is lacking, those estimates and statistics have been avoided.

The complete data set used for this work can be found on the author's website at www.drmichaelfrawley.com. As explained, missing firms were located in a variety of primary sources. Tables C.1, C.2, and C.3 on the website provide a listing by county for each state based on the kind of primary source, either the census, city/county directories, newspaper and journal advertisements, the R. G. Dun credit reports, or local histories, in which a concern was first located. The maps of missing firms in chapter 2 are based on this county-level information. The importance of ownership type to industrial development in the Gulf South was discussed in chapter 2 through various tables and maps at the state level to show where firms of various ownership forms were located in the region. Tables C.4, C.5, and C.6, again on the website, show the breakdown by county of ownership form for each state reviewed in this work. To get the estimated values of the various factors of production and output in the process described here, the following industrial line of business information sheets was created. Each sheet shows how many of each firm type were listed in the census, how many were found in other primary sources, and estimates of the capital, raw materials used, employees, wage bills, and production for all of the missing firms. There are no sheets included here for any line of business that did not have any missing firms discovered for it. All of this can be found on the author's website.

In the end, the entire 1860 Census needs to be reevaluated, not just the manufacturing census discussed in detail here. If there were manufacturers missing from the census, then there most likely were workers or other people who should have been listed as manufacturing workers, missing from the census. The population census asked people their occupations, but few listed any kind of manufacturing labor. Perhaps the mass of people who were listed in the census as "laborer" worked at these firms. Perhaps much of this work was seasonal, as discussed earlier, and workers listed themselves as farmers, as that is what they felt they did for a living. Thus, while the population census missed some people, as all of the censuses have, the error most likely was not in the number of people missed, but in how their occupation appeared in the population census. All that can be said at this point is that the number of people listed in the population census as industrial workers does not match even the lowest estimate of industrial workers the region must have possessed. But as the manufacturing census does not list individual workers, and the population census is, at best, hit-or-miss on occupations, this discrepancy will not be determined with any great deal of accuracy. Thus, if the manufacturing census had errors, it stands to reason that the population census did as well. Moreover, the slave census does not tell whether slaves performed industrial labor, which they did, creating even more problems with determining the true extent of industrial labor in the region. While this study has belabored, at times, the errors of the census, these errors are something that historians are not going to be able to fix, no matter how detailed their work in the field.

# NOTES

## CHAPTER ONE

1. Laura Wood Roper, *F.L.O.: A Biography of Frederick Law Olmsted* (Baltimore: Johns Hopkins University Press, 1973), 84.

2. Roper, *F.L.O.*, 84.

3. Frederick Law Olmsted, *The Cotton Kingdom* (New York: Mason Brothers, 1861), 381–82.

4. Olmsted, *The Cotton Kingdom*, 214.

5. Olmsted, *The Cotton Kingdom*, 219–21.

6. Olmsted, *The Cotton Kingdom*, 291–93.

7. Olmsted, *The Cotton Kingdom*, 301.

8. Olmsted, *The Cotton Kingdom*, 336.

9. Olmsted, *The Cotton Kingdom*, 423.

10. Vicki Vaughn Johnson, *The Men and* the *Vision of the Southern Commercial Conventions* (Columbia: University of Missouri Press, 1992), 112.

11. Hinton Rowan Helper, *The Impending Crisis of the South: How to Meet It* (New York: Burdick Brothers, 1857), 23.

12. Helper, *The Impending Crisis of the South*, 335.

13. Olmsted, *The Cotton Kingdom*, 38. Olmsted's travel books paint a picture of a South that is backward because of its dependence on slave labor. Most southerners are depicted as ignorant, violent, dirty, and uneducated, supporting the stereotypes of an unindustrial South. For example, the only mill Olmsted mentions in the Gulf South is a "rude corn mill" in Southeast Louisiana.

14. *Agricultural and Manufacturing Census Records of Fifteen Southern States for the Years 1850, 1860, 1870, and 1880* (Chapel Hill: University of North Carolina Library, 1962), microfilm, 8, located at the Mississippi State Archives in Jackson, Mississippi, hereafter cited as *Mississippi Schedule of Manufacturers*. All punctuation, spelling, and grammar in quotations will remain as written in the original documents.

15. Ronald L. Lewis, *Coal, Iron, and Slaves: Industrial Slavery in Maryland and Virginia, 1715–1865* (Westport, CT: Greenwood Press, 1979), 3.

16. Thomas Prentice Kettell, *Southern Wealth and Northern Profits* (New York: George W. & John A. Wood, 1860), 62.

17. Kettell, *Southern Wealth and Northern Profits*, 172–73.

18. Thomas Prentice Kettell in James De Bow, *Industrial Resources, Statistics, &c. of*

*the United States and More Particularly of the Southern and Western States* (New York: Appleton, 1852), 3:53.

19. "A Mississippi Planter," *De Bow's Review* 2 (February 1850): 100.

20. "A Mississippi Planter," 99.

21. De Bow, *Industrial Resources*, 1:80.

22. John Cairnes, *The Slave Power: Its Character, Career, and Probable Designs* (London: Macmillan, 1863), 66.

23. Cairnes, *The Slave Power*, 71.

24. *Weekly Telegraph*, October 2, 1860.

25. *West Alabamian*, June 6, 1860.

26. *Weekly Telegraph*, April 17, 1860; *Daily Confederation*, June 15, 1860.

27. Gavin Wright, *The Political Economy of the Cotton South: Households, Markets, and Wealth in the Nineteenth Century* (New York: W.W. Norton, 1978), 8; Hugh Aitken, *Did Slavery Pay?* (Boston: Houghton Mifflin, 1971), 329. Aitken explains that a society needs the ability to "transform itself" in order to industrialize, and that the presence of slavery kept the South from being able to transform into a more modern economy.

28. Florida was excluded from this study, because even though it is a Gulf South state, in 1860 it had only 185 firms, a negligible industrial base. Moreover, the state's sparse settlement inhibited even the beginning of industrialization. Louisiana will be discussed briefly, but because its Manufacturing Census Schedules are lost, an in-depth study of the state could not be made.

29. Walter Buenger, *Secession and the Union in Texas* (Austin: University of Texas Press, 1984), 16. Buenger explains that while Texas was a special case, Texans identified closely with Alabama and Mississippi because of the developing slave-based cotton economy. See also Andrew Torget, "Cotton Empire: Slavery and the Texas Borderlands, 1820–1837" (PhD diss., University of Virginia, 2009). Torget concurs in this view and demonstrates that Texas was fully integrated into the Gulf South's slave economy.

30. While the border South was developing manufacturing before the war, the Deep South was not seen as an industrializing area. See James Huston, "The Pregnant Economics of the Border South, 1840–1860: Virginia, Kentucky, Tennessee, and the Possibilities of Slave Labor Expansion," in Diane Barnes, Brian Schoen, and Frank Towers, eds., *The Old South's Modern Worlds: Slavery, Region, and Nation in the Age of Progress* (Oxford: Oxford University Press, 2011), 123; and Richard Goff, *Confederate Supply* (Durham, NC: Duke University Press, 1969), 4. Both Huston and Goff contend that beyond the Piedmont and New Orleans there was little or no industry anywhere else in the Lower South.

31. John Friedmann, *Regional Development Policy: A Case Study of Venezuela* (Cambridge, MA: MIT Press, 1966), 9, 22.

32. Friedmann, *Regional Development Policy*, 43. Friedmann also explains that these centers of concentration will stimulate development in the surrounding area, something maps will display.

33. Sam Bowers Hilliard, *Atlas of Antebellum Southern Agriculture* (Baton Rouge: LSU Press, 1984), 1.

34. Hilliard, *Atlas of Antebellum Southern Agriculture*, 3.

35. Fred Bateman and Thomas Weiss, "Manufacturing in the Antebellum South," in Paul Uselding, ed., *Research in Economic History* (Greenwich, CT: JAI Press, 1976), 1:3.

36. For an example of a comparison to the North, see Richard Graham, "Slavery and Economic Development: Brazil and the United States South in the Nineteenth Century," *Comparative Studies in Society and History* 23 (October 1981): 620; or Marc Egnal, *Clash of Extremes: The Economic Origins of the Civil War* (New York: Hill and Wang, 2009). More recent work is turning away from northern comparisons to put the South in an Atlantic perspective; see Anthony Kaye, "The Second Slavery: Modernity in the Nineteenth-Century and the Atlantic World," *Journal of Southern History* 75 (August 2009): 627–50.

37. Paul Paskoff, "Measures of War: A Quantitative Examination of the Civil War's Destructiveness in the Confederacy," *Civil War History* 54 (2008): 35–62.

38. For a discussion on war running down industry in the South, see Mary DeCredico, *Patriotism for Profit: Georgia's Urban Entrepreneurs and the Confederate War Effort* (Chapel Hill: University of North Carolina Press, 1990), xvi. Further, Union forces did destroy any major industrial concerns they could reach. For example, the Mississippi state penitentiary was burned because of its extensive textile works. Inspection Records, November 1863, Mississippi State Penitentiary Records, Mississippi Department of Archives and History.

39. C. Vann Woodward, *Origins of the New South, 1877–1913* (Baton Rouge: LSU Press, 1971).

40. Edward Pollard, *The Lost Cause: A New History of the War of the Confederates* (New York: E. B. Treat, 1866), 131.

41. Pollard, *The Lost Cause*, 41.

42. Gaines M. Foster, *Ghosts of the Confederacy: Defeat, the Lost Cause, and the Emergence of the New South* (Oxford: Oxford University Press, 1985).

43. Ulrich B. Phillips, *American Negro Slavery* (New York: D. Appleton, 1918). Also see Charles W. Ramsdell, *The Natural Limits of Slavery Expansion* (Indianapolis: Bobbs-Merrill, 1929).

44. Phillips, *American Negro Slavery*, 397.

45. Phillips, *American Negro Slavery*, 395. Phillips was not wrong, as slaves increased in value greatly in the decade leading up to the war.

46. Broadus Mitchell, "The Rise of Cotton Mills in the South," *Johns Hopkins University Studies in Historical and Political Science* 39 (1921): 27, 46; Charles and Mary Beard, *The Rise of American Civilization* (New York: Macmillan, 1930), 657–63. The Beards found many reasons that slavery and slave owners held back the antebellum South, from investment of outsiders, to slave owners, to labor. Furthermore, the Beards were not the only ones to point out that a tribesman's point of view may have affected southern life. See also Grady McWhinney, *Cracker Culture: Celtic Ways in the Old South* (Tuscaloosa: University of Alabama Press, 1988). McWhinney's work makes the same point based on southerners' Celtic background.

47. Emory Hawk, *Economic History of the South* (New York: Prentice-Hall, 1934), 278. Hawk's view would slowly be adapted over time by other historians to create a South with no real industry because it was being compared to a highly industrial North.

48. Eugene D. Genovese, *The Political Economy of Slavery* (New York: Vintage Books, 1967).

49. Genovese, *The Political Economy of Slavery*, 20.

50. For works that follow Genovese's example of slavery holding back development, see John Ashworth, *Slavery, Capitalism, and Politics in the Antebellum Republic: The Coming of the Civil War, 1850–1861* (Cambridge: Cambridge University Press, 2007); Robin Blackburn, *The Making of New World Slavery: From the Baroque to the Modern, 1492–1800* (London: Verso, 1997); Douglas Egerton, "Markets Without a Market Revolution: Southern Planters and Capitalism," *Journal of the Early Republic* 16 (Summer 1996): 207–21; and Raimondo Luraghi, *The Rise and Fall of the Plantation South* (New York: Franklin Watts, 1978). Bertram Wyatt-Brown also addresses this anti-industrial South in his work; see *Southern Honor: Ethics & Behavior in the Old South* (Oxford: Oxford University Press, 1982).

51. Douglass C. North, *The Economic Growth of the United States, 1790–1860* (New York: W.W. Norton, 1966), 67, 113.

52. North, *The Economic Growth of the United States*, 126.

53. Alfred Conrad and John Meyer, *The Economics of Slavery* (Chicago: Aldine Publishing, 1964); Robert William Fogel and Stanley L. Engerman, *Time on the Cross: The Economics of American Negro Slavery* (Boston: Little, Brown, 1974); Yasukichi Yasuba, "The Profitability and Viability of Plantation Slavery in the United States," in *Did Slavery Pay*, ed. Hugh G. J. Aitken (Boston: Houghton Mifflin, 1971). Cliometrics is the study of historical data using econometric methodology.

54. Alfred Conrad and John Meyer, "The Economics of Slavery in the Ante Bellum South," *Journal of Political Economy* 66 (April 1958): 119–20.

55. Robert William Fogel, *Without Consent or Contract: The Rise and Fall of American Slavery* (New York: Norton, 1989), 103.

56. Richard Wade, *Slavery in the Cities: The South 1820–1860* (Oxford: Oxford University Press, 1964), viii; Robert S. Starobin, *Industrial Slavery in the Old South* (Oxford: Oxford University Press, 1970), 231.

57. Claudia Dale Goldin, *Urban Slavery in the American South, 1820–1860: A Quantitative History* (Chicago: University of Chicago Press, 1976).

58. There have also been many recent studies focused on industry in other small areas of the antebellum South, such as Tom Downey, *Planting a Capitalist South: Masters, Merchants and Manufacturers in the Southern Interior, 1790–1860* (Baton Rouge: LSU Press, 2006); and Michael Gagnon, *Transition to an Industrial South: Athens, Georgia, 1830–1870* (Baton Rouge: LSU Press, 2012). John Hebron Moore, *The Emergence of the Cotton Kingdom in the Old Southwest* (Baton Rouge: LSU Press, 1988); J. Mills Thornton, *Politics and Power in a Slave Society: Alabama, 1800–1860* (Baton Rouge: LSU Press, 1978); Joseph

Reidy, *From Slavery to Agrarian Capitalism in the Cotton Plantation South: Central Georgia, 1800–1880* (Chapel Hill: University of North Carolina Press, 1992); Mary DeCredico, *Patriotism for Profit*. DeCredico's work may not seem to fit here, as she focuses more on Georgia during the Civil War, but it does give some attention to prewar industrial development in Georgia. W. David Lewis, "The Emergence of Birmingham as a Case Study of a Continuity between the Antebellum Planter Class and Industrialization in the 'New South,'" *Agricultural History* 68 (Spring 1994): 62–79. Also see, for information on Vicksburg, Christopher Morris, *Becoming Southern: The Evolution of a Way of Life: Warren County and Vicksburg, Mississippi, 1770–1860* (Oxford: Oxford University Press, 1995). For San Antonio, an example from Texas, see Raymond Boryczka, "The Busiest Man in Town: John Herman Kampmann and the Urbanization of San Antonio, Texas, 1848–1885," *Southwestern Historical Quarterly* 115 (April 2012): 329–63; William Thomas, *The Iron Way: Railroads, the Civil War, and the Making of Modern America* (New Haven, CT: Yale University Press, 2011).

59. John McCardell, *The Idea of a Southern Nation: Southern Nationalists and Southern Nationalism, 1830–1860* (New York: W.W. Norton, 1979); James McPherson, *Ordeal by Fire: The Civil War and Reconstruction* (New York: McGraw-Hill, 1992), 31.

60. McPherson, *Ordeal by Fire*, 30–31; Egnal, *Clash of Extremes*, 283.

61. Gavin Wright, *Old South, New South: Revolutions in the Southern Economy Since the Civil War* (Baton Rouge: LSU Press, 1996), 24–25.

62. Fred Bateman and Thomas Joseph Weiss, *A Deplorable Scarcity: The Failure of Industrialization in the Slave Economy* (Chapel Hill: University of North Carolina Press, 1981).

63. See Fred Bateman and Thomas Weiss, "Comparative Regional Development in Antebellum Manufacturing," *Journal of Economic History* 35 (March 1975); and Fred Bateman, Thomas Weiss, and James Foust, "The Participation of Planters in Manufacturing in the Antebellum South," *Agricultural History* 48 (April 1974): 277.

64. Bateman and Weiss, *A Deplorable Scarcity*, 5.

65. Bateman and Weiss, *A Deplorable Scarcity*, 4, 5, 10, 13.

66. Bateman and Weiss, *A Deplorable Scarcity*, 23.

67. Bateman and Weiss, *A Deplorable Scarcity*, 98; Bateman and Weiss, "Comparative Regional Development," 184–85; quote from Fred Bateman, Thomas Weiss, and James Foust, "The Participation of Planters in Manufacturing," 277.

68. Bateman and Weiss, *A Deplorable Scarcity*, chapter 2.

69. Bateman and Weiss, *A Deplorable Scarcity*, 51–58.

70. Bateman and Weiss, *A Deplorable Scarcity*, 69.

71. Bateman and Weiss, "Comparative Regional Development," 200.

72. Bateman and Weiss, "Comparative Regional Development," 201.

73. Bateman and Weiss, *A Deplorable Scarcity*, 148–50; Bateman and Weiss, "Comparative Regional Development," 156. See also Bonnie Martin, "Slavery's Invisible Engine: Mortgaging Human Property," *Journal of Southern History* 76 (November 2010): 817–66.

Martin's work shows that slaves themselves were used as security for loans to keep capital flowing in the South.

74. Bateman and Weiss, *A Deplorable Scarcity,* 70.

75. Bateman and Weiss, *A Deplorable Scarcity,* 121, 77. Slaves were capital that moved with their owners so they could be used to support local development while allowing employment for idle hands during off-planting seasons, something James De Bow pointed out in the 1850s. The interaction of labor has received much attention in recent years; see Jacqueline Jones, "Labor and the Idea of Race in the American South," *Journal of Southern History* 75 (August 2009): 613–26; and John J. Zaborney, *Slave for Hire: Renting Enslaved Laborers in Antebellum Virginia* (Baton Rouge: LSU Press, 2012).

76. Walter Johnson, "The Pedestal and the Veil: Rethinking the Capitalism/Slavery Question," *Journal of the Early Republic* 24 (Summer 2004): 300.

77. Bateman and Weiss, *A Deplorable Scarcity,* 77; Theodore Kornweibel, "Railroads and Slavery," *Railroad History* 189 (Fall–Winter 2003): 34.

78. Charles Dew, *Ironmaker to the Confederacy: Joseph R. Anderson and the Tredegar Iron Works* (New Haven, CT: Yale University Press, 1966), 3.

79. Bateman and Weiss, *A Deplorable Scarcity,* 31.

80. Bateman and Weiss, *A Deplorable Scarcity,* 31. Furthermore, slaves could be mortgaged to gain liquid assets. See Bonnie Martin, "Slavery's Invisible Engine."

81. Stanley Engerman, "Chicken Little, Anna Karenina, and the Economics of Slavery: Two Reflections on Historical Analysis, with Examples Drawn Mostly from the Study of Slavery," *Social Science History* 17 (Summer 1993): 161–71; John Bezis-Selfa, "A Tale of Two Ironworks: Slavery, Free Labor, Work, and Resistance in the Early Republic," *William and Mary Quarterly* 56 (October 1999): 677–700.

82. Bateman and Weiss, *A Deplorable Scarcity,* 158–60.

83. Bateman and Weiss, *A Deplorable Scarcity,* 162; Bateman, Foust, and Weiss, "Participation of Planters," 291–92; Bateman and Weiss, "Manufacturing in the Antebellum South," 38–39. Using the same data set, Bateman and Weiss would reprint their conclusions in many forms, thus reaching a wide audience and implanting this theory deeply in the historiography of the subject.

84. Bateman and Weiss, "Manufacturing in the Antebellum South," 39. Bateman and Weiss make a direct connection between their views and Eugene Genovese's work on planters being precapitalist and not modern, and again these views have become very accepted over time as they fit so neatly with the popular view of the antebellum South.

85. Bateman and Weiss, "Manufacturing in the Antebellum South," 2.

86. Bateman and Weiss, *A Deplorable Scarcity,* 165.

87. Bateman and Weiss, *A Deplorable Scarcity,* 93, 166. Household production could add as much as 10 percent to southern manufacturing production, while plantation production, such as cotton ginning, rice cleaning, and sugar refining, added $216.1 million and 100,000 workers to southern industry. But Bateman and Weiss believe that "these activities are not part of a true 'industrial sector' in the commercial and developmental

sense." Bateman and Weiss, "Manufacturing in the Antebellum South," 40.

88. Bateman and Weiss, *A Deplorable Scarcity*, 13, 23–26, 167–70. For example, Bateman and Weiss found that the published census summary listed 102 firms for a certain county, while the manuscript schedules enumerated 104 firms. Also, Bateman and Weiss did not think that the missing records from Louisiana and Georgia affect in any way their conclusions on Southern industry, even though these states were two of the most industrialized in the region; *A Deplorable Scarcity*, 25.

89. Bateman and Weiss, *A Deplorable Scarcity*, 171.

90. Bateman and Weiss, *A Deplorable Scarcity*, 146.

91. Herbert Gutman, *Slavery and the Numbers Game* (Urbana: University of Illinois Press, 1975), 60, 70. Gutman shows the problems with using sampling. His attacks, though, focus on Fogel and Engerman's *Time on the Cross*, going into great detail about the book's sample deficiencies, which could have been avoided, such as a sample being too small to be representative, problems that *A Deplorable Scarcity* also possesses.

92. Richard Vedder and Lowell Gallaway, "Profitability of Antebellum Manufacturing: Some New Estimates," *Business History Review* 54 (Spring 1980): 95–96, 103.

93. L. Diane Barnes, "Industry and Its Laborers, Free and Slave in Late-Antebellum Virginia," in Diane Barnes, Brian Schoen, and Frank Towers, eds., *The Old South's Modern Worlds: Slavery, Region, and Nation in the Age of Progress* (Oxford: Oxford University Press, 2011), 190.

94. Stanley Engerman, "A Reconsideration of Southern Economic Growth, 1770–1860," *Agricultural History* 49 (April 1975): 350.

95. Bateman and Weiss, *A Deplorable Scarcity*, 59.

96. R. Ogilvie Buchanan, *The Pastoral Industries of New Zealand* (London: George Philip & Son, Ltd., 1935), 70.

97. Harold Williamson, ed., *The Growth of the American Economy: An Introduction to the Economic History of the United States* (New York: Prentice-Hall, 1944), 2.

98. Bateman and Weiss, *A Deplorable Scarcity*, 23.

99. Richard Brown, *Modernization: The Transformation of American Life, 1600–1865* (New York: Hill and Wang, 1976), 4.

100. John Majewskei, *Modernizing a Slave Economy: The Economic Vision of the Confederate Nation* (Chapel Hill: University of North Carolina Press, 2009), 16–17.

101. Lewis, *Coal, Iron, and Slaves*; Steven G. Collins, "System in the South: John W. Mallet, Josiah Gorgas, and Uniform Production at the Confederate Ordnance Department," *Technology and Culture* 40 (July 1999): 517–44; Steven G. Collins, "System, Organization, and Agricultural Reform in the Antebellum South, 1840–1860," *Agricultural History* 75 (Winter 2001): 1–27. Collins's work especially shows that there were many in the South who had the same views on modernization that northerners had, and that they readily accepted new technologies and ideas that would help them to run their businesses and plantations as efficiently as possible. Jonathan Wells, "The Southern Middle Class," *Journal of Southern History* 75 (August 2009): 651–62. Wells presents a dynamic middle

class forming before the war that was a driving force after the conflict ended. Anthony Kaye, in his work, shows a "second slavery" that was modern and capitalistic well before the war. See Kaye, "The Second Slavery," 633.

102. Johnson, *Men and the Vision of the Southern Commercial Conventions*, 120. Gregg "borrowed" this line from Henry C. Carey, as it was the title of a journal that Carey published in the 1840s.

## CHAPTER TWO

1. Congressional Globe, 36th Congress, 2nd Session (15 January 1861), 391.

2. Texas, vol. 2, p. 32, R. G. Dun & Co. Credit Report Volumes.

3. Reagan did realize the importance of Texas to the Confederate war effort. He spends time explaining how he pushed for the relief of Vicksburg in cabinet meetings so that men and supplies from the western half of the Confederacy could still reach the places where they were needed. John Reagan, *Memoirs: With Special Reference to Secession and the Civil War* (New York: Neale Publishing, 1906), 151–54.

4. James De Bow, *Industrial Resources, Statistics, &c. of the United States and More Particularly of the Southern and Western States* (New York: Appleton, 1852), 1:114.

5. William Gregg, *Essays on Domestic Industry: An Inquiry into the Expediency of Establishing Cotton Manufacturers in South Carolina* (Charleston: Burges & James, 1845; reprint, Graniteville, SC: Graniteville Co., 1941), 34 (page citations are to the reprint edition).

6. Peter Stearns, *The Industrial Revolution in World History* (Boulder, CO: Westview Press, 1993), 2.

7. Brian Schoen, *The Fragile Fabric of Union: Cotton, Federal Politics, and the Global Origins of the Civil War* (Baltimore: Johns Hopkins University Press, 2009), 207.

8. Southern newspapers constantly ran advertisements at this time for the latest technological improvements that budding industrialists could use. Most of these machines were northern-made and were being sold by merchants in New Orleans to southern firm owners. But it is interesting to note that there are also many advertisements for southern-made copies of these machines.

9. J. M. Edmunds, *Manufacturers of the United States in 1860: Compiled from the Original Returns of the Eighth Census, under the Direction of the Secretary of the Interior* (Washington, DC: Government Printing Office, 1865), vii.

10. Broadus Mitchell, "The Rise of Cotton Mills in the South," *Johns Hopkins University Studies in Historical and Political Science* 39 (1921): 11.

11. Census Office, *Eighth Census, United States—1860: Instructions to U.S. Marshals* (Washington: Geo. W. Bowman, Public Printer, 1860), 10. There are many problems with the census itself. For example, Bateman and Weiss estimated that adding household production to the total of output in the South could have added 10 percent to southern manufacturing in 1860. See Fred Bateman and Thomas Joseph Weiss, *A Deplorable Scarcity: The Failure of Industrialization in the Slave Economy* (Chapel Hill: University of North

Carolina Press, 1981), 93–94. Vera Lea Dugas found a great deal of manufacturing taking place outside of factories in Texas on the eve of the war, and the money that was kept in Texas by this manufacturing would help to fund further industrial enterprises. See "Texas Industry, 1860–1880," *Southwestern Historical Quarterly* 59 (October 1955): 153. Stanley Engerman has also pointed out that items made in quantity on southern plantations such as flour, soap, liquor, clothing, and shoes should have been added to the manufacturing totals of the South. Moreover, as Engerman noted, cotton ginning should have been counted as manufacturing. See "A Reconsideration of Southern Economic Growth, 1770–1860," 357–58.

12. Census Office, *Eighth Census, United States—1860: Instructions to U.S. Marshals* (Washington, DC: Geo. W. Bowman, Public Printer, 1860), 24.

13. For a detailed discussion of these sources, see Appendix A—Sources.

14. Census Office, *Eighth Census, United States—1860*, 25.

15. Edmunds, *Manufacturers of the United States in 1860*, 2.

16. James D. Norris, *R. G. Dun & Co. 1841–1900: The Development of Credit-Reporting in the Nineteenth Century* (Westport, CT: Greenwood Press, 1978), 44–45.

17. See *Daily Confederation*, February 1, 1860.

18. See the *Natchez Daily Courier*, July 1860, for one example of a practice that became widespread throughout the Gulf South over the rest of the year.

19. Richard Griffin, "Cotton Manufacture in Alabama to 1865," 296. Griffin explains that the *Tuscaloosa Monitor* reported the extent of cotton manufacturing in the local area and the eighteen factories producing products. Of course, not all newspapers printed articles that supported industry in the South. For example, the *Daily Confederation*, of Montgomery, Alabama, printed an article that asserted that manufacturers continually asked for handouts from the government while good "agricultural, producing people" did not want the government to do anything but leave them alone. *Daily Confederation*, June 10, 1859. The *Texas State Gazette* of Austin made much the same point as it talked of the inequality of the tariffs that supported northern business at the expense of southern farmers. *Texas State Gazette*, June 20, 1857.

20. *South Western Baptist*, February 23, 1860. This advertisement appeared in newspapers throughout northern and eastern Alabama.

21. *Weekly Houston Telegraph*, July 6, 1959; *The Vicksburg Whig*, May 19, 1860.

22. *The Vicksburg Whig*, April 28, 1860.

23. *Vicksburg Whig*, August 14, 1857, Reading-Pierson Vertical File, McCardell Library, Old Courthouse Museum, Vicksburg, MS.

24. It was not just newspapers that businesses used to promote their companies. Copper, tin, and sheet iron manufacturer R. A. Smith of Jackson, Mississippi, printed its advertisements on envelopes used by many Confederate soldiers to send letters home during the war. See Humphrey's Collection, Folder 1, Mississippi Department of Archives and History.

25. Chapman and Battle, H. P. Chapman and J. F. Battle, *Picturesque Vicksburg: A*

*Description of the Resources and Prospects of that City and the Famous Yazoo Delta, Its Agriculture and Commercial Interests, To Which is Attached a Series of Sketches of Representative Industries: Profoundly Illustrated* (Vicksburg, MS: Vicksburg Printing and Publishing, 1895), 124, 166.

26. Mississippi, vol. 21, p. 91F, R. G. Dun & Co. Credit Report Volumes.

27. Mississippi, vol. 21, p. 42B, R. G. Dun & Co. Credit Report Volumes.

28. Mississippi, vol. 2, pp. 20, 47, 66, R. G. Dun & Co. Credit Report Volumes.

29. Mississippi, vol. 2, p. 18, R. G. Dun & Co. Credit Report Volumes.

30. Texas, vol. 15b, pp. 25, 53, R. G. Dun & Co. Credit Report Volumes.

31. Texas, vol. 15b, pp. 25, 53, R. G. Dun & Co. Credit Report Volumes.

32. Alabama, vol. 2, p. 12, R. G. Dun & Co. Credit Report Volumes.

33. For 1860 value of production, see 1860 Manufacturing Census Schedules for Autauga County, Alabama. For the production values for 1857–1859, see *Southern Statesman*, April 28, 1860. For more information on Daniel Pratt and his Prattville factories, see Curtis Evans, *The Conquest of Labor: Daniel Pratt and Southern Industrialization* (Baton Rouge: LSU Press, 2001).

34. Randall M. Miller, "Daniel Pratt's Industrial Urbanism: The Cotton Mill Town in Ante-bellum Alabama," *Alabama Historical Quarterly* 34 (Spring 1972): 13.

35. William D. McCain, *The Story of Jackson: A History of the Capital of Mississippi, 1821–1851* (Jackson, MS: J. F. Hyer Publishing, 1953), 1:313.

36. Mississippi, vol. 9, p. 52, R. G. Dun & Co. Credit Report Volumes.

37. Mississippi, vol. 9, p. 1, R. G. Dun & Co. Credit Report Volumes.

38. Mississippi, vol. 9, p. 85, R. G. Dun & Co. Credit Report Volumes.

39. Alabama, vol. 8, p. 7, R. G. Dun & Co. Credit Report Volumes.

40. Texas, vol. 16, p. 185, R. G. Dun & Co. Credit Report Volumes.

41. Alabama, vol. 8, p. 7, R. G. Dun & Co. Credit Report Volumes.

42. Alabama, vol. 10, pp. 132 and 87, R. G. Dun & Co. Credit Report Volumes.

43. Alabama, vol. 2, p. 6, R. G. Dun & Co. Credit Report Volumes.

44. Alabama, vol. 10, p. 116, R. G. Dun & Co. Credit Report Volumes.

45. McCain, *Story of Jackson*, 1:83.

46. Mississippi State Penitentiary Account Sheets, RG 29, Mississippi Department of Archives and History, 1860. The records of the Penitentiary show how much each shop in the facility brought in for various months in 1860. For example, the cotton factory put out $2,244.36 in June 1860, $1,693.32 in July 1860, and $846.64 in November 1860. There are also returns for the wood shop, shoe shop, and smith shop that show that each unit was an important part of the prison factory.

47. *Southern Messenger*, March 21, 1860. Other products listed were: wheat fans, well buckets, cabinet ware, and five- and ten-gallon kegs. The factory was leased by Burrows, Holt, and Company.

48. W. & D. Richardson, *The Texas Almanac for 1860, with Statistics, Historical and Biographical Sketches, &c. Relating to Texas* (Galveston: *Galveston News*, 1860), 201–2.

49. Abigail Holbrook, "A Glimpse of Life on Antebellum Slave Plantations in Texas," *Southwestern Historical Quarterly* 76 (April 1973): 371–72.

50. Louisiana also had a state prison factory where slaves were incarcerated along with white prisoners. The prisoners made clothing that was sold on the open market and, in a speech before the state legislature in March 1857, Senator Buffington predicted that "the day is not far distant, when we will see every inhabitant of the South clothed in fabrics made by our own slave labor." *Official Reports of the Senate of Louisiana*, 3rd Legislature, 2nd Session, 1857, 36–39.

51. Texas, vol. 3, p. 120B, R. G. Dun & Co. Credit Report Volumes.

52. Mississippi, vol. 2, p. 59, R. G. Dun & Co. Credit Report Volumes.

53. Alabama, vol. 2, p. 9, R. G. Dun & Co. Credit Report Volumes.

54. Mississippi, vol. 9, p. 78, R. G. Dun & Co. Credit Report Volumes.

55. 1860 Population Census Schedules, Claiborne County, Mississippi.

56. 1860 Population Census Schedules, Claiborne County, Mississippi.

57. Alabama, vol. 10, p. 106, R. G. Dun & Co. Credit Report Volumes.

58. Fred Bateman and Thomas Weiss, "Manufacturing in the Antebellum South," *Research in Economic History* 1 (October 1976): 14. Bateman and Weiss elaborate on this point in *A Deplorable Scarcity*, 157–63.

59. *Trinity Advocate*, Palestine, Texas, June 8, 1859.

60. The idea that planters were the people in the antebellum South with the most capital to invest was covered in detail by William Scarborough. See his book *Masters of the Big House: Elite Slaveholders of the Mid-Nineteenth Century South* (Baton Rouge: LSU Press, 2003),218.

61. Value in today's currency determined using www.measuringworth.com.

62. Alabama, vol. 17, p. 100, R. G. Dun & Co. Credit Report Volumes.

63. Mississippi, vol. 4, p. 30H, R. G. Dun & Co. Credit Report Volumes. Harris was missed by both the manufacturing and population census.

64. Frederick Law Olmsted, *The Cotton Kingdom: A Traveller's Observations of Cotton and Slavery in the American Slave States* (New York: Mason Brothers, 1861), 117–21.

65. Bateman and Weiss, *A Deplorable Scarcity*, 113, 160.

66. Alabama, vol. 11, p. 66, R. G. Dun & Co. Credit Report Volumes.

67. For more information on industrial firms that used slave labor, see William Gregg, *Essays on Domestic Industry*; Curtis Evans, *The Conquest of Labor*; and Charles Dew, *Ironmaker to the Confederacy: Joseph R. Anderson and the Tredegar Iron Works* (New Haven, CT: Yale University Press, 1966).

## CHAPTER THREE

1. *Daily Confederation*, February 26, 1859.

2. Charles Dew, *Ironmaker to the Confederacy: Joseph R. Anderson and the Tredegar Iron Works* (New Haven, CT: Yale University Press, 1966), 3.

3. Robert Royal Russel, *Economic Aspects of Southern Sectionalism, 1840–1861* (Urbana: University of Illinois Press, 1924), 235. J. Mills Thornton said much the same thing in his work, *Politics and Power in a Slave Society: Alabama, 1800–1860* (Baton Rouge: LSU Press, 1978).

4. Harold D. Woodman, "The Profitability of Slavery: A Historical Perennial," *Journal of Southern History* 29 (August 1963). Historians today still make these claims. While individual examples of industrial success existed, such as Daniel Pratt's gin factories in Alabama and William Gregg's textile works in South Carolina, most believe that the South still had to import most of its industrial needs.

5. H. P. Chapman and J. F. Battle, *Picturesque Vicksburg: A Description of the Resources and Prospects of that City and the Famous Yazoo Delta, Its Agriculture and Commercial Interests, To Which is Attached a Series of Sketches of Representative Industries: Profoundly Illustrated* (Vicksburg, MS: Vicksburg Printing and Publishing, 1895), 2. Chapman and Battle go on to say that all the area needed was the capital to drive development. Capital may have been a problem in the postwar South, but before the war there was enough capital available for manufacturing, as chapter 5 will show.

6. Chapman and Battle, *Picturesque Vicksburg*, 15, 310.

7. Douglass C. North, *The Economic Growth of the United States 1790–1860* (New York: W.W. Norton, 1966), 122–23.

8. Henry Hughes, *Treatise on Sociology, Theoretical and Practical* (Philadelphia: Lippincott, Grambo, 1854), 170.

9. *Jacksonville Republican*, Jan. 12, 1860.

10. James Oakes, *Slavery and Freedom: An Interpretation of the Old South* (New York: Alfred A. Knopf, 1990).

11. Raimondo Luraghi, *The Rise and Fall of the Plantation South* (New York: Franklin Watts, 1978), 57.

12. State Gazette (Austin, TX), June 30, 1860.

13. Russel, *Economic Aspects of Southern Sectionalism*, 207.

14. This is the old Charles Beard argument of almost a century ago, an argument that will not go away; for example, Marc Egnal, in his work *Clash of Extremes*, makes this same argument yet again. See Egnal, *Clash of Extremes: The Economic Origins of the Civil War* (New York: Hill and Wang, 2009), 10.

15. Thornton, *Politics and Power in a Slave Society*, 31. Also see Robert William Fogel and Stanley L. Engerman, *Time on the Cross: The Economics of American Negro Slavery* (Boston: Little, Brown, 1974) 198–99.

16. Charles S. Davis, *The Cotton Kingdom in Alabama* (Montgomery: Alabama State Department of Archives and History, 1939), 45; Donald A. Reynolds, *Texas Terror: The Slave Insurrection Panic of 1860 and the Secession of the Lower South* (Baton Rouge: LSU Press, 2007), 24–26. In 1860 the region underwent pronounced drought that caused crop failures and economic problems for many plantations.

17. J. D. B. De Bow, *The Industrial Resources, Statistics, &c. of the United States and More Particularly of the Southern and Western States* (New York: Appleton, 1852), 1:45.

18. As Davis Smiley explains, "the climate and its alleged offspring, the plantation, the planter, the staple crop, and the Negro, all set in a rural scene surrounded by primitive folkways, have provided students with the ingredients for a central theme." Davis Smiley, "The Quest for the Central Theme in Southern History," *South Atlantic Quarterly* 71 (Summer 1972): 318. Randolph Campbell, in his work *Empire for Slavery*, also comments on this natural advantage of climate, as do many other historians who only look at the visible surface of the southern landscape. Randolph Campbell, *An Empire for Slavery: The Peculiar Institution in Texas, 1821–1865* (Baton Rouge: LSU Press, 1989), 78–81.

19. Michael Williams, "Industrial Impacts on the Forests of the United States, 1860–1920," *Journal of Forest History* 31 (July 1987): 110.

20. Williams, "Industrial Impacts on the Forests of the United States," 51.

21. Emory Hawk, *Economic History of the South* (New York: Prentice-Hall, 1934), 20–21; R. V. Reynolds, *Fuel Wood Used in the United States, 1630–1930* (Washington, DC: United States Department of Agriculture, 1942), 9. In the decade leading up to the Civil War, the eastern Gulf states used 88,100 billion boardfeet of wood for fuel, while the Lower Mississippi Valley states used 82,490 billion boardfeet.

22. Sam H. Schurr and Bruce C. Netschert, *Energy in the American Economy, 1850–1975* (Baltimore: Johns Hopkins Press, 1960), 52.

23. Schurr and Netschert, *Energy in the American Economy*, 46–47.

24. Alfred Chandler, "Anthracite Coal and the Beginnings of the Industrial Revolution in the United States," *Business History Review* 46 (Summer 1972): 179–80; Hawk, *Economic History of the South*, 18.

25. Harold Williamson, ed., *The Growth of the American Economy: An Introduction to the Economic History of the United States* (New York: Prentice-Hall, 1944), 7.

26. De Bow, *Industrial Resources*, 1:61.

27. Ethal Armes, *The Story of Coal and Iron in Alabama* (Birmingham: Birmingham Chamber of Commerce, 1910), 68–69. The first president of the ACMC was John Storrs and was based out of Montevallo. James Day, "Dealing in Black Diamonds: Joseph Squire and Alabama's Early Coal-Mining Operations," *Alabama Review* 64 (2011): 6.

28. Armes, *The Story of Coal and Iron*, 149.

29. Joyce Jackson, "History of the Shelby Iron Company, 1861–1868" (thesis, University of Alabama, 1948), 1–2.

30. De Bow, *Industrial Resources*, 1:60–61; Day, "Dealing in Black Diamonds," 4. This vein ran through St. Clair, Jefferson, Shelby, and Bibb counties. William Phineas Browne and Philip J. Weaver owned companies that mined in this field, known as the Cahaba Field, and supplied coal to Selma, Montgomery, Marion, Uniontown, and Mobile. Browne also owned a rolling mill in Bibb County named "Bright-Hope." See Day, "Dealing in Black Diamonds," 7.

31. Sean Patrick Adams, "The US Coal Industry in the Nineteenth Century," accessed September 17, 2013, http://eh.net/encyclopedia/article/adams.industry.coal.us.

32. Hawk, *Economic History of the South*, 15–16.

33. Weymouth T. Jordan, *Ante-Bellum Alabama: Town and Country* (Tuscaloosa: University of Alabama Press, 1987), 145.

34. Jackson, "History of the Shelby Iron Company," 3–4.

35. Armes, *The Story of Coal and Iron*, 27–29.

36. Armes, *The Story of Coal and Iron*, 83.

37. J. P. Lesley, *The Iron Manufacturer's Guide to the Furnaces, Forges, and Rolling Mills of the United States* (New York: John Wiley Publishers, 1859), 595. Alabama coal and iron production was centered on a group of counties, made up of: Franklin, Blount, Jefferson, Walker, Tuscaloosa, Bibb, Shelby, Talladega, Calhoun, Cherokee, Lauderdale, and Lamar. See Armes, *The Story of Coal and Iron*, 40. Alabama had four main mineral regions: the Highland Rim, full of brown ore; the Cumberland Plateau, with Red Mountain ore and two great coal fields, the Black Warrior Field and the Lookout Mountain Field; the Appalachian Valley, containing two more coal fields, the Coosa and the Cahaba, along with large amounts of brown ore; and finally the Ashland Plateau, which was a mix of many different types of iron ore and other minerals. See Armes, *The Story of Coal and Iron*, xxix. Cherokee County also was the only place in the state to mine dyestone fossil ores. See Lesley, *Iron Manufacturer's Guide*, 631.

38. Armes, *The Story of Coal and Iron*, 78–79.

39. Lesley, *Iron Manufacturer's Guide*, 759.

40. Alabama, vol. 20, p. 73, R. G. Dun & Co. Credit Report Volumes, Baker Library Historical Collections, Harvard Business School.

41. Olmsted, *The Cotton Kingdom* (New York: Mason Brothers, 1861), 114–15.

42. Alabama, vol. 17, p. 145, R. G. Dun & Co. Credit Report Volumes, Baker Library Historical Collections, Harvard Business School.

43. De Bow, *Industrial Resources*, 1:57.

44. De Bow, *Industrial Resources*, 1:59–60.

45. Harriett E. Amos Doss, "Cotton City, 1813–1860, in Michael V. R. Thomason, *Mobile: The New History of Alabama's First City* (Tuscaloosa: University of Alabama Press, 2001), 88.

46. Alabama, vol. 17, p. 92, R. G. Dun & Co. Credit Report Volumes.

47. William Scarborough, *Masters of the Big House: Elite Slaveholders of the Mid-Nineteenth Century South* (Baton Rouge: LSU Press, 2003), 226. For Alabama, the total of all coal and iron mined and processed is not completely known, because a great deal of this production was never recorded in a systematic way. This was a problem in all industrial processes of the antebellum South, not just coal and iron production. See Armes, *The Story of Coal and Iron in Alabama*, 121. Further, J. P. Lesley, in his enumeration of iron manufacturers, listed no furnaces in Alabama that made use of local deposits of coal.

48. John Hebron Moore, *The Emergence of the Cotton Kingdom in the Old Southwest* (Baton Rouge: LSU Press, 1988), 205.

49. Mississippi, vol. 20, pp. 296, 236a, R. G. Dun & Co. Credit Report Volumes; Mississippi, vol. 2, p. 223, R. G. Dun & Co. Credit Report Volumes.

50. *Jackson Daily News,* March 14, 1860.

51. DeBow, *Industrial Resources*, 1:325.

52. *Alamo Express*, October 1, 1860.

53. Randolph Campbell, *Gone to Texas: A History of the Lone Star State* (Oxford: Oxford University Press, 2003), 212.

54. Texas, vol. 15b, p. 25, R. G. Dun & Co. Credit Report Volumes; Texas, vol. 4, p. 133, R. G. Dun & Co. Credit Report Volumes; Texas, vol. 2, p. 18, R. G. Dun & Co. Credit Report Volumes.

55. Texas, vol. 2, p. 36, R. G. Dun & Co. Credit Report Volumes.

56. De Bow, *Industrial Resources*, 1:338–40.

57. De Bow, *Industrial Resources*, 1:233.

58. De Bow, *Industrial Resources*, 1:233.

59. Jackson, "History of the Shelby Iron Company," 12.

60. Mississippi Planter, "Production and Manufacture of Cotton," *De Bow's Review* 7 (February 1850): 101.

61. *Trinity Advocate,* September 23, 1857.

62. John P. Campbell, *Southern Business Directory and General Commercial Advertiser* (Charleston: Press of Walker and James, 1854), 7.

63. This statement is based on the actual distribution of the raw material costs in each industry for firms reported in the census. See Appendix B—Methods, for a more detailed explanation.

64. Jordan, *Ante-Bellum Alabama,* 158–59. Pratt was also a Know Nothing for a time, and he supported John Bell, the Constitutional Unionist, in the 1860 presidential election.

65. Jordan, *Ante-Bellum Alabama,* 158. It is important to note, though, that Henry Walker Collier, the one-time chief justice and governor of Alabama, supported Alabama's industrial development and helped get laws passed to support manufacturing. See Richard W. Griffin, "Cotton Manufacture in Alabama to 1865," *Alabama Historical Quarterly* 18 (Fall 1956): 299.

66. Randall M. Miller, "Daniel Pratt's Industrial Urbanism: The Cotton Mill Town in Ante-bellum Alabama," *Alabama Historical Quarterly* 34 (Spring 1972): 13. . Some politicians and editors in the South attacked Pratt for these ideas. They claimed he was pushing for artificial support of industry. This was something, they argued, that northerners did, and should not be copied by the South. Pratt was also northern-born, and some in the South held that against him and used it to attack industrial development in the region. Curtis Evans made the same point in his work, especially when discussing Pratt's political activism. See Curtis Evans, *The Conquest of Labor: Daniel Pratt and Southern Industrialization* (Baton Rouge: LSU Press, 2001), 194–96.

67. Miller, "Daniel Pratt's Industrial Urbanism," 33.

68. *State Gazette,* January 30, 1860.

69. Chapman and Battle, *Picturesque Vicksburg,* 42.

70. Mississippi Planter, "Production and Manufacture of Cotton," *De Bow's Review* (February 1850): 100.

## CHAPTER FOUR

1. Ronald L. Lewis, *Coal, Iron, and Slaves: Industrial Slavery in Maryland and Virginia, 1715–1865* (Westport, CT: Greenwood Press, 1979), 49. For a brief but insightful discussion of the role of the South's transportation system in the region's development, as well as that of its rapidly emerging telegraph network, see Laird Bergad, "American Slave Markets during the 1850s," in Davis Eltis, Frank D. Lewis, and Kenneth L. Sokoloff, eds., *Slavery in the Development of the Americas* (Cambridge: Cambridge University Press, 2004), 228. Scott Marler, in his work *Merchants' Capital: New Orleans and the Political Economy of the Nineteenth-Century South,* argues the same thing. Merchants did not divert their capital to railroads as they were not sure that they would get the return on their investments. See Scott Marler, *Merchants' Capital: New Orleans and the Political Economy of the Nineteenth-Century South* (New York: Cambridge University Press, 2013).

2. Richard Brown, *Modernization: The Transformation of American Life, 1600–1865* (New York: Hill and Wang, 1976), 3–4.

3. James De Bow, *Industrial Resources, Statistics, &c. of the United States and More Particularly of the Southern and Western States* (New York: Appleton, 1852), 1:80.

4. John Lauritz Larson, *Internal Improvements: National Public Works and the Promise of Popular Government in the Early United States* (Chapel Hill: University of North Carolina Press, 2001), 257.

5. William McCain and Charlotte Capers, *Memoirs of Henry Tillinghast Ireys* (Jackson: Mississippi Department of Archives and History, 1954), 54.

6. John C. Calhoun, *Annals of Congress,* 14th Congress, 2nd Session, 851–960. This was a speech in support of the Bonus Bill and building canals with government support. Some, like John Binder, argue that transportation caused the war as the West united with the East in opposition to the South. See John J. Binder, "The Transportation Revolution and Antebellum Sectional Disagreement," *Social Science History* 35 (Spring 2011).

7. Charles S. Davis, *The Cotton Kingdom in Alabama* (Montgomery: Alabama State Department of Archives and History, 1939), 1.

8. Davis, *Cotton Kingdom in Alabama,* 25. Geography not only influenced the economy of the state, but its politics as well, and that influence explains why the state's regions had different ideas on state support for industrial endeavors. Charles Summersell, *Mobile: History of a Seaport Town* (University: University of Alabama Press, 1949), 16.

9. Summersell, *Mobile: History of a Seaport Town,* 16. See also Davis, *Cotton Kingdom,* 1.

10. Alabama, vol. 17, p. 92, R. G. Dun & Co. Credit Report Volumes, Baker Library Historical Collections, Harvard Business School.

11. Alabama, vol. 17, p. 236, R. G. Dun & Co. Credit Report Volumes.

12. Richard W. Griffin, "Cotton Manufacture in Alabama to 1865," *Alabama Historical Quarterly* 18 (Fall 1956): 290.

13. William Martin, "Internal Improvements in Alabama," *Johns Hopkins University Studies in Historical and Political Science* 20 (April 1902): 33.

14. Alabama, Vol 11., pp. 76, 80, R. G. Dun & Co. Credit Report Volumes.

15. Sam Bowers Hilliard, *Atlas of Antebellum Southern Agriculture* (Baton Rouge: LSU Press, 1984), 7–8. In the state this fall line separates the Piedmont from the Coastal Plain, which was not just a major geographical border, but a political, social, and economic one as well, much like the divisions in Alabama.

16. Mississippi, vol. 2, pp. 15, 20, 66, R. G. Dun & Co. Credit Report Volumes.

17. A. Ray Stephens and William M. Holmes, *Historical Atlas of Texas* (Norman: University of Oklahoma Press, 1989), 4.

18. Randolph Campbell, *Gone to Texas: A History of the Lone Star State* (Oxford: Oxford University Press, 2003), 209.

19. Campbell, *Gone to Texas*, 211.

20. Walter Buenger, *Secession and the Union in Texas* (Austin: University of Texas Press, 1984), 10.

21. Stephens and Holmes, *Historical Atlas of Texas*, 90. Stephens lists many small industrial centers in Texas in 1860, including: Paris, Dallas, Mount Pleasant, Jefferson, Marshall, Tyler, Rusk, Waco, Austin, San Antonio, Hempstead, Houston, and the Huntsville Penitentiary.

22. Texas, vol. 15b, p. 84, R. G. Dun & Co. Credit Report Volumes.

23. Texas, vol. 15b, pp. 56, 25, R. G. Dun & Co. Credit Report Volumes.

24. Bradley Bond, *Political Culture in the Nineteenth-Century South: Mississippi 1830–1900* (Baton Rouge: Louisiana State University Press, 1995), 31–32.

25. Mississippi, vol. 21, pp. 61, 42b, 28, R. G. Dun & Co. Credit Report Volumes.

26. Mississippi, vol. 21, p. 32, R. G. Dun & Co. Credit Report Volumes.

27. Weymouth T. Jordan, *Ante-Bellum Alabama: Town and Country* (Tuscaloosa: University of Alabama Press, 1987), 58–59.

28. Alabama, vol. 20, p. 42, R. G. Dun & Co. Credit Report Volumes.

29. Campbell, *Gone to Texas*, 211. In reality, this description fits well for any road built before the war almost anywhere in the nation.

30. Campbell, *Gone to Texas*, 211.

31. Campbell, *Gone to Texas*, 190–96. Texas had some special problems, though, with this network. Cartmen ran ox-carts between San Antonio and Indianola to move goods, and most of these cartmen were Mexicans who had moved into the area before Texan Independence. Anglos began trying to compete with these Mexican cartmen, but they

could not meet the prices that the Mexicans set. This would lead, in 1857, to the "Cart War" between the Anglo and Mexican teamsters, with a great deal of violence on both sides, which was not stopped until San Antonio businessmen had to step in as transportation costs began to rise. A few companies came to dominate most of the transportation in the state, most notably the stagecoach line run by Sawyer & Risher. See Llerna Friend, "The Texan of 1860," *Southwestern History Quarterly* 62 (July 1958): 5.

32. Campbell, *Gone to Texas,* 190–96.

33. Texas, vol. 3, pp. 117, 101, R. G. Dun & Co. Credit Report Volumes.

34. Carter Goodrich, *Government Promotion of American Canals and Railroads, 1800–1890* (New York: Columbia University Press, 1960), 7–8.

35. Milton S. Heath, "North American Railroads: Public Railroad Construction and the Development of Private Enterprise in the South before 1861," *Journal of Economic History* 10 (1950): 44.

36. Larson, *Internal Improvements,* 226.

37. Larson, *Internal Improvements,* 238.

38. Larson, *Internal Improvements,* 233.

39. De Bow, *Industrial Resources,* 1:391.

40. Larson, *Internal Improvements,* 238.

41. Heath, "North American Railroads," 41–42. Alabama was able to pull together a total of $7,341,012, while Mississippi gathered $5,668,322, from federal, state, county, and municipal sources to fund their railroad building efforts.

42. The Public Debt of Alabama in 1851 was $10,385,938, Mississippi $7,271,707, and Texas $11,050,201. De Bow, *Industrial Resources,* 1:433.

43. Brian Schoen, "The Burdens and Opportunities of Interdependence: The Political Economics of the Planter Class," in *The Old South's Modern Worlds: Slavery, Region, and Nation in the Age of Progress* (Oxford: Oxford University Press, 2011), 77.

44. Albert Fishlow, *American Railroads and the Transformation of the Antebellum Economy* (Cambridge, MA: Harvard University Press, 1965), 9.

45. James A. Ward, "A New Look at Antebellum Southern Railroad Development," *Journal of Southern History* 39 (August 2009): 419–20. Also see James Huston, *The Panic of 1857 and the Coming of the Civil War* (Baton Rouge: LSU Press, 1987), 216–17.

46. Ward, "A New Look at Antebellum Southern Railroad Development", 411. George Rogers Taylor and Irene Neu make the same point that commercial interests in seaboard cities and towns pushed railroad development as a way to draw inland trade to them. See George Rogers Taylor and Irene Neu, *The American Railroad Network, 1861–1890* (Cambridge, MA: Harvard University Press, 1956), 41. Also see William Thomas, *The Iron Way: Railroads, the Civil War, and the Making of Modern America* (New Haven, CT: Yale University Press, 2011).

47. *A New Map of Mississippi with its Roads and Distances,* Mississippi Department of History and Archives, 1859. Many maps were printed during the period showing the distance between cities on steamboat routes and showing where railroads connected with them.

48. Ward, "A New Look," 411. Moreover, many of these lines did not run on the same gauge. So, while a network may look complete on a map, railroads would have to stop at a depot, unload all they were carrying, load it onto a different train on a different gauge track, then move on to the next line and repeat the process. Taylor and Neu, *The American Railroad Network*, 43–45.

49. James Huston, "The Pregnant Economies of the Border South, 1840–1860: Virginia, Kentucky, Tennessee, and the Possibilities of Slave-Labor Expansion," in *The Old South's Modern Worlds: Slavery, Region, and Nation in the Age of Progress*, ed. L. Diane Barnes, Brian Schoen, and Frank Towers (Oxford: Oxford University Press, 2011), 123.

50. U. B. Phillips, *Life and Labor in the Old South* (Boston: Little, Brown, 1929), 146.

51. This development is highlighted well in Barnes, Schoen, and Towers's *The Old South's Modern Worlds*, especially Frank Towers's contribution, which explains that southern consumption of products, because of slavery pushed the development of a few cities rather than numerous small towns, which then could be connected by rail and water links. See Frank Towers, "The Southern Path to Modern Cities: Urbanization of the Slave States," in Barnes, Schoen, and Towers, *The Old South's Modern Worlds: Slavery, Region, and Nation in the Age of Progress* (Oxford: Oxford University Press, 2011), 152–54.

52. Steven G. Collins, "Organizing the South: Railroads, Plantations, and War" (PhD diss., Louisiana State University, 1999), 40.

53. Aaron W. Marrs, *Railroads in the Old South: Pursuing Progress in a Slave Society* (Baltimore: Johns Hopkins University Press, 2009), 197.

54. For example, the amount of miles in the South Atlantic states tripled from 1851 to 1861, increasing from 1,650 miles to almost 5,400 miles. Robert C. Black, *The Railroads of the Confederacy* (Chapel Hill: University of North Carolina Press, 1998), 2.

55. Ward, "A New Look," 420. Southerners were also supporters of a transcontinental railroad. They realized its economic importance, as long as it connected to a major southern city, and leaders like John C. Calhoun publicly called for its construction. See Larson, *Internal Improvements*, 242.

56. Collins, "Organizing the South," 34.

57. Martin, "Internal Improvements in Alabama," 31. Also see Goodrich, *Government Promotion*, 156–58. Local and private funds were the most important sources of funding in Alabama.

58. Martin, "Internal Improvements in Alabama," 64.

59. J. Mills Thornton, *Politics and Power in a Slave Society: Alabama, 1800–1860* (Baton Rouge: LSU Press, 1978), 108–10.

60. Thornton, *Politics and Power in a Slave Society*, 68.

61. De Bow, *Industrial Resources*, 1:459.

62. Harriett E. Doss, "Cotton City," 87, in Michael V. R. Thomason, *Mobile: The New History of Alabama's First City* (Tuscaloosa: University of Alabama Press, 2001).

63. Alan Smith Thompson, "Mobile, Alabama, 1850–1861: Economic, Political, Physical, and Population Characteristics" (PhD diss., University of Alabama, 1979), 84–87.

64. Goodrich, *Government Promotion*, 170–71.

65. Henry S. Tanner, *Canals and Railroads of the United States* (New York: T. R. Tanner & J. Disturnell, 1840), 182.

66. Alabama, vol. 17, p. 165, R. G. Dun & Co. Credit Report Volumes.

67. De Bow, *Industrial Resources*, 1:446.

68. De Bow, *Industrial Resources*, 1:476.

69. Alabama, vol. 20, p. 97, R. G. Dun & Co. Credit Report Volumes.

70. Alabama, vol. 20, p. 140, R. G. Dun & Co. Credit Report Volumes.

71. Alabama, vol. 17, p. 119, R. G. Dun & Co. Credit Report Volumes.

72. Tanner, *Canals and Railroads of the United States*, 182. Extending the entire transportation network of the region was always the goal of railroad promoters as it was much easier to extend what was available rather than to replace it.

73. Tanner, *Canals and Railroads of the United States.*

74. Tanner, *Canals and Railroads of the United States.*

75. Tanner, *Canals and Railroads of the United States*; also see Jordan, *Ante-Bellum Alabama: Town and Country*, 36. The railroad ran for 35 miles.

76. Tanner, *Canals and Railroads of the United States*, 182.

77. Clanton Williams, *The Early History of Montgomery and Incidentally of the State of Alabama* (University, AL: Confederate Publishing Company, 1979), 99.

78. Tanner, *Canals and Railroads of the United States*, 180–82.

79. Tanner, *Canals and Railroads of the United States.*

80. Thornton, *Politics and Power in a Slave Society*, 280.

81. Armes, *The Story of Coal and Iron in Alabama*, 104. The two halves of the state would not be completely brought together until the Alabama Central Railroad was finally completed after the end of the Civil War, as a gap in the line existed until then.

82. Bond, *Political Culture in the Nineteenth-Century South*, 110.

83. Goodrich, *Government Promotion*, 159.

84. For example, the Memphis and St. Louis Packet Company, which would later become the Anchor Line, ran to Vicksburg by the start of the war. See H. P. Chapman, H. P. and J. F. Battle, *Picturesque Vicksburg: A Description of the Resources and Prospects of that City and the Famous Yazoo Delta, Its Agriculture and Commercial Interests, To Which is Attached a Series of Sketches of Representative Industries: Profoundly Illustrated* (Vicksburg, MS: Vicksburg Printing and Publishing, 1895), 77.

85. Goodrich, *Government Promotion*, 160.

86. *Jackson Daily News*, March 26, 1860.

87. Mississippi, vol. 21, p. 91c, R. G. Dun & Co. Credit Report Volumes.

88. De Bow, *Industrial Resources*, 1:459. The reason that De Bow mentions this conference so often in his work was that he was a major industrial and railroad booster for the South and was an important figure in the Commercial Convention movement.

89. De Bow, *Industrial Resources*, 1:476.

90. De Bow, *Industrial Resources*, 1:44.

91. De Bow, *Industrial Resources*, 1:44.

92. Tanner, *Canals and Railroads of the United States*, 184.

93. Tanner, *Canals and Railroads of the United States*, 189.

94. Tanner, *Canals and Railroads of the United States*, 184. This was a 54-mile-long road.

95. Tanner, *Canals and Railroads of the United States*, 184.

96. Tanner, *Canals and Railroads of the United States*, 184.

97. Buenger, *Secession and the Union in Texas*, 17.

98. US Census Compilation for 1860, Schedule E, 230.

99. Stephens and Holmes, *Historical Atlas of Texas*, 51.

100. De Bow, *Industrial Resources*, 1:477.

101. Buenger, *Secession and the Union in Texas*, 11.

102. Campbell, *Gone to Texas*, 212.

103. De Bow, *Industrial Resources*, 1:459.

104. Friend, "The Texan of 1860," 5.

105. Goodrich, *Government Promotion*, 161–62.

106. Texas, vol. 15b, p. 56, R. G. Dun & Co. Credit Report Volumes.

107. Texas, Vol 15b, p. 83, R. G. Dun & Co. Credit Report Volumes.

108. Texas, vol. 15b, p. 84, R. G. Dun & Co. Credit Report Volumes.

109. Texas, vol. 30, p. 56, R. G. Dun & Co. Credit Report Volumes.

110. Thomas, *The Iron Way*, 34.

111. Ward, "A New Look at Antebellum Southern Railroad Development," 419.

112. DeCredico, *Patriotism for Profit*, 73. DeCredico cites only three southern companies that made railroad equipment before the start of the Civil War: Tredegar in Richmond, the Nashville Manufacturing Company, and the Forest City Foundry in Augusta, Georgia. But as time went on, many railroads began building cars for themselves. These three may have been the only three advertising that they were making equipment for general sale, but the roads themselves made what they could for internal use.

113. Theodore Kornweibel, "Railroads and Slavery," *Railroad History* 189 (Fall–Winter 2003): 36.

114. Theodore Kornweibel, "Railroads and Slavery," 34. James Huston also discusses the use of slave labor in an industrial economy and shows that the South did make sure of this labor force. See James Huston, *Calculating the Value of the Union: Slavery, Property Rights, and the Economic Origins of the Civil War* (Chapel Hill: University of North Carolina Press, 2003).

115. Collins, "Organizing the South," 42–43.

116. R. G. Morris, Esq., "Slave Labor Upon Public Works at the South," *De Bow's Review* 17 (July 1854): 78–79.

117. LMVC, Edward G. Parker papers, 1859.

118. Lewis, *Coal, Iron, and Slaves*, 87.

## CHAPTER FIVE

1. *New Orleans Bee*, January 11, 1860.

2. *Macon Telegraph*, August 18, 1828.

3. James De Bow, *Industrial Resources, Statistics, &c. of the United States and More Particularly of the Southern and Western States* (New York: Appleton, 1852), 1:28.

4. See Appendix B—Methods, for a more detailed explanation of how missing data was estimated.

5. De Bow, *Industrial Resources*, 1:58.

6. See Map 5.9 for the location of the slave population in the Gulf South in 1860.

7. Frederick Law Olmsted, *The Cotton Kingdom* (New York: Mason Brothers, 1861), 381–82; Charles and Mary Beard, *The Rise of American Civilization* (New York: Macmillan, 1930), 669–71; Fred Bateman and Thomas Joseph Weiss, *A Deplorable Scarcity: The Failure of Industrialization in the Slave Economy* (Chapel Hill: University of North Carolina Press, 1981), 31–32.

8. William Scarborough, *Masters of the Big House: Elite Slaveholders of the Mid-Nineteenth Century South* (Baton Rouge: LSU Press, 2003), 218.

9. The basic procedure followed was to calculate the lower 25 percent, the middle 50 percent, and the upper 25 percent of capital investment of manufacturing firms in each industry reported by the census. Then these figures were multiplied by the number of firms not reported by the census in each of the corresponding industries. For a more detailed explanation see Appendix B—Methods.

10. Grady McWhinney, *Cracker Culture: Celtic Ways in the Old South* (Tuscaloosa: University of Alabama Press, 1988), 253. William Miller argued that southerners did not have many opportunities to find industrial work and that they could keep themselves sustained through hunting and fishing. But as this work shows, there were jobs out there if southerners wanted them, and many did. See William Miller, "Slavery and the Population of the South," *Southern Economic Journal* 28 (July 1961): 49.

11. Randall M. Miller, "Daniel Pratt's Industrial Urbanism: The Cotton Mill Town in Ante-bellum Alabama," *Alabama Historical Quarterly* 34 (Spring 1972): 29.

12. John Cairnes, *The Slave Power: Its Character, Career, and Probable Designs* (London: Macmillan, 1863), 147. Of course, the degraded class that Cairnes was talking about consisted of the slaves who existed in all parts of the antebellum South. Cairnes goes into great detail about how slavery made it impossible for white men to do the same kinds of work. See p. 148.

13. Between 1850 and 1860 the number of manufacturing employees grew by 43.43 percent in Alabama, 37.58 percent in Mississippi, and 72.42 percent in Texas. See US Census, 1850 and 1860, Population. David Ward explains this transition and why southern whites were seeking industrial work especially in and around William Gregg's Graniteville factories. Ward argues that the positions of many poor whites were tenuous at best, and while the head of the household may have worked a farm, children, and in-

creasingly wives, found work in the factory to supplement household income. In time this would grow into dependence on this industrial labor. See David C. Ward, "Industrial Workers in the Mid-Nineteenth Century South: Family and Labor in The Graniteville (SC) Textile Mill," *Labor History* 28 (Summer 1987): 342.

14. Jacqueline Jones, "Labor and the Idea of Race in the American South," *Journal of Southern History* 75 (August 2009): 615.

15. William Gregg, "Domestic Industry—Manufactures at the South," *De Bow's Review* 8 (February 1850): 134, taken from Paul Paskoff and Daniel Wilson, eds., *The Cause of the South: Selections from De Bow's Review, 1846–1867* (Baton Rouge: LSU Press, 1982), 94.

16. Bateman and Weiss, while finding far fewer industrial employees than this study does, also found that less than 1 percent of the population worked in industrial pursuits. Bateman and Weiss, *Deplorable Scarcity*, 4.

17. In Madison County, Alabama, at the Bell Factory, the census schedule records that the employees listed by the marshals were slaves.

18. Robert S. Starobin, *Industrial Slavery in the Old South* (Oxford: Oxford University Press, 1970), 189. Daniel Pratt is a prime example of this. In his first run for state representative, in 1855, he was defeated because of his Whig political views, but in 1860, he was elected to the State House of Representatives because his importance and political clout had grown. Curtis Evans, *The Conquest of Labor: Daniel Pratt and Southern Industrialization* (Baton Rouge: LSU Press, 2001), 137–38, 211–12.

19. Ward, "Industrial Workers," 334.

20. Randolph Campbell, *An Empire for Slavery: The Peculiar Institution in Texas, 1821–1865* (Baton Rouge: LSU Press, 1989), 212. Campbell explains that only 1 percent of the Texas population worked in industry and that the state should have done more, importing paper and textiles when cotton and wood were available all over Texas. Of course, the actual relative significance of the manufacturing workforce in the Gulf South was, for various reasons, considerably greater. Women, for example, did not work in most industries, especially the heavier lines in manufacturing. Also, employers generally preferred to hire younger male workers rather than older men, because young men were stronger and healthier. All in all, such considerations meant that the number of manufacturing workers as a percentage of the available workforce was considerably greater than at first meets the eye. The 17,582 manufacturing workers reported by the census for Alabama, Mississippi, and Texas represented 2.91 percent of the male and female population of 604,018 in those states between the ages of 15 and 50. That figure's relative size was still greater if calculated as the proportion of just the male population in that age group. US Census, 1860 Population Schedules, for Alabama, Mississippi, and Texas.

21. See Appendix C, available at drmichaelfrawley.com, for a breakdown of employees by line of business.

22. *In and About Vicksburg: An Illustrated Guide Book to the City of Vicksburg, Mississippi* (Vicksburg: Gibraltar Publishing, 1890), 181.

23. 1860 Population Census Schedules for Warren County, Mississippi. The value of Hoffman's real estate in today's money is calculated using www.measuringworth.com.

24. 1860 Manufacturing Census Schedules for Alabama.

25. US Census, 1860 Population Schedules, Autauga County, Alabama.

26. Miller, "Pratt's Industrial Urbanism," 11. For more information on the founding of Prattville, see Evans, *The Conquest of Labor*, 17–18.

27. Weymouth T. Jordan, *Ante-Bellum Alabama: Town and Country* (Tuscaloosa: University of Alabama Press, 1987), 149.

28. Jordan, *Ante-Bellum Alabama*, 148.

29. Carville Earle, *Geographical Inquiry and American Historical Problems* (Stanford, CA: Stanford University Press, 1992), 321. Gavin Wright argues the same thing in his work as he delves into the seasonality of labor, the problems of moving from field to factory, and the effect that cotton had on wages. Gavin Wright, *Old South, New South: Revolutions in the Southern Economy Since the Civil War* (Baton Rouge: LSU Press, 1996).

30. Earle, *Geographical Inquiry*, 316.

31. Ward, "Industrial Workers," 334.

32. J. M. Edmunds, *Manufactures of the United States in 1860: Compiled from the Original Returns of the Eighth Census, under the Direction of the Secretary of the Interior* (Washington: Government Printing Office, 1865), xii.

33. 1860 Manufacturing Census Schedules for Autauga and Bibb Counties, Alabama.

34. Olmsted, *Cotton Kingdom*, 396.

35. Tom Terrill, Edmond Ewing, and Pamela White, "Eager Hands: Labor for Southern Textiles, 1850–1860," *Journal of Economic History* 36 (March 1976): 84.

36. Carville Earle and Ronald Hoffman, "Foundation of the Modern Economy: Agriculture and the Costs of Labor in the United States and England, 1800–60," *American Historical Review* 85 (December 1980): 1077.

37. Karl Marx, *Capital* (reprint, New York: Penguin Books, 1990), 1:711.

38. There are many blank counties on Map 4.13 in Texas. But these counties had been created by the state government before people had moved there. Thus we can consider these counties to be unsettled.

39. Jones, "Labor and the Idea of Race," 615. Jones states that "slave labor was relatively inflexible and expensive to maintain during the slack season of production." This seems to be a strong argument for the use of slaves in industrial concerns wherever possible. Ralph Anderson and Robert Gallman also commented on this idea as they believed that slavery created a need for full employment and pushed forward plantation diversity. See Ralph Anderson and Robert Gallman, "Slaves as Fixed Capital: Slave Labor and Southern Industrial Development," *Journal of American History* 64 (June 1977): 45–46.

40. William Harper, *Memoir on Slavery* (Charleston: James S. Burges Publisher, 1838), 53.

41. De Bow, *Industrial Resources*, 1:313.

42. De Bow, *Industrial Resources*, 1:11–12. Slaves were good agricultural laborers, but

there would be a limit to the number of people agriculture could support, and when that limit was reached they would have to be put to some other work. See Harper, *Memoir on Slavery*, 53. The problem of an expanding slave population was something that southerners recognized very early on. See De Bow, *Industrial Resources*, 1:313.

43. De Bow, *Industrial Resources*, 1:339.

44. Jones, "Labor and the Idea of Race," 615.

45. Bonnie Martin found large networks of credit based on slave property operating all over frontier areas of the antebellum South. See Bonnie Martin, "Slavery's Invisible Engine: Mortgaging Human Property," *Journal of Southern History* 76 (November 2010): 818, 865. For further information about the use of slaves as collateral, see Richard Kilbourne, *Debt, Investment, Slaves: Credit Relations in East Feliciana Parish, Louisiana* (Tuscaloosa: University of Alabama Press, 1995), quote on p. 5.

46. The Dun reports list many cases of slave ownership by industrial owners such as $15,000 in slaves owned by Edwin Reese of Green County, Alabama and the $5,000 in slaves that Robert Logan owned in Chambers County, Alabama. These slaves were good collateral for any credit a northern firm extended. See Alabama, vol. 11, p. 174, R. G. Dun & Co. Credit Report Volumes, Baker Library Historical Collections, Harvard Business School; and Alabama, vol. 6, p. 126, R. G. Dun & Co. Credit Report Volumes.

47. W. David Lewis, "The Emergence of Birmingham as a Case Study of a Continuity between the Antebellum Planter Class and Industrialization in the 'New South,'" *Agricultural History* 68 (Spring 1994): 63.

48. John Hebron Moore, *The Emergence of the Cotton Kingdom in the Old Southwest* (Baton Rouge: LSU Press, 1988), 222.

49. Moore, *Emergence of the Cotton Kingdom*, 223.

50. William Gregg, *Essays on Domestic Industry: An Inquiry into the Expediency of Establishing Cotton Manufacturers in South Carolina* (Graniteville, SC: Graniteville Company, 1941), 48–49. Also see Jones, "Labor and the Idea of Race," 615.

51. Charles Dew, *Ironmaker to the Confederacy: Joseph R. Anderson and the Tredegar Iron Works* (New Haven, CT: Yale University Press, 1966), 3.

52. De Bow, *Industrial Resources*, 1:79.

53. Randall Miller, "Cotton Mill Movement in Antebellum Alabama" (PhD diss., Ohio State University, 1971), 219. Curtis Evans also discussed the use of slave labor by Pratt. He argued that Pratt used slave labor for the same reason that William Gregg did, to have greater control over his workforce. See Evans, *The Conquest of Labor*, 80–83.

54. Theodore Kornweibel, "Railroads and Slavery," *Railroad History* 189 (Fall–Winter 2003): 36.

55. Komweibel, "Railroads and Slavery," 34.

56. John Parker, *His Promised Land* (New York: W.W. Norton, 1996), 7–8.

57. Parker, *His Promised Land*, 68.

58. Parker, *His Promised Land*, 67.

59. Parker, *His Promised Land*, 66–67.

60. According to James Huston, some northerners also feared industrial slave labor, such as Parker's, because it challenged the free labor–driven model of industrialization. See James L. Huston, "Property Rights in Slavery and the Coming of the Civil War," *Journal of Southern History* 65 (May 1999): 271.

61. *De Bow's Review* 26 (May 1859): 600.

62. Arnold Rose argues that slaves dominated the unskilled and skilled labor markets. See *The Negro in America* (Boston: Beacon Press, 1948), 101–2. This, of course, was an overstatement, and Rose does not have the data to back up this assertion, but slave labor was very important to the South, and as in all the examples given here, it was also important to industrial development in the region. Of course, many others have looked at this idea, including Fogel and Engerman, Gavin Wright, and Bateman and Weiss, all of whom have been discussed in detail earlier in this work. These historians concluded that slavery was extremely profitable, and that these profits could be turned to things other than agriculture. But they all also state that manufacturing, for one reason or another, did not receive the investment it should have. This discussion considers the problem from another angle, to add to our understanding of capital investment in areas with large slave ownership.

63. Harold D. Woodman, "The Profitability of Slavery: A Historical Perennial," *Journal of Southern History* 29 (August 1963): 321.

64. R Sq Linear shows how close the data is to the regression line, so the higher the number, the better the data fits in with the model presented. In this case, a 0.109 shows a strong correlation between the two variables presented.

65. Wright, *Old South, New South,* 124.

66. Scarborough, *Masters of the Big House,* 409.

67. Douglas R. Egerton, "Markets without a Market Revolution: Southern Planters and Capitalism," *Journal of the Early Republic* 16 (Summer 1996): 220–21. Eugene Genovese explains the same thing in his work on this subject, that paternalism allowed the economy to expand, but not develop. See Genovese, *The Political Economy of Slavery: Studies in the Economy & Society of the Slave South* (New York: Pantheon Books, 1965).

68. Edward Pessen, "How Different from Each Other Were the Antebellum North and South," *American Historical Review* 85 (December 1980): 1125.

69. U. B. Phillips, *Life and Labor in the Old South* (Boston: Little, Brown, 1929), 395.

70. Stanley Lebergott, *The Americans: An Economic Record* (New York: W.W. Norton, 1984), 136. Also see Douglass C. North, *The Economic Growth of the United States, 1790–1860* (New York: W.W. Norton, 1966), 128.

71. Vicki Vaughn Johnson, *The Men and the Vision of the Southern Commercial Conventions, 1845–1871* (Columbia: University of Missouri Press, 1992), 119.

72. John Majewski, *Modernizing a Slave Economy: The Economic Vision of the Confederate Nation* (Chapel Hill: University of North Carolina Press, 2009),.6–14.

73. De Bow, *Industrial Resources,* 1:113.

CHAPTER SIX

1. *Daily Confederation*, 19 May 1858.

2. William Gregg, *Essays on Domestic Industry: An Inquiry into the Expediency of Establishing Cotton Manufacturers in South Carolina* (Graniteville, SC: Graniteville Company, 1941), 6–7. Douglass North, in his work on American economic growth before 1860, observed that "residentiary industry failed to develop because a local market did not grow." See North, *The Economic Growth of the United States, 1790–1860* (New York: W.W. Norton, 1966).

3. Mr. Marshall, "We Must Diversify Our Industry," *De Bow's Review* 24 (March 1858): 261.

4. *The Navarro Express*, June 2, 1860.

5. Hubert Spangler, "In Memorium of the Spanglers," n.p., 1937, Spangler Vertical File, McCardell Library, Old Courthouse Museum, Vicksburg, Mississippi.

6. *In and About Vicksburg: An Illustrated Guide Book to the City of Vicksburg, Mississippi, Its History, Its Appearance, Its Business Houses: To Which is Added a Description of the Resources and Progress of the State of Mississippi, as an Investing Field for Immigration and Capital* (Vicksburg: The Gibraltar Publishing Co., 1890), 189. Klein's concern was also listed in the census records.

7. George Rogers Taylor and Irene Neu, *The American Railroad Network, 1861–1890* (Cambridge, MA: Harvard University Press, 1956), 45.

8. 1860 US Census Manufacturing Schedules. Weymouth Jordan discusses the gin industry in his work. See Weymouth T. Jordan, *Ante-Bellum Alabama: Town and Country* (Tuscaloosa: University of Alabama Press, 1987), 152.

9. In 1860, Alabama had twenty-four iron firms according to the manufacturing census schedules.

10. J. P. Lesley, in his guide to iron manufacturing in the United States, lists many different firms that were producing iron in Alabama and explained that many of them were taking advantage of transportation avenues, such as railroads and rivers, to begin exporting this production to other areas. See Lesley, *The Iron Manufacturer's Guide to the Furnaces, Forges, and Rolling Mills of the United States (New York: John Wiley Publishers, 1859)*, 78–19, 194–96.

11. Walter Buenger explained that lumber mills were the most prevalent form of manufacturing in the South before the war and that people had a great deal of their industrial interactions with these firms. See Walter Buenger, *Secession and the Union in Texas* (Austin: University of Texas Press, 1984), 13.

12. Census of 1860 Manufacturing Schedules.

13. The conversion to today's currency was done using measuringworth.com.

14. According to the 1860 census schedules for Alabama, Mississippi, and Texas, the average blind, sash, and door firm produced $17,701 and an average foundry put out $28,232. The average firm in the Gulf South produced $7,241 in 1860.

15. See Table 2.6 for a listing of missed firms by organization type.

16. Mississippi, vol. 17, p. 33, R. G. Dun & Co. Credit Report Volumes, Baker Library Historical Collections, Harvard Business School.

17. Mississippi, vol. 21, p. 19, R. G. Dun & Co. Credit Report Volumes.

18. Edward Pollard, *The Lost Cause: A New History of the War of the Confederates* (New York: E. B. Treat, 1866), 101.

19. Brian Schoen, *The Fragile Fabric of Union: Cotton, Federal Politics, and the Global Origins of the Civil War* (Baltimore: Johns Hopkins University Press, 2009), 208.

20. Paul Paskoff, *Industrial Evolution: Organization, Structure, and Growth of the Pennsylvania Iron Industry, 1750–1860* (Baltimore: Johns Hopkins Press, 1983), 3.

21. James D. Norris, *R. G. Dun & Co. 1841–1900: The Development of Credit-Reporting in the Nineteenth Century* (Westport, CT: Greenwood Press, 1978), 22.

22. Gavin Wright, *Slavery and American Economic Development* (Baton Rouge: LSU Press, 2006), 80–81.

23. Harriet Amos, *Cotton City: Urban Development in Antebellum Mobile* (University: University of Alabama Press, 1985), 213. Amos explains in detail that Mobile was by any conceivable measure the leading industrial county in Alabama. Also, Mobile was a major export center for the Gulf South and in the decade before the war, a large variety of goods passed through the city bound for other areas. See Jordan, *Antebellum Alabama*, 18.

24. Frederick Law Olmsted, *The Cotton Kingdom* (New York: Mason Brothers, 1861), 214.

25. Beringer argued that public and private industrial efforts made the region less dependent on imports. Richard Beringer, Herman Hattaway, Archer Jones, and William N. Still Jr., *Why the South Lost the Civil War* (Athens: University of Georgia Press, 1986), 63.

26. Alabama, vol. 17, p. 204, R. G. Dun & Co. Credit Report Volumes.

27. Alan Smith Thompson, "Mobile, Alabama, 1850–1861: Economic, Political, Physical, and Population Characteristics" (PhD diss., University of Alabama, 1979), 269. Stanley Engerman concluded that the problems faced by southern industry arose because the local market was too small. But if industrial production was larger than previously believed, then the market was larger and southern industry may not have been held back by market size. See Stanley Engerman, "A Reconsideration of Southern Economic Growth, 1770–1860," *Agricultural History* 49 (April 1975): 359.

28. Thompson, "Mobile, Alabama," 286.

29. Mississippi, vol. 2, p. 66, R. G. Dun & Co. Credit Report Volumes.

30. Mississippi, vol. 21, p. 28, R. G. Dun & Co. Credit Report Volumes.

31. Alabama, vol. 2, p. 113, R. G. Dun & Co. Credit Report Volumes.

32. See Appendix B—Methods—to see how this estimate was determined.

33. US Bureau of the Census, *Historical Statistics of the United States, Colonial Times to 1970, Bicentennial Edition, Part 1* (Washington: US Government Printing Office, 1975), 209.

34. The conversion of 1860 dollars to 2013 dollars, which is the closest to today that can be currently determined, was done using the currency converter on www.measuringworth.com.

35. *Texas State Gazette*, June 15, 1860.

36. See Appendix B—Methods—to see how this estimate was determined.

37. US Bureau of the Census, *Historical Statistics of the United States*, 209.

38. The conversion to today's money was done using www.measuringworth.com.

39. According to Edward Pessen, antebellum investors did not plan their investments; rather, they just invested in whatever would turn a profit, and a "'rational' investment was the one likely to pay off." See Edward Pessen, "How Different from Each Other Were the Antebellum North and South?" *The American Historical Review* 85 (December 1980): 1126. William Scarborough also discussed the investment patterns of southerners in his work *Masters of the Big House*. See William Scarborough, *Masters of the Big House: Elite Slaveholders of the Mid-Nineteenth Century South* (Baton Rouge: LSU Press, 2003), 217–37.

40. The values listed in Table 5.9 for capital, output, and ratio of output to capital for agricultural implements concerns owned by partnerships is not an average. There was only one firm of that type listed in the census, and thus the values in the table are for that one concern.

41. Bateman and Weiss also looked at rate of return for the firms in their sample and found that investment of capital in manufacturing was profitable. But there are problems with judging what values to use when determining something like the ratio of output to capital. For example, slaves owned as part of a firm's holdings may not be included in capital investment, and therefore the ratio could look much different. See Bateman and Weiss, *A Deplorable Scarcity* (Chapel Hill: University of North Carolina Press, 1981), 126–27 and 195–97.

42. Mississippi, vol. 4, p. 37, R. G. Dun & Co. Credit Report Volumes.

43. Mississippi, vol. 4, p. 37, R. G. Dun & Co. Credit Report Volumes. This is a rare instance where a Dun reporter actually recorded amounts of production.

44. Bateman and Weiss, *A Deplorable Scarcity*, 109–13. Of course, Bateman and Weiss stated that people with capital neglected this kind of investment opportunity even though it was profitable. Moreover, Bateman and Weiss also discussed some of the other costs of doing business that needed to be considered. See 195–97.

45. Scarborough, *Masters of the Big House*, 428. Scarborough (p. 219) also explained that planters invested in banking, manufacturing, railroads, steamboats, land speculation, and many other things.

46. Gregory Clark, *A Farewell to Alms: A Brief Economic History of the World* (Princeton, NJ: Princeton University Press, 2007), 67

47. Historians continue to say that southerners did not make good industrial workers. For example, as Richard Brown argued, the southern workforce was held back by poor ed-

ucation, a lack of immigration, and slavery. See Brown, *Modernization: The Transformation of American Life, 1600–1865* (New York: Hill and Wang, 1976), 145–47.

48. *Independent Monitor,* April 22, 1846, cited in Tom Terrill, Edmond Ewing, and Pamela White, "Eager Hands: Labor for Southern Textiles, 1850–1860," *Journal of Economic History* 36 (March 1976): 87.

49. US Census Compendium for 1860.

50. The top 25 percent of companies does have a lower output per worker than we would expect it to have. But this was most likely because of the small number of firms that are in the category.

51. US Census Compendium for 1860.

52. George Fitzhugh, *Sociology for the South, or, The Failure of Free Society* (Richmond, VA: A. Morris, 1854), 203.

53. J. D. B. De Bow, *The Industrial Resources, Statistics, &c., of the United States and More Particularly of the Southern and Western States* (New York: Appleton, 1852), 1:28.

54. William Cooper, *Liberty and Slavery: Southern Politics to 1860* (New York: Knopf, 1983), 253.

## EPILOGUE

1. Fred Bateman and Thomas Weiss, "Manufacturing in the Antebellum South," in Paul Uselding, ed., *Research in Economic History* (Greenwich, CT: JAI Press, 1976), 1.

2. Brian Schoen, *The Fragile Fabric of Union: Cotton, Federal Politics, and the Global Origins of the Civil War* (Baltimore: Johns Hopkins University Press, 2009), 206.

3. Laurence Shore explains that many people in the region wanted more support for industry. See Lawrence Shore, *Southern Capitalists: The Ideological Leadership of an Elite, 1832–1885* (Chapel Hill: University of North Carolina Press, 1986), 61.

4. Darrett Rutman, "The Village South," in Darrett B. Rutman and Anita Rutman, *Small Worlds, Large Questions: Explorations in Early American Social History, 1600–1850* (Charlottesville: University Press of Virginia, 1994), 271.

5. Robert William Fogel and Stanley L. Engerman, *Time on the Cross: The Economics of American Negro Slavery* (Boston: Little, Brown, 1974), 6.

6. Fogel and Engerman, *Time on the Cross,* 250.

7. Gavin Wright, *Slavery and American Economic Development* (Baton Rouge: LSU Press, 2006), 124.

8. Gavin Wright, *Slavery and American Economic Development* (Baton Rouge: LSU Press, 2006), 124.

9. Stanley Engerman, "A Reconsideration of Southern Economic Growth, 1770–1860," *Agricultural History* 49 (April 1975): 351. Engerman went on to argue that most economies in European countries were still based on large economic sectors, just as the South, and even the North, were.

10. Raimondo Luraghi argued that, "To enter the war with a minimum probability of survival, the Confederacy, obviously, had to industrialize—or die." The results of the war seem to prove his case. See Raimondo Luraghi, *The Rise and Fall of the Plantation South* (New York: Franklin Watts, 1978), 110–11.

11. For more information on the blockade, see Lance E. Davis and Stanley L. Engerman, *Naval Blockades in Peace and War: An Economic History Since 1750* (Cambridge: Cambridge University Press, 2006); Mark Thornton and Robert B. Ekelund Jr., *Tariffs, Blockades, and Inflation: The Economics of the Civil War* (Wilmington, DE: Scholarly Resources, 2004).

12. *Panola Star*, November 29, 1860.

13. The Dun reports show this. In all entries on the eve of war, the local reporters make no mention of fears of war or of businesses founded to meet expected war needs.

14. Letter of George Dobson to his wife, December 9, 1861, Humphrey's (David Colin) Collection, Mississippi Department of Archives and History.

15. John Ashworth has stated that the South had the economic strength to fight four years of war. He had, however, very little statistical data upon which to base this assumption. See Ashworth, *Slavery, Capitalism, and Politics in the Antebellum Republic: The Coming of the Civil War, 1850–1861* (Cambridge: Cambridge University Press, 2007), 16.

16. The Confederate government did not purchase everything offered to it, and many large and important firms, such as the Phoenix Iron Works in New Orleans, the Selma Powder Works, and William Gregg's Graniteville Mill were all turned down by the Confederacy at one point or another. See Richard Goff, *Confederate Supply* (Durham, NC: Duke University Press, 1969), 12.

17. Mary DeCredico, *Patriotism for Profit: Georgia's Urban Entrepreneurs and the Confederate War Effort* (Chapel Hill: University of North Carolina Press, 1990), xvi.

18. *Vicksburg Whig*, May 13, 1861.

19. Unidentified obituary of A. B. Reading, Reading-Pierson Vertical File, McCardell Library, Old Courthouse Museum, Vicksburg, Mississippi.

20. John Hebron Moore, *The Emergence of the Cotton Kingdom in the Old Southwest* (Baton Rouge: LSU Press, 1988), 225.

21. Ethel Armes, *The Story of Coal and Iron in Alabama* (Birmingham: Birmingham Chamber of Commerce, 1910), 134–35.

22. Arthur W. Bergeron Jr., *Confederate Mobile* (Baton Rouge: LSU Press, 1991), 16–17.

23. Larry Daniel and Riley Gunter, *Confederate Cannon Foundries* (Union City, TN: Pioneer Press, 1977), 89.

24. Goff, *Confederate Supply*, 15.

25. Ben Wynne, *Mississippi's Civil War: A Narrative History* (Macon, GA: Mercer University Press, 2006), 101. Life in the town was based around the mill.Once it was gone there was no reason for people to stay, and Bankston became a ghost town.

26. Inspection Records, November 1863, Mississippi State Penitentiary Records, Mississippi Department of Archives and History.

27. Alabama, vol. 10, p. 87, R. G. Dun & Co. Credit Report Volumes, Baker Library Historical Collections, Harvard Business School.

28. Harold S. Wilson, *Confederate Industry: Manufacturers and Quartermasters in the Civil War* (Jackson: University Press of Mississippi, 2002), 215. Mary DeCredico made the same point about people wearing out by the end of the war in her work on Georgia. See *Patriotism for Profit*, 152–54.

29. Alabama, vol. 12, p. 125, R. G. Dun & Co. Credit Report Volumes.

30. Mississippi, vol. 9, p. 78, R. G. Dun & Co. Credit Report Volumes.

31. Alabama, vol. 11, pp. 11 and 76, R. G. Dun & Co. Credit Report Volumes.

32. For a map of the counties in the South that saw conflict during the Civil War, see Paul Paskoff, "Measures of War: A Quantitative Examination of the Civil War's Destructiveness in the Confederacy," *Civil War History* 54 (2008): 43.

33. Paskoff, "Measures of War," 58. While Paskoff does not discuss the impact of the war on industrial concerns specifically, he does make the point that the level of destruction in the South was much lower than believed. There is no reason to think that industrial concerns did not also have a lower level of destruction.

34. Weymouth T. Jordan, *Ante-Bellum Alabama: Town and Country* (Tuscaloosa: University of Alabama Press, 1987), 160.

35. Schoen, *Fragile Fabric of Union*, 207.

36. DeCredico, *Patriotism for Profit*, 12.

37. Other historians have pushed the start back already. See Ronald L. Lewis, *Coal, Iron, and Slaves: Industrial Slavery in Maryland and Virginia, 1715–1865* (Westport, CT: Greenwood Press, 1979); Steven G. Collins, "System in the South: John W. Mallet, Josiah Gorgas, and Uniform Production at the Confederate Ordnance Department," *Technology and Culture* 40 (July 1999): 517–44; Steven G. Collins, "System, Organization, and Agricultural Reform in the Antebellum South, 1840–1860," *Agricultural History* 75 (Winter 2001): 1–27.

38. Hinton Rowan Helper, *The Impending Crisis of the South: How to Meet It* (New York: Burdick Brothers, 1857), 22–34.

39. Fred Bateman and Thomas Joseph Weiss, *A Deplorable Scarcity: The Failure of Industrialization in the Slave Economy* (Chapel Hill: University of North Carolina Press, 1981), 163.

40. Engerman, "Southern Economic Growth," 354.

41. Richard Brown, *Modernization: The Transformation of American Life, 1600–1865* (New York: Hill and Wang, 1976), 152.

42. Stanley Engerman explained that "the growth in Southern manufacturing was quite rapid, although somewhat slower than in the North during this period of its most rapid growth." See Engerman, "Southern Economic Growth," 357.

43. As stated earlier, most historians understand that slavery did not hold back southern development. As David Eltis explained, "Nevertheless, arguments that slavery stymied the development of the Americas, both before and after its abolition, tend to rely more on hopeful constructions of social development then on hard empirical evidence of how slave

societies functioned." See Davis Eltis, Frank D. Lewis, and Kenneth L. Sokoloff, eds., *Slavery in the Development of the Americas* (Cambridge: Cambridge University Press, 2004), especially chapter 4, for a further discussion of slavery and industry in the Gulf South.

44. Bateman and Weiss, *A Deplorable Scarcity*, 158.

## APPENDIX A

1. Eighth Census, United States—1860: Instructions to US Marshals.

2. *The Civilian & Gazette*, September 18, 1860.

3. J. D. B. De Bow, *The Industrial Resources, Statistics, &c. of the United States and More Particularly of the Southern and Western States* (New York: Appleton, 1852), 1:192.

4. Ronald L. Lewis, *Coal, Iron, and Slaves: Industrial Slavery in Maryland and Virginia, 1715– 1865* (Westport, CT: Greenwood Press, 1979), 180.

5. Michael Gagnon, *Transition to an Industrial South: Athens, Georgia, 1830–1870* (Baton Rouge: LSU Press, 2012), 53. Vera Dugas saw the same thing in Texas: there were more people listed with an industrial profession than there were industrial firms to employ them. Dugas assumed that this meant there was a large amount of production going on outside of factories, but the evidence in this work seems to run in the face of Dugas's idea. See Vera Lea Dugas, "Texas Industry, 1860–1880," *Southwestern Historical Quarterly* 59 (October 1955): 152–53.

6. Richard K. Vedde and Lowell E. Gallaway, "The Profitability of Antebellum Manufacturing: Some New Estimates," *Business History Review* 54 (Spring 1980): 95.

7. Robert William Fogel, *Without Consent or Contract: The Rise and Fall of American Slavery* (New York: Norton, 1989), 103; Fred Bateman and Thomas Joseph Weiss, *A Deplorable Scarcity: The Failure of Industrialization in the Slave Economy* (Chapel Hill: University of North Carolina Press, 1981), 95–96. Bateman and Weiss estimated that plantation production could have added as much as $216.1 million in industrial production to the antebellum South's ledgers. Moreover, James Huston argued that some lines of business that were counted as industrial by the census should not have been because they had little to do with the development of the factory system, such as wheelwrights, millers, and coopers. See James L. Huston, "Property Rights in Slavery and the Coming of the Civil War," *Journal of Southern History* 65 (May 1999): 254.

8. Darrett B. Rutman, "The Village South," in Darrett B. Rutman and Anita H. Rutman, *Small Worlds, Large Questions: Explorations in Early American Social History, 1600–1850* (Charlottesville: University Press of Virginia, 1994), 237.

9. L. Diane Barnes, Brian Schoen, and Frank Towers, eds., *The Old South's Modern Worlds: Slavery, Region, and Nation in the Age of Progress* (Oxford: Oxford University Press, 2011), 153.

10. Bateman and Weiss were, of course, two historians who did work on antebellum southern industry and assumed that the census was complete. See Bateman and Weiss, *A Deplorable Scarcity*, 166.

11. James D. Norris, *R. G. Dun & Co., 1841–1900: The Development of Credit-Reporting in the Nineteenth Century* (Westport, CT: Greenwood Press, 1978), 61–63.

12. Norris, *R. G. Dun & Co.*, xvi.

13. Noris, *R. G. Dun & Co.*, 63.

14. Noris, *R. G. Dun & Co.*, 66.

15. Noris, *R. G. Dun & Co.*, 34.

16. Lewis Tappen, *Business Circular*, 1842, quoted in Norris, *R. G. Dun & Company*, 22.

17. Norris, *R. G. Dun & Company*, 10.

18. See, for one example, H. P. Chapman and J. F. Battle, *Picturesque Vicksburg: A Description of the Resources and Prospects of that City and the Famous Yazoo Delta, Its Agriculture and Commercial Interests, To Which is Attached a Series of Sketches of Representative Industries: Profoundly Illustrated* (Vicksburg, MI: Vicksburg Printing and Publishing Co., 1895).

## APPENDIX B

1. J. D. B. De Bow, *The Industrial Resources, Statistics, &c. of the United States and More Particularly of the Southern and Western States* (New York: Appleton, 1852), 1:9.

2. A shapefile is a term used in GIS to denote the computer file that contains the outlines and positioning for various geographic areas. For this work a shapefile with the outlines of the counties in Alabama, Mississippi, and Texas in 1860 is used. Each county in the file has a number assigned to it, which allows data from other sources to be matched to a specific county in the file. This process is called geocoding.

3. See Appendix C—Data, which is available on drmichaelfrawley.com, for both organizational and line of business breakdowns of Gulf South industry.

4. An attempt was made in chaper 2 to review advertising as a way to determine the scale of a business. But this was done through looking at ads in available sources, especially in newspapers, and was used to justify their inclusion in the list of firms, not as a way to determine profitability. But as was argued, any firm that could afford to advertise at the rate listed were most likely profitable.

# BIBLIOGRAPHY


## Primary Sources

### MANUSCRIPT COLLECTIONS

Baker Library Historical Collection—Harvard University
R. G. Dun Credit Reports, 1860

Lower Mississippi Valley Collection—Louisiana State University
Edward G. Parker Letter, 1859

McCardle Library, Old Courthouse Museum—Vicksburg, MS
G. R. Reading, Pierson Vertical File
Paxton Vertical File
Spangler Vertical File

Mississippi Department of Archives and History—Jackson, MS
A New Map of Mississippi with its Roads and Distances, 1859
Humphrey's Collection
Mississippi State Penitentiary Account Sheets, 1860, Record Group 29

## *Newspapers and Periodicals*

*Alabama Beacon* (Greensboro, AL)
*Alabama Reporter* (Talladega, AL)
*Alabama State Sentinel* (Selma, AL)
*Alamo Express* (Brazoria, TX)
*Amite Democrat* (Liberty, MS)
*The Autauga Citizen* (Prattville, AL)
*Brandon Republic* (Brandon, MS)
*Cahaba Gazette* (Cahaba, AL)
*Carrollton Democrat* (Carrollton, MS)
*The Central Enquirer* (Selma, AL)
*The Chronicle* (Hayneville, AL)

*The Civilian and Gazette* (Galveston, TX)
*Clarke County Democrat* (Grove Hill, AL)
*Commonwealth* (Canton, MS)
*Daily Confederation* (Montgomery, AL)
*Daily State Sentinel* (Selma, AL)
*Dallas Herald* (Dallas, TX)
*De Bow's Review*
*The Democrat* (Huntsville, AL)
*Democrat and Planter* (Columbia, TX)
*The Democratic Watchtower* (Talladega, AL)
*Eastern Clarion* (DeSoto, MS)
*Florence Gazette* (Florence, AL)
*Hayneville Chronicle* (Hayneville, AL)
*The Independent (Gainesville, AL)*
*Independent American* (Montgomery, AL)
*The Independent Monitor* (Talladega, AL)
*Independent Observer* (Eutaw, AL)
*Indianola Courier* (Indianola, TX)
*Jacksonville Republican* (Jacksonville, AL)
*Lexington Advertiser* (Lexington, MS)
*Macon Beacon* (Macon, MS)
*Macon Telegraph* (Macon, GA)
*Montgomery Weekly Post* (Montgomery, AL)
*Natchez Weekly Courier* (Natchez, MS)
*Navarro Express* (Corsicana, TX)
*New Orleans Bee* (New Orleans, LA)
*Oxford Intelligence* (Holly Springs, MS)
*Pickens Republican* (Pickens, AL)
*Ranchero* (Corpus Christi, TX)
*Selma Morning Reporter* (Selma, AL)
*Selma Weekly Reporter* (Selma, AL)
*The South Alabamian* (Greenville, AL)
*Southern Advocate* (Huntsville, AL)
*Southern Champion* (Claiborne, AL)
*Southern Cultivator*
*Southern Intelligencer* (Austin, TX)
*Southern Messenger* (Greenville, AL)
*Southern Planter*

*Southern Statesman* (Prattville, AL)
*South Western Baptist* (Tuskegee, AL)
*Spirit of the South* (Eufaula, AL)
*The Standard* (Clarksville, TX)
*State Gazette* (Austin, TX)
*Sunny South* (Aberdeen, MS)
*The Watchman* (Hayneville, AL)
*Universalist Herald* (Greenville, AL)
*Weekly Southern Era* (Opelika, AL)
*Weekly Southern Star* (Macon, MS)
*Weekly Telegraph* (Houston, TX)
*West Alabamian* (Carrollton, AL)
*Yazoo Democrat* (Yazoo City, MS)

## Government Documents

*Agricultural and Manufacturing Census Records of Fifteen Southern States for the Years 1850, 1860, 1870, and 1880.* Chapel Hill: University of North Carolina Library, 1962.

Annals of Congress, 14th Congress, 2nd Session (1816). Census Office. *Eighth Census, United States—1860: Instructions to U.S. Marshals.* Washington, DC: Geo. W. Bowman, Public Printer, 1860.

Congressional Globe, 36th Congress, 2nd Session (1861).

Edmunds, J. M. *Manufactures of the United States in 1860: Compiled from the Original Returns of the Eighth Census, under the Direction of the Secretary of the Interior.* Washington: Government Printing Office, 1865.

Reynolds, R. V. *Fuel Wood Used in the United States, 1630–1930* (Circular No. 641). Washington: United States Department of Agriculture, 1942.

US Bureau of the Census. *Historical Statistics of the United States, Colonial Times to 1970, Bicentennial Edition.* Washington: Government Printing Office, 1975.

## Primary Books and Pamphlets

Cairnes, John E. The Slave Power: Its Character, Career, and Probable Designs. London: Macmillan, 1863.

Campbell, John P. *The Southern Business Directory and General Commercial Advertiser.* Charleston: Press of Walker & James, 1854.

Chapman, H. P., and J. F. Battle. *Picturesque Vicksburg: A Description of the Re-*

*sources and Prospects of that City and the Famous Yazoo Delta, Its Agriculture and Commercial Interests, To Which is Attached a Series of Sketches of Representative Industries: Profoundly Illustrated.* Vicksburg, MS: Vicksburg Printing and Publishing, 1895.

Clarke, H. C. *A General Directory of the City of Vicksburg.* Vicksburg: H. C. Clarke Publishers, 1860.

De Bow, J. D. B. *The Industrial Resources, Statistics, &c., of the United States and More Particularly of the Southern and Western States.* 3 vols. New York: Appleton, 1852.

Farrow & Dennett. *Directory for the City of Mobile for 1861.* Mobile: Farrow & Dennett, 1861.

Fitzhugh, George. *Sociology for the South, or, The Failure of Free Society.* Richmond, VA: A. Morris, 1854.

French, B. F. *History of the Rise and Progress of the Iron Trade of the United States From 1621 to 1857.* New York: Wiley & Halsted, 1858.

Gregg, William. *Essays on Domestic Industry: An Inquiry into the Expediency of Establishing Cotton Manufacturers in South Carolina.* Graniteville: Graniteville Company, 1941.

Harper, William. *Memoir on Slavery.* Charleston: James S. Burges Publisher, 1838.

Helper, Hinton Rowan. *The Impending Crisis of the South: How to Meet It.* New York: Burdick Brothers, 1857.

Hughes, Henry. *Treatise on Sociology, Theoretical and Practical.* Philadelphia: Lippincott, Grambo, 1854.

*In and About Vicksburg: An Illustrated Guide Book to the City of Vicksburg, Mississippi, Its History, Its Appearance, Its Business Houses: To Which is Added a Description of the Resources and Progress of the State of Mississippi, as an Investing Field for Immigration and Capital.* Vicksburg, MS: Gibraltar Publishing, 1890.

Kettell, Thomas Prentice. *Southern Wealth and Northern Profits.* New York: George W. & John A. Wood, 1860.

Lesley, J. P. *The Iron Manufacturer's Guide to the Furnaces, Forges, and Rolling Mills of the United States.* New York: John Wiley Publishers, 1859.

Mears & Turnbull. *The Montgomery Directory of 1859–60.* Montgomery: Advertiser Book and Job Printing Office, 1859.

Olmsted, Frederick Law. *The Cotton Kingdom: A Traveller's Observations of Cotton and Slavery in the American Slave States.* New York: Mason Brothers, 1861.

Parker, John. *His Promised Land.* Edited by Stuart Sprague. New York: W.W. Norton, 1996.

Power, J. L. *Professional and Business Directory of the City of Jackson, Mississippi.* Jackson: J. L. Power Publishing, 1860.

Richardson, W. & D. *The Texas Almanac for 1860, with Statistics, Historical and Biographical Sketches, &c. Relating to Texas.* Galveston: Galveston News, 1860.

Tanner, Henry S. *Canals and Railroads of the United States.* New York: T. R. Tanner & J. Disturnell, 1840.

Tharin, W. C. *A Directory of Marengo County for 1860–61.* Mobile: Farrow & Dennett, 1861.

## Secondary Sources

BOOKS

Aitken, Hugh G. J., ed. *Did Slavery Pay?* Boston: Houghton Mifflin, 1971.

Amos, Harriet E. *Cotton City: Urban Development in Antebellum Mobile.* University: University of Alabama Press, 1985.

Armes, Ethel. *The Story of Coal and Iron in Alabama.* Birmingham: Birmingham Chamber of Commerce, 1910.

Ashworth, John. *Slavery, Capitalism, and Politics in the Antebellum Republic: The Coming of the Civil War, 1850–1861.* Cambridge: Cambridge University Press, 2007.

Barnes, L. Diane, Brian Schoen, and Frank Towers, eds. *The Old South's Modern Worlds: Slavery, Region, and Nation in the Age of Progress.* Oxford: Oxford University Press, 2011.

Bateman, Fred, and Thomas Joseph Weiss. *A Deplorable Scarcity: The Failure of Industrialization in the Slave Economy.* Chapel Hill: University of North Carolina Press, 1981.

Beard, Charles and Mary. *The Rise of American Civilization.* New York: Macmillan, 1930.

Bergeron, Arthur W. Jr. *Confederate Mobile.* Baton Rouge: LSU Press, 1991.

Beringer, Richard E., Herman Hattaway, Archer Jones, and William N. Still Jr. *Why the South Lost the Civil War.* Athens: University of Georgia Press, 1986.

Black, Robert C. *The Railroads of the Confederacy.* Chapel Hill: University of North Carolina Press, 1998.

Blackburn, Robin. *The Making of New World Slavery: From the Baroque to the Modern, 1492–1800.* London: Verso, 1997.

Bond, Bradley. *Political Culture in the Nineteenth-Century South: Mississippi 1830–1900.* Baton Rouge: LSU Press, 1995.

Brown, Richard D. *Modernization: The Transformation of American Life, 1600–1865*. New York: Hill and Wang, 1976.

Buchanan, R. Ogilvie. *The Pastoral Industries of New Zealand*. London: George Philip & Son, Ltd., 1935.

Buenger, Walter L. *Secession and the Union in Texas*. Austin: University of Texas Press, 1984.

Campbell, Randolph. *An Empire for Slavery: The Peculiar Institution in Texas, 1821–1865*. Baton Rouge: LSU Press, 1989.

———. *Gone to Texas: A History of the Lone Star State*. Oxford: Oxford University Press, 2003.

Clark, Gregory. *A Farewell to Alms: A Brief Economic History of the World*. Princeton, NJ: Princeton University Press, 2007.

Conrad, Alfred, and John Meyer. *The Economics of Slavery*. Chicago: Aldine Publishing, 1964.

Cooper, William J. *Liberty and Slavery: Southern Politics to 1860*. New York: Knopf, 1983.

Daniel, Larry, and Riley Gunter. *Confederate Cannon Foundries*. Union City, TN: Pioneer Press, 1977.

Davis, Charles S. *The Cotton Kingdom in Alabama*. Montgomery: Alabama State Department of Archives and History, 1939.

Davis, Lance E., and Stanley L. Engerman. *Naval Blockades in Peace and War: An Economic History Since 1750*. Cambridge: Cambridge University Press, 2006.

DeCredico, Mary A. *Patriotism for Profit: Georgia's Urban Entrepreneurs and the Confederate War Effort*. Chapel Hill: University of North Carolina Press, 1990.

Delfino, Susanna, and Michele Gillespie, eds. *Global Perspectives on Industrial Transformation in the American South*. Columbia: University of Missouri Press, 2005.

———. *Technology, Innovation, and Southern Industrialization: From Antebellum Era to the Computer Age*. Columbia: University of Missouri Press, 2008.

Delfino, Susanna, Michele Gillespie, and Louis Kyriakoudes, eds. *Southern Society and Its Transformations, 1790–1860*. Columbia: University of Missouri Press, 2011.

Dew, Charles. *Ironmaker to the Confederacy: Joseph R. Anderson and the Tredegar Iron Works*. New Haven, CT: Yale University Press, 1966.

Downey, Tom. *Planting a Capitalist South: Masters, Merchants and Manufacturers in the Southern Interior, 1790–1860*. Baton Rouge: LSU Press, 2006.

Earle, Carville. *Geographical Inquiry and American Historical Problems.* Stanford, CA: Stanford University Press, 1992.

Egnal, Marc. *Clash of Extremes: The Economic Origins of the Civil War.* New York: Hill and Wang, 2009.

Eltis, Davis, Frank D. Lewis, and Kenneth L. Sokoloff, eds. *Slavery in the Development of the Americas.* Cambridge: Cambridge University Press, 2004.

Evans, Curtis. *The Conquest of Labor: Daniel Pratt and Southern Industrialization.* Baton Rouge: LSU Press, 2001.

Fishlow, Albert. *American Railroads and the Transformation of the Antebellum Economy.* Cambridge, MA: Harvard University Press, 1965.

Fogel, Robert William. *Without Consent or Contract: The Rise and Fall of American Slavery.* New York: Norton, 1989.

Fogel, Robert William, and Stanley L. Engerman. *Time on the Cross: The Economics of American Negro Slavery.* Boston: Little, Brown, 1974.

Foster, Gaines. *Ghosts of the Confederacy: Defeat, the Lost Cause, and the Emergence of the New South.* Oxford: Oxford University Press, 1987.

Friedmann, John. *Regional Development Policy: A Case Study of Venezuela.* Cambridge: MIT Press, 1966.

Gagnon, Michael. *Transition to an Industrial South: Athens, Georgia, 1830–1870.* Baton Rouge: LSU Press, 2012.

Genovese, Eugene D. *The Political Economy of Slavery: Studies in the Economy & Society of the Slave South.* New York: Pantheon Books, 1965.

Goff, Richard D. *Confederate Supply.* Durham, NC: Duke University Press, 1969.

Goldin, Claudia Dale. *Urban Slavery in the American South, 1820–1860: A Quantitative History.* Chicago: University of Chicago Press, 1976.

Goodrich, Carter. *Government Promotion of American Canals and Railroads, 1800–1890.* New York: Columbia University Press, 1960.

Gray, Lewis Cecil, and Esther Katherine Thompson. *History of Agriculture in the Southern United States to 1860.* Washington, DC: Carnegie Institution of Washington, 1933.

Gutman, Herbert. *Slavery and the Numbers Game.* Urbana: University of Illinois Press, 1975.

Hawk, Emory. *Economic History of the South.* New York: Prentice-Hall, 1934.

Hilliard, Sam Bowers. *Atlas of Antebellum Southern Agriculture.* Baton Rouge: LSU Press, 1984.

———. *Hog Meat and Hoecake.* Carbondale: Southern Illinois University Press, 1972.

Huston, James. *Calculating the Value of the Union: Slavery, Property Rights, and the Economic Origins of the Civil War.* Chapel Hill: University of North Carolina Press, 2003.

———. *The Panic of 1857 and the Coming of the Civil War.* Baton Rouge: LSU Press, 1987.

Johnson, Vicki Vaughn. *The Men and the Vision of the Southern Commercial Conventions, 1845–1871.* Columbia: University of Missouri Press, 1992.

Jordan, Weymouth T. *Ante-Bellum Alabama: Town and Country.* Tuscaloosa: University of Alabama Press, 1987.

Kilbourne, Richard Holcombe Jr. *Debt, Investment, Slaves: Credit Relations in East Feliciana Parish, Louisiana.* Tuscaloosa: University of Alabama Press, 1995.

Larson, John Lauritz. *Internal Improvements: National Public Works and the Promise of Popular Government in the Early United States.* Chapel Hill: University of North Carolina Press, 2001.

Lebergott, Stanley. *The Americans: An Economic Record.* New York: W.W. Norton, 1984.

Lewis, Ronald L. *Coal, Iron, and Slaves: Industrial Slavery in Maryland and Virginia, 1715– 1865.* Westport, CT: Greenwood Press, 1979.

Luraghi, Raimondo. *The Rise and Fall of the Plantation South.* New York: Franklin Watts, 1978.

Majewski, John. *Modernizing a Slave Economy: The Economic Vision of the Confederate Nation.* Chapel Hill: University of North Carolina Press, 2009.

Marler, Scott. *Merchants' Capital: New Orleans and the Political Economy of the Nineteenth- Century South.* New York: Cambridge University Press, 2013.

Marrs, Aaron W. *Railroads in the Old South: Pursuing Progress in a Slave Society.* Baltimore: Johns Hopkins University Press, 2009.

Marx, Karl. *Capital.* Reprint. New York: Penguin Books, 1990.

McCain, William D. *The Story of Jackson: A History of the Capital of Mississippi, 1821–1851.* 2 vols. Jackson: J. F. Hyer Publishing, 1953.

McCain, William, and Charlotte Capers. *Memoirs of Henry Tillinghast Ireys.* Jackson: Mississippi Department of Archives and History, 1954.

McCardell, John. *The Idea of a Southern Nation: Southern Nationalists and Southern Nationalism, 1830–1860.* New York: W. W. Norton, 1979.

McPherson, James M. *Ordeal by Fire: The Civil War and Reconstruction.* 2nd ed. New York: McGraw-Hill, 1992.

McWhiney, Grady. *Cracker Culture: Celtic Ways in the Old South.* University: University of Alabama Press, 1988.

Moore, John Hebron. *The Emergence of the Cotton Kingdom in the Old Southwest.* Baton Rouge: LSU Press, 1988.

Morris, Christopher. *Becoming Southern: The Evolution of a Way of Life, Warren County and Vicksburg, Mississippi, 1770–1860.* Oxford: Oxford University Press, 1995.

National Bureau of Economic Research. *Output, Employment, and Productivity in the United States After 1800.* Studies in Income and Wealth. New York: Columbia University Press, 1966.

———. *Trends in the American Economy in the Nineteenth Century.* Princeton, NJ: Princeton University Press, 1960.

Norris, James D. *R. G. Dun & Co., 1841–1900: The Development of Credit-Reporting in the Nineteenth Century.* Westport, CT: Greenwood Press, 1978.

North, Douglass C. *The Economic Growth of the United States 1790–1860.* New York: W.W. Norton, 1966.

Oakes, James. *Slavery and Freedom: An Interpretation of the Old South.* New York: Alfred A. Knopf, 1990.

Paskoff, Paul. *Industrial Evolution: Organization, Structure, and Growth of the Pennsylvania Iron Industry, 1750–1860.* Baltimore: Johns Hopkins Press, 1983.

Paskoff, Paul F., and Daniel J. Wilson, eds. *The Cause of the South: Selections from De Bow's Review, 1846–1867.* Baton Rouge: LSU Press, 1982.

Phillips, Ulrich B. *American Negro Slavery.* New York: D. Appleton, 1918.

———. *Life and Labor in the Old South.* Boston: Little, Brown, 1929.

Pollard, Edward Alfred. *The Lost Cause: A New History of the War of the Confederates.* New York: E. B. Trent, 1866.

Ramsdell, Charles W. *The Natural Limits of Slavery Expansion.* Indianapolis: Bobbs-Merrill, 1929.

Reidy, Joseph. *From Slavery to Agrarian Capitalism in the Cotton Plantation South: Central Georgia, 1800–1880.* Chapel Hill: University of North Carolina Press, 1992.

Reynolds, Donald A. *Texas Terror: The Slave Insurrection Panic of 1860 and the Secession of the Lower South.* Baton Rouge: LSU Press, 2007.

Roper, Laura Wood. *FLO: A Biography of Frederick Law Olmsted.* Baltimore: Johns Hopkins University Press, 1973.

Rose, Arnold. *The Negro in America.* Boston: Beacon Press, 1948.

Russel, Robert Royal. *Economic Aspects of Southern Sectionalism, 1840–1861.* Urbana: University of Illinois Press, 1924. Reprint, New York: Russell & Russell, 1960.

Rutman, Darrett B., and Anita H. Rutman. *Small Worlds, Large Questions: Explorations in Early American Social History, 1600–1850*. Charlottesville: University Press of Virginia, 1994.

Scarborough, William. *Masters of the Big House: Elite Slaveholders of the Mid-Nineteenth Century South*. Baton Rouge: LSU Press, 2003.

Schoen, Brian. *The Fragile Fabric of Union: Cotton, Federal Politics, and the Global Origins of the Civil War*. Baltimore: Johns Hopkins University Press, 2009.

Schurr, Sam H., and Bruce C. Netschert. *Energy in the American Economy, 1850–1975*. Baltimore: Johns Hopkins Press, 1960.

Shaw, Ronald E. *Canals for a Nation: The Canal Era in the United States, 1790–1860*. Lexington: University of Kentucky Press, 1990.

Shore, Laurence. *Southern Capitalists: The Ideological Leadership of an Elite, 1832–1885*. Chapel Hill: University of North Carolina Press, 1986.

Sledge, John S. *An Ornament to the City: Old Mobile Ironwork*. Athens: University of Georgia Press, 2006.

Starobin, Robert S. *Industrial Slavery in the Old South*. New York: Oxford University Press, 1970.

Stearns, Peter. *The Industrial Revolution in World History*. Boulder, CO: Westview Press, 1993.

Stephens, A. Ray, and William M. Holmes. *Historical Atlas of Texas*. Norman: University of Oklahoma Press, 1989.

Summersell, Charles. *Mobile: History of a Seaport Town*. University: University of Alabama Press, 1949.

Taylor, George Rogers. *The Transportation Revolution, 1815–1860*. New York: Harper Torchbooks, 1951.

Taylor, George Rogers, and Irene D. Neu. *The American Railroad Network, 1861–1890*. Cambridge, MA: Harvard University Press, 1956.

Thomas, William. *The Iron Way: Railroads, the Civil War, and the Making of Modern America*. New Haven, CT: Yale University Press, 2011.

Thomason, Michael, ed. *Mobile: The New History of Alabama's First City*. Tuscaloosa: University of Alabama Press, 2001.

Thornton III, J. Mills. *Politics and Power in a Slave Society: Alabama, 1800–1850*. Baton Rouge: LSU Press, 1978.

Thornton, Mark, and Robert B. Ekelund Jr. *Tariffs, Blockades, and Inflation: The Economics of the Civil War*. Wilmington, DE: Scholarly Resources, 2004.

Towers, Frank. *The Urban South and the Coming of the Civil War*. Charlottesville: University of Virginia Press, 2004.

Uselding, Paul, ed. *Research in Economic History*, vol. 1. Greenwich, CT: JAI Press, 1976.

Wade, Richard C. *Slavery in the Cities: The South 1820–1860*. Oxford: Oxford University Press, 1964.

Wells, Jonathan Daniel. *The Origins of the Southern Middle Class, 1800–1861*. Chapel Hill: University of North Carolina Press, 2004.

Williams, Clanton. *The Early History of Montgomery and Incidentally of the State of Alabama*. University: Confederate Publishing Company, 1979.

Williamson, Harold F., ed. *The Growth of the American Economy: An Introduction to the Economic History of the United States*. New York: Prentice-Hall, 1944.

Wilson, Harold S. *Confederate Industry: Manufacturers and Quartermasters in the Civil War*. Jackson: University Press of Mississippi, 2002.

Woodward, C. Vann. *Origins of the New South, 1877–1913*. Baton Rouge: LSU Press, 1971.

Wright, Gavin. *Old South, New South: Revolutions in the Southern Economy Since the Civil War*. Baton Rouge: LSU Press, 1996.

———. *The Political Economy of the Cotton South: Households, Markets, and Wealth in the Nineteenth Century*. New York: W.W. Norton, 1978.

———. *Slavery and American Economic Development*. Baton Rouge: LSU Press, 2006.

Wyatt-Brown, Bertram. *Southern Honor: Ethics & Behavior in the Old South*. Oxford: Oxford University Press, 1982.

Wynne, Ben. *Mississippi's Civil War: A Narrative History*. Macon, GA: Mercer University Press, 2006.

Zaborney, John J. *Slaves for Hire: Renting Enslaved Laborers in Antebellum Virginia*. Baton Rouge: LSU Press, 2012.

## Articles

Adams, Sean. "US Coal Industry in the Nineteenth Century." EH.Net Encyclopedia, edited by Robert Whaples. January 23, 2003. http://eh.net/encyclopedia/article/adams.industry.coal.us.

Anderson, Ralph V., and Robert E. Gallman. "Slaves as Fixed Capital: Slave Labor and Southern Economic Development." *Journal of American History* 64 (June 1977): 24–46.

Bateman, Fred, James Foust, and Thomas Weiss. "The Participation of Planters in Manufacturing in the Antebellum South." *Agricultural History* 48 (April 1974): 277–97.

Bateman, Fred, and Thomas Weiss. "Comparative Regional Development in Antebellum Manufacturing." *Journal of Economic History* 35 (March 1975): 182–208.

———. "Manufacturing in the Antebellum South." *Research in Economic History* 1 (October 1976): 1–44.

Bender, John J. "The Transportation Revolution and Antebellum Sectional Disagreement." *Social Science History* 35 (Spring 2011): 19–57.

Bezis-Selfa, John. "A Tale of Two Ironworks: Slavery, Free Labor, Work, and Resistance in the Early Republic." *William and Mary Quarterly* 56 (October 1999): 677–700.

Boryczka, Raymond. "The Busiest Man in Town: John Herman Kampmann and the Urbanization of San Antonio, Texas, 1848–1885." *Southwestern Historical Quarterly* 115 (April 2012): 329–63.

Chandler, Alfred. "Anthracite Coal and the Beginnings of the Industrial Revolution in the United States." *Business History Review* 46 (Summer 1972): 141–81.

Collins, Steven G. "System in the South: John W. Mallet, Josiah Gorgas, and Uniform Production at the Confederate Ordnance Department." *Technology and Culture* 40 (July 1999): 517–44.

———. "System, Organization, and Agricultural Reform in the Antebellum South, 1840–1860." *Agricultural History* 75 (Winter 2001): 1–27.

Conrad, Alfred, and John Meyer. "The Economics of Slavery in the Ante Bellum South." *Journal of Political Economy* 66 (April 1958): 95–130.

Day, James Sanders. "Dealing in Black Diamonds: Joseph Squire and Alabama's Early Coal- Mining Operations." *Alabama Review* 64 (2011): 3–29.

Downey, Tom. "Riparian Rights and Manufacturing in Antebellum South Carolina: William Gregg and the Origins of the 'Industrial Mind.'" *Journal of Southern History* 65 (February 1999): 77–108.

Dugas, Vera Lea. "Texas Industry, 1860–1880." *Southwestern Historical Quarterly* 59 (October 1955): 151–83.

Earle, Carville, and Ronald Hoffman. "The Foundation of the Modern Economy: Agriculture and the Costs of Labor in the United States and England, 1800–60." *American Historical Review* 85 (December 1980): 1055–94.

Egerton, Douglas R. "Markets without a Market Revolution: Southern Planters and Capitalism." *Journal of the Early Republic* 16 (Summer 1996): 207–21.

Engerman, Stanley L. "A Reconsideration of Southern Economic Growth, 1770–1860." *Agricultural History* 49 (April 1975): 343–61.

———. "Chicken Little, Anna Karenina, and the Economics of Slavery: Two

Reflections on Historical Analysis, with Examples Drawn Mostly from the Study of Slavery." *Social Science History* 17 (Summer 1993): 161–71.

Friend, Llerena B. "The Texan of 1860." *Southwestern History Quarterly* 62 (July 1958): 1–17.

Graham, Richard. "Slavery and Economic Development: Brazil and the United States South in the Nineteenth Century." *Comparative Studies in Society and History* (October 1981): 620–55.

Griffin, Richard W. "Cotton Manufacture in Alabama to 1865." *Alabama Historical Quarterly* 18 (Fall 1956): 289–308.

Heath, Milton S. "North American Railroads: Public Railroad Construction and the Development of Private Enterprise in the South before 1861." *Journal of Economic History* 10 (1950): 40–53.

Holbrook, Abigail. "A Glimpse of Life on Antebellum Slave Plantations in Texas." *Southwestern Historical Quarterly* 76 (April 1973): 361–383.

Huston, James L. "Property Rights in Slavery and the Coming of the Civil War." *Journal of Southern History* 65 (May 1999): 249–86.

Johnson, Walter. "The Pedestal and the Veil: Rethinking the Capitalism/Slavery Question." *Journal of the Early Republic* 24 (Summer 2004): 299–308.

Jones, Jacqueline. "Labor and the Idea of Race in the American South." *Journal of Southern History* 75 (August 2009): 613–26.

Kaye, Anthony. "The Second Slavery: Modernity in the Nineteenth-Century and the Atlantic World." *Journal of Southern History* 75 (August 2009): 627–50.

Kornweibel, Theodore. "Railroads and Slavery." *Railroad History* 189 (Fall–Winter 2003): 34–59.

Lewis, W. David. "The Emergence of Birmingham as a Case Study of Continuity between the Antebellum Planter Class and Industrialization in the 'New South.'" *Agricultural History* 68 (Spring 1994): 62–79.

Martin, Bonnie. "Slavery's Invisible Engine: Mortgaging Human Property." *Journal of Southern History* 76 (November 2010): 817–66.

Martin, William. "Internal Improvements in Alabama." *Johns Hopkins University Studies in Historical and Political Science* 20 (April 1902): 9–87.

Miller, Randall M. "Daniel Pratt's Industrial Urbanism: The Cotton Mill Town in Ante-bellum Alabama." *Alabama Historical Quarterly* 34 (Spring 1972): 5–36.

Miller, William L. "Slavery and the Population of the South." *Southern Economic Journal* 28 (July 1961): 46–54.

Mitchell, Broadus. "The Rise of Cotton Mills in the South." *Johns Hopkins University Studies in Historical and Political Science* 39 (1921): 1–281.

Paskoff, Paul. "Measures of War: A Quantitative Examination of the Civil War's Destructiveness in the Confederacy." *Civil War History* 54 (2008): 35–62.

Pessen, Edward. "How Different from Each Other Were the Antebellum North and South?" *American Historical Review* 85 (December 1980): 1119–49.

Smiley, David. "The Quest for the Central Theme in Southern History." *South Atlantic Quarterly* 71 (Summer 1972): 307–25.

Terrill, Tom, Edmond Ewing, and Pamela White. "Eager Hands: Labor for Southern Textiles, 1850–1860." *Journal of Economic History* 36 (March 1976): 84–99.

Vandiver, Frank. "The Shelby Iron Company in the Civil War: A Study of Confederate Industry." *Alabama Review* 1 (1948): 12–25.

Vedder, Richard K., and Lowell E. Gallaway. "The Profitability of Antebellum Manufacturing: Some New Estimates." *Business History Review* 54 (Spring 1980): 92–103.

Ward, David C. "Industrial Workers in the Mid-Nineteenth Century South: Family and Labor in The Graniteville (SC) Textile Mill." *Labor History* 28 (Summer 1987): 328–48.

Ward, James A. "A New Look at Antebellum Southern Railroad Development." *Journal of Southern History* 39 (August 1973): 409–20.

Wells, Jonathan. "The Southern Middle Class." *Journal of Southern History* 75 (August 2009): 651–62.

Williams, Michael. "Industrial Impacts on the Forests of the United States, 1860–1920." *Journal of Forest History* 31 (July 1987): 108–21.

Woodman, Harold D. "The Profitability of Slavery: A Historical Perennial." *Journal of Southern History* 29 (August 1963): 303–25.

**Dissertations/Theses**

Collins, Steven G. "Organizing the South: Railroads, Plantations, and War." PhD diss., Louisiana State University, 1999.

Jackson, Joyce. "History of the Shelby Iron Company, 1862–1868." Thesis, University of Alabama, 1948.

Miller, Randall. "Cotton Mill Movement in Antebellum Alabama." PhD diss., Ohio State University, 1971.

Thompson, Alan Smith. "Mobile, Alabama, 1850–1861: Economic, Political, Physical, and Population Characteristics." PhD diss., University of Alabama, 1979.

Torget, Andrew Jonathan. "Cotton Empire: Slavery and the Texas Borderlands, 1820–1837." PhD diss., University of Virginia, 2009.

# INDEX

Page numbers in italics refer to figures and tables